EBURY PRESS

INDIA'S MOST FEARLESS 2

Shiv Aroor is an editor and anchor with India Today television, with experience of over a decade covering the Indian military. He has reported from conflict zones that include Kashmir, India's North-east, Sri Lanka and Libya. For the latter, he won two awards for war reporting. As a political reporter on TV, he was also recently awarded for his coverage of the 2018 state elections in his home state, Karnataka. Aroor also runs the popular award-winning military news and analysis site, Livefist, on which he frequently tells the stories of India's military heroes.

Rahul Singh has covered defence and military affairs at the *Hindustan Times* for over a decade, in a career spanning twenty years. Apart from extensive and deep reporting from the world of the Indian military, including several newsbreaks that have set the national news agenda over the years, Singh has reported from conflict zones including Kashmir, the North-east and war-torn Congo.

PRAISE FOR *INDIA'S MOST FEARLESS 1*

'If our nation is to be stronger, the stories of these heroes must spread far, wide and never be forgotten.'—General Bipin Rawat, Chief of the Army Staff

'India's new generation will find it impossible to forget these riveting military tales.'—Air Chief Marshal B.S. Dhanoa, Chief of the Air Staff

'Inspirational accounts of extraordinary courage, fearlessness and heroism of our valiant soldiers under extreme adversity—a must-read.'—Admiral Sunil Lanba, Chief of the Naval Staff

INDIA'S
MOST
FEARLESS
2

More Military Stories *of*
Unimaginable Courage
and Sacrifice

SHIV AROOR | RAHUL SINGH

EBURY
PRESS

An imprint of Penguin Random House

EBURY PRESS

USA | Canada | UK | Ireland | Australia
New Zealand | India | South Africa | China

Ebury Press is part of the Penguin Random House group of companies
whose addresses can be found at global.penguinrandomhouse.com

Published by Penguin Random House India Pvt. Ltd
7th Floor, Infinity Tower C, DLF Cyber City,
Gurgaon 122 002, Haryana, India

Penguin
Random House
India

First published in Ebury Press by Penguin Random House India 2019

Copyright © Shiv Aroor and Rahul Singh 2019
Illustrations by Sandeep Unnithan

ISBN 9780143443155

Typeset in Bembo Std by Manipal Digital Systems, Manipal
Printed at Replika Press Pvt. Ltd, India

www.penguin.co.in

MIX
Paper from
responsible sources
FSC® C016779

Contents

Forewords

'Either I will come back after hoisting the tricolour, or I will come back wrapped in it, but I will be back for sure.'

—Captain Vikram Batra, Param Vir Chakra

These immortal words of one of India's bravest warriors encapsulate the spirit of the Indian Armed Forces. Our fine men and women epitomize the highest standards of honour, courage and commitment. They meet the myriad challenges of our volatile security environment with an unflinching sense of purpose, fully prepared to make any sacrifice required to protect the nation.

Over the last four decades, there have been innumerable acts of valour by our men and women from the three services. Many a times, in challenging situations at sea, one has seen extraordinary feats being performed to overcome seemingly insurmountable odds. Similarly, stories about the heroic acts by our soldiers and air warriors, against the enemy and in protection of the citizenry, abound. These chronicles are an affirmation of the strength of our ethos, conviction and resolve.

This sequel to *India's Most Fearless* offers the reader a poignant insight into a few such instances. The willingness and confidence of the individuals to surmount all fear and push the limits of the possible, described in each of these stories in the book, will leave an indelible mark. The stories about our heroic submariners give a unique insight into the obscure, hostile and unforgiving realm in which these silent warriors operate.

Readers will undoubtedly gain a deeper understanding of the culture of our forces, as well as an appreciation of the sacrifices made in the defence of the nation. In this day of incessant 'Breaking News' and short-lived societal memory, accounts such as these serve to rekindle our memory of those who made enormous sacrifices for India's security and our tomorrow . . . 'lest we forget'.

Our heroes, through their sacrifices and bravery, have continued to strengthen the very foundations of our great nation. By remembering them, we ensure that their example continues to guide us in all walks of life.

Jai Hind.

Admiral Sunil Lanba
PVSM, AVSM, ADC
Chairman, Chiefs of Staff Committee, and
Chief of the Naval Staff

'Always do everything you ask of those you command.'

—General George S. Patton, Jr

3 June 1999 seems like yesterday to me. I remember taking off from Srinagar with my Flight Commander in a pair of MiG-21 jets, soaring over the Drass-Kargil heights and dropping 250 kg bombs on Tiger Hill. Our squadron had moved from Punjab to the Kashmir Valley a fortnight earlier to help hunt down and destroy the enemy intruder positions.

Being deployed for war was a dream. As difficult and dangerous it was, this was what my squadron and I had trained tirelessly for. What could be more fulfilling than to be called upon to do what you had joined the Indian Air Force for?

Those few weeks threw up some of India's best known and most beloved heroes. Men whose actions have deservedly won them a valuable price in public memory. But as I have always held, India has never needed a full-scale war or conflict for its heroes to step up. In a country that faces threats from across the spectrum, the demand for courage and gallantry remains high. History is rife with acts of courage and valour by the three services.

Air power and employment of the Air Force is frequently seen as an indisputable act of hostility in a conflict. The nature of military aviation and the many other roles of the Indian Air Force mean that our men and women are uninterruptedly in difficult and demanding lines of duty. From a fighter cockpit that's on fire, to a transport plane headed to a dangerously small airfield high up on a mountain, from daring helicopter rescues during floods to the extensive ground operations that occupy thousands of our ranks, it does not stop.

In *India's Most Fearless 2*, you will gain insight into the
story of an air warrior, amongst others, in a role that you would
not normally associate with the Indian Air Force as you know
it: Anti-Terror Operations. The other accounts, equally, must
occupy us with questions not only about the will to survive
and the skill of our three services, but also about what it takes
to make peace with one's own likely demise, if in the bargain
many more lives are saved.

My compliments to the authors for the sequel, for very
aptly highlighting the valour of our heroes once again.

Jai Hind.

Air Chief Marshal B.S. Dhanoa
PVSM, AVSM, YSM, VM, ADC
Chief of the Air Staff

The wide readership of the first book, *India's Most Fearless*, has been a source of great satisfaction to the Army fraternity. The book undoubtedly brings to light the bravery against all odds of a few of the 'heroes' of Indian Army, amongst many such stories of unparalleled guts, glory and courage.

The book and its popularity is an affirmation that despite many distractions in our modern and hyper-connected society, millions are still interested in the stories of our men and women in uniform. The soldiers keep themselves professionally abreast and ensure that they are available for the 'call of duty' at all times to uphold the sovereignty and integrity of our great nation.

Our men and women in uniform have never let the nation down in the highest traditions of the Armed Forces. After having seen the entire spectrum of challenges in which Indian Army soldiers operate, I can say with conviction that we will continue to put the nation first, always and every time.

We are grateful to the citizens of our nation who continue to acknowledge the bravery and sacrifice of our men and women in uniform in any manner they can, through messages, cards, letters, social media or even standing ovations at public places. We are sanguine of the continued support of our countrymen in the times to come.

Compliments to the authors for having continued with the sequel to highlight the actions of our 'heroes'.

Jai Hind.

General Bipin Rawat
PVSM, UYSM, AVSM, YSM, SM, VSM, ADC
Chief of the Army Staff

Prologue

Just after 3.30 a.m. on 26 February 2019, climbing abruptly to 27,000 feet in dark airspace over Pakistan-occupied Kashmir (PoK), an Indian Air Force (IAF) pilot flying in a single-seat Mirage 2000 fighter jet pushed a button on his flight-stick. A few feet below him, from the rumbling belly of his aircraft, an Israeli-made bomb silently detached itself and dropped away to begin a journey—first gliding and then careening—towards a target over 70 km away. The bomb, fed with satellite coordinates and an on-board guidance chip, had all the information it needed to hurtle to its destination.

The Mirage 2000 was far from home. It had taken off from the Gwalior air force base over 1000 km away earlier that night along with at least six more Mirage jets from the three squadrons based there. Over the hour the jets flew over central India and into the northern sector. Following in their wake, five more Mirage 2000 jets took off in the darkness from an air base in Punjab.

The dozen Mirages, flying in three separate and unequal formations, weren't alone in the air. Two airborne early warning jets, an Embraer Netra from the Bathinda air base and a higher performance Phalcon jet from Agra were already in the air, their powerful radars and sensors on full alert to the mission ahead. Communications between aircraft were kept to a minimum. This was a mission with almost no room for deviation unless absolutely necessary. And it needed to last for as little time as possible.

As the three Mirage formations flew in a circuit at low altitude, very much in the manner of night flying training sorties conducted by squadrons, ten jets more roared off the tarmac from two more air bases, including Sukhoi Su-30 MKI fighters from the forward air base at Halwara. It was this pack of Su-30s that would play a crucial role in what came next.

With a total of twenty-two IAF fighters in the air, the jets slowly mixed their formations to create three separate packs— two mixed packs of Mirage 2000 and Su-30 fighters. And a third pack comprised only of Su-30s. While it's tempting to think of these three packs as neat little jet formations in the sky, it was nothing quite like that. The jets in each pack flew tens of kilometres from each other, and were only bound by a loose common flightpath and mission profile.

Shortly after 3 a.m., the mission began with a pre-planned deception.

The third fighter pack, consisting of big, heavy Su-30 jets, turned south, heading out of Punjab and into the Rajasthan sector, all the while ensuring it remained prominent and visible to Pakistani radars on the other side of the international border. Turning around over Jodhpur, the fighters began provocatively flying in the direction of the international border north of the Chandan firing ranges, their noses pointed towards a Pakistani city that couldn't possibly have been on a higher alert at the time—Bahawalpur, 250 km to the north, the city that was home to the Jaish-e-Mohammad's (JEM's) headquarters and largest terror training facilities. The IAF planners had counted on Pakistan's 'hair-trigger' state of alert to provoke a reaction. It happened within minutes.

The Pakistan Air Force scrambled a group of F-16 jets from the Mushaf air base in Sargodha about 320 km to the north of Bahawalpur. Just as the jets were getting airborne and moving south to fend off any possible attack by the Indian Su-30s, the second IAF pack, comprising Mirage 2000s and Su-30s, broke away from its circuit and turned south over Jammu along a radial pointed towards Sialkot and Lahore in Pakistan, both large and commercially important cities. This second pack split further, with one part flying along a radial that would pass through Pakistan's Okara and lead once again to Bahawalpur.

The twin air manoeuvres from two directions doubled the air threat to the 'capital city' of the JeM. More F-16s departed Sargodha to engage with this second Indian threat. Pakistan's instantaneous scrambling of fighters wasn't surprising to Indian radar controllers and sensor operators on the two airborne early warning jets. The country's air defences would have been on their highest state of readiness since the 26/11 Mumbai terror attacks, an act of carnage terrible enough that it got India to seriously consider retaliatory air strikes for the first time.

And now, for twelve days without pause, Pakistan's military had cranked its alertness levels to maximum.

Eleven days earlier, at 9.30 a.m. on 15 February 2019, the chiefs of the Indian armed forces and intelligence agencies, top ministers and the National Security Advisor arrived at Delhi's leafy 7, Lok Kalyan Marg compound where the Prime Minister of India lives and sometimes operates from. It was far from a routine weekly meeting for the Prime Minister to take stock of national security.

Eighteen hours earlier, 800 kilometres north, in the Lethapora area of Jammu and Kashmir's Pulwama district, a vehicle packed with explosives and driven by a young man named Adil Ahmad Dar, had managed to snake between vehicles of a large convoy of Srinagar-bound trucks carrying 2500 troops from the Central Reserve Police Force (CRPF), and rammed it. The explosion killed forty troops, spattering the highway with their blood and body parts. Minutes after the blast, a stream of pictures of the mangled vehicles and sickening carnage taken from mobile phones of locals and first responders flooded social media.

With the Pakistan–administered JeM terror group claiming responsibility for the attack, the Prime Minister had convened this meeting of the Cabinet Committee on Security (CCS) solely to assess how India could respond. Forty minutes later, the meeting was finished. Asked if air strikes on a terror target were a viable option, IAF Chief Air Chief Marshal Birender Singh Dhanoa responded in the affirmative, also briefing the Cabinet Committee that the country's jets would be ready to strike with confirmed targets in a matter of days. He was given two weeks.

From 16–20 February, the IAF worked with intelligence agencies at the operations room in Delhi's Vayu Bhawan. With National Security Advisor Ajit Doval receiving a daily update on proceedings, the deliberations were honed by satellite imagery, human intelligence from the ground in Pakistan and PoK, and photographs from a pair of Heron drones flying daily missions along the Line of Control (LoC).

On 21 February, the IAF presented a classified set of 'target tables' to the government via the National Security Advisor.

The first in the list of seven separate target options was a JeM terror training compound that sat on a hill called Jabba Top outside the city of Balakot in Pakistan's Khyber-Pakhtunkhwa province. The IAF recommended Balakot, just 100 km from Pakistan's capital Islamabad, since it was a secluded target with the lowest probability of non-terrorist casualties. The two other 'viable' targets presented to the government were in PoK—Muzzafarabad, 23 km south-east of Balakot, and Chakothi about 70 km away. But these two, along with Bahawalpur, carried not just the risk of collateral damage, but a slightly higher chance of being hindered by Pakistani air defences. Among the remaining options was Muridke, north of Lahore, the city that held the headquarters of that other dreaded India-focused terror group, the Lashkar-e-Taiba (LeT). This too was deemed a highly risky target to consider.

By midnight on 22 February, a highly controlled chain of command decided that the Indian jets would strike the first target in the list—the one outside Pakistan's Balakot. Every man and woman in the secret chain was aware that if such a mission went through, it would be India's first air strike on Pakistani soil since the 1971 war. What amplified the mission ahead was that the two countries weren't at war in 2019. Could such a mission change that?

There was another important reason why Balakot was chosen. Unlike Muzzafarabad and Chakothi, Balakot was in Pakistan and not PoK. As an international message, an air strike on sovereign Pakistani soil—as opposed to PoK, which India considers its own territory—would make all the difference in the world.

The target dossier submitted to the government also contained pages of data detailing the latest intelligence assessments of the kind of damage that could be caused to terrorist infrastructure in each case. In the case of Balakot, apart from satellite imagery and some medium-grade electronic intelligence, the Indian intelligence agencies had also been able to procure invaluable human inputs from Balakot town. The intelligence, obtained from Indian 'assets' on the ground, provided invaluable shape to the target, and was the original source of a number that would later be the subject of much controversy and debate. India's assets in Balakot had reported that there would be at least 300 terrorists and terror trainees on site at Jabba Top at any given time. In other words, a facility that was known to house a significant enough number of handlers, terrorist recruits and ideologues, to justify a high-risk air strike from airspace peppered with and primed for anti-air defence.

As a fully intelligence-based operation, it was imperative that India chose targets that involved not just terror infrastructure, but the presence of a significant number of terrorists at any given time. Apart from the National Technical Research Organization's (NTRO) signal intelligence inputs, it was this human intelligence that helped guide and lock India's choice of target.

It wasn't the first time India was using such human assets for an offensive operation in hostile territory. In September 2016, during the Indian Army Special Forces 'surgical strikes' in PoK, Indian assets[1] in the JeM had confirmed the terror launch pads as viable targets, revealed first in the first book of the India's Most Fearless series.

A data analyst with one of India's intelligence agencies told the authors, 'An operation of this kind is very difficult without human intelligence on the ground. It would have been a huge risk to do so without a conclusive word to corroborate your other inputs, whether satellite or electronic.'

An Army officer who served on the composite intelligence team that formulated the target packages during the 2016 trans-LoC strikes says, 'The question is not about whether ground assets were used or not. They 100 per cent were. The

---

[1] See *India's Most Fearless 1* (New Delhi: Penguin Random House India, 2017).

only question, might I add that nobody needs to ever know about, is whether these were the same assets that helped in 2016 or similar assets—or assets of a totally different kind. That will hopefully remain guesswork. Let films and books (!) do the guessing.'

On 24 February, pilots of the Mirage 2000 squadrons in Gwalior were briefed about the mission. That same day, aircraft would be airborne over central India for a short mock air drill alongside a Phalcon AWACS jet and Ilyushin-78M mid-air refuelling tanker from Agra. The jets taking part in the drill didn't return to Gwalior, instead landing at a base in Punjab. They would remain at the base all of the next day.

The IAF was about to take a violent break from history, but in Delhi, every effort was made to ensure that it was business as usual. On the night of 25 February, hours before the Mirages took to the air on their mission, the IAF hosted a customary farewell banquet for the outgoing chief of the Western Air Command, Air Marshal C. Hari Kumar— he was retiring three days later. The sit-down dinner was organized at the Akash Air Force Officer's mess near Delhi's India Gate, where just a few hours earlier Prime Minister Narendra Modi had inaugurated the country's National War Memorial.

In his speech, IAF Chief Dhanoa regaled the audience with stories of how he and Air Marshal Hari Kumar had gone to the same school—Rashtriya Indian Military College (RIMC), Dehradun—and were from the same house. It was a typical military evening of mirth and nostalgia. The banquet had over eighty senior air force officers in attendance. But only a handful of them, IAF chief Dhanoa and Air Marshal Hari Kumar included, were in the 'need-to-know' loop on what was about to happen. Those who *weren't* in that loop confirm to the authors that there was absolutely no indication that evening that some of their service personnel were about to soar out across the border to drop bombs inside Pakistan.

After farewell speeches and dessert, the banquet wound up at 11 p.m. IAF Chief Dhanoa was driven back to his official residence on Delhi's Akbar Road. He tells the authors he received a final update on preparations before turning in for a quick couple of hours of rest—everything was in control by a team he knew he could trust his life with. Thirty minutes before the Mirages took off from Gwalior, Dhanoa woke up to plug back into the secret proceedings.

Four kilometres away at 7, Lok Kalyan Marg, Prime Minister Modi was awake too. He received his final pre-mission brief 20 minutes before the jets departed Gwalior. There would be communication silence for the next half hour—covering the most crucial part of the mission. The intrusion.

As the second and third fighter packs flew menacing flight paths on the Jodhpur–Bahawalpur and Jammu–Sialkot radials, the first pack, comprising six Mirage 2000 jets, crossed the LoC at low altitude in the Keran sector in Kupwara. Flying over the Athmuqam town in PoK, the six jets spread out further and climbed, crossing between 12–15 km into hostile airspace.

With the Jabba Top hill now in effective range, and given the all clear from radar controllers in the Phalcon jet, the aircraft dropped their bombs one by one. Five munitions from five aircraft dropped away in the cold dark, whooshing west out of PoK and into sovereign Pakistani airspace.

Tracking the weapons as they closed in on Jabba Top, pilots in the air and controllers on the ground knew history had already been made. The IAF weaponry was about to hit targets on Pakistani soil for the first time in over forty-seven years—and, crucially, for the first time when the two countries weren't involved in a full-blown war. The very act of pushing the button and letting those bombs loose was a message, the IAF leadership would tell pilots in a debrief later.

Seconds after the weapons release, a warning call went out to the Mirages as they tracked the bombs screaming towards their targets using infrared sensors. Three Pakistani jets had been scrambled from the Minhas air base in Pakistan's Kamra town, just over 60 km north-west of Islamabad. Tracked by the Indian Phalcon jet, the Pakistani fighters, believed to be Chinese-origin JF-17 Thunder jets, flew at full throttle towards PoK. It was near impossible for Pakistani defences to know that Indian bombs were headed towards Balakot.

With Pakistani jets inbound, Indian controllers on the Phalcon jet instructed the Mirage pilots to turn around immediately, drop altitude quickly and return across the LoC. With the Pakistani jets well over 50 km away, the six jets would cross back between Chowkibal and the Leepa Valley, flying close to Chakothi, one of the targets that had been considered but dropped in favour of Balakot.

The intrusion into hostile airspace had lasted only a few minutes. The six Mirages, their backs watched by the Phalcon jet, landed safely in Srinagar. The other Mirages and Su-30s from the second and third pack would also be summoned back to bases in Punjab. A debrief of the full mission would later affirm that the second and third packs had very ably lured Pakistani 'first responder' F-16s away from the area of attack to the north, and kept them engaged and 'on edge' until the strike mission was complete. The Netra early warning jet from Bathinda would record the deception, providing compelling battlespace imagery for post-mission discussions.

Thirty hours after the air strikes on Balakot, the historic mission would be overshadowed briefly by Pakistan's retaliation attempt over the LoC in the Sunderbani sector near Jammu, using a pack of fighters that included F-16s, Mirage IIIs and JF-17s from the Sargodha and Rafiqui air bases. While the Balakot air strikes had passed without the names of any of the Indian pilots or personnel involved reaching the media, one name would per force become public the following morning. Wing Commander Abhinandan Varthaman, in his MiG-21 Bison jet, would be shot down while chasing a Pakistani intruder back across the LoC. With its pilot repatriated to India barely 48 hours later, the IAF would publicly credit Varthaman with having shot down a Pakistani F-16 jet during the air joust, triggering an uninterrupted storm of claims and counterclaims, with questions likely to linger indefinitely.

The true history of that late winter week, however, would be in the work done in darkness by a group of IAF pilots—many of them young—who, under instructions, had flown into the most hostile airspace imaginable, to conduct a mission never done before. Each of those pilots will have known the risks and the substantial chances that they could be shot down by ground fire or surface-to-air missiles in an area that was on high alert. Just how the Indian Mirages managed to make their way so deep into PoK unchecked will likely be a low-profile introspection within Pakistan's military. Just as the events of the following morning will be one for the IAF.

While the authors have interviewed several officers involved or familiar with the 26 February mission, the pilots must remain nameless. At the time that this book is published, the historic air strike on Balakot remains a classified operation.

Introduction

At 2.45 p.m. on 11 January 2019, just as we had finished writing much of this book, an improvised explosive device (IED) was remotely detonated at the LoC in Nowshera, north of Jammu, an area infamous for Pakistani ceasefire violations and infiltration attempts. Two Indian Army personnel on patrol were instantly killed in the explosion, believed to be the work of a hybrid infiltration unit comprising Pakistan Army commandos and terrorists, better known as the Border Action Team (BAT).

The soldier killed in the blast was Rifleman Jiwan Gurung, twenty-four years old and at the start of his life. The officer, Major Sashidharan Vijay Nair, wasn't much older—thirty-three. For a few days after the incident, their deaths would merely add to the familiar statistics of mortality from that part of the country. But within four days, by 15 January, journalists would discover a numbing back story that would push the deceased Major into the news headlines.

The back story would radiate from a young figure in a wheelchair first seen at the Pune war memorial and later at the city's Vaikunth cremation ground. Maj. Sashidharan had met and fallen in love with Trupti six years ago. Only months into their engagement, Trupti was diagnosed with an autoimmune disease of the central nervous system that manifests itself with progressively intensifying symptoms that can be managed but never cured. On the threshold of marriage, friends and family are said to have advised Maj. Sashidharan—then twenty-seven—to reconsider his future. Friends say that even Trupti told her fiancé she would understand if he were to break off the engagement and move on with his life.

Maj. Sashidharan would hear none of it. Trupti and he were married a few weeks later. Months after the wedding, Trupti suffered another serious health setback that rendered her paralysed from the waist down, permanently consigning her to a wheelchair. The young officer would devote himself to Trupti, ensuring that they never missed out on the army life he had signed up for. Days before his death, while on leave in Pune, he had calmed a worried Trupti about being deployed at the LoC.

In life as in death, said a news report about him.

But would Maj. Sashidharan be more than a flag-draped casket on the inside pages of a newspaper had it not been for these details about his personal life? What if they had never been discovered? What about the soldier, young Rifleman Gurung, who died with him? Does he too have a crushing back story that burnishes his heroism? Is such a back story even necessary to amplify the heroism of those who put their lives on the line as a matter of daily routine? These aren't loaded black-and-white questions, but ones we have continuously grappled with through the writing of this book, the second in the India's Most Fearless series.

A month after the explosion that killed Maj. Sashidharan and Rifleman Gurung, on 14 February, an election-bound India was shatteringly interrupted by a suicide vehicle attack on a convoy of the CRPF in Jammu and Kashmir's

Pulwama. For a country that has become inured to periodic Pakistan–sponsored terrorist attacks, there was an immediate and unmissable 'enough is enough' air. Few could tell quite why this attack had proven so uniquely numbing—India had suffered bloodier attacks at Pakistan's hands before. Was it the terrifying nature of the attack? Was it a country that had already raised the bar on punitive responses with its strikes inside PoK in 2016? Did looming elections play a role as critics would later allege? Whatever it was, twelve days later, India would cross a new red line with a historic air attack on a terror facility of the JeM inside Pakistan.

The Balakot operation has already attained mythical status even as India and Pakistan fight an uninterrupted stream of claims and counterclaims. While that has always been the nature of the beast between the two countries, the operation itself remains classified in India, with the barest of details ever emerging officially. And that means there is a good chance that the names of over a dozen of those fighter pilots who were assigned the historic and enormously dangerous task of flying into Pakistani airspace in darkness, will never be known with certainty. The prologue to this book carries an account of the Balakot air strikes based on conversations with many of those involved, but who cannot be named. From radar operators, mission support pilots and planners, their work will linger, possibly forever, in the shadows.

Like them, there are hundreds on land, in the air and at sea, who cannot be named because of the nature of their feats.

In the course of writing *India's Most Fearless 1* and *2,* if there's one unshakeable truth that we have come upon, it is this: if you look hard enough, every soldier has a shattering back story. But, like in the case of Maj. Sashidharan, does it take their deaths for such stories to bubble to the surface?

Jim Morrison of The Doors may have been right when
he said:

> Death makes angels of us all
> And gives us wings
> Where we had shoulders
> Smooth as raven's claws.

('A Feast of Friends', The Doors)

But it is equally true that the stories of our soldiers are there
to be told if only someone were willing to ask. As in the first
book of this series, many of the heroes in *India's Most Fearless
2* are no longer alive. But as you will hopefully discover as you
turn the pages, death was only a final flourish in lives lived
with constant heroism.

What this journey started out as was two guys who've
spent their entire careers as journalists listening to stories of
military valour deciding it was time to begin documenting
them. Not out of any lofty sense of responsibility, but simply
because these are stupendous stories that everyone needs to
hear. Since the first *India's Most Fearless* was published in 2017,
a common response we receive from readers is, thanks for the
inspiration. Any thanks, we always tell them, is due only to
the heroes, their comrades and their families. We haven't for
a moment chosen to tell these stories with the intention to
inspire. We have done so because they were amazing stories
for us personally. If inspiration is the inevitable effect of these
stories, then thanks is due only to the men we've written
about.

The book you hold in your hands takes forward the legacy
we didn't imagine would take so powerful a root when the
first *India's Most Fearless* was released in 2017. Neither of us

fathomed that stories of military heroes would be read by so many people in so many languages and with a thirst for more. The book you are (hopefully) about to read is the result of thousands of messages from readers urging us to write about more heroes and their amazing feats.

When we announced this book early in 2019, one reader sent us a message saying, 'The India's Most Fearless series can never end, because India will never run out of heroes.' This is the truth, but a disturbing one. It has never escaped our minds for a moment that it is India's uniquely difficult security atmosphere that creates opportunities for military heroism—the Balakot strikes will serve as a numbing reminder to a generation of Indians that wasn't born when India and Pakistan last locked horns in Kargil. And in many ways, it does mean there will be a steady flow of acts of courage from our frontlines and disturbed areas. But not for a moment is *India's Most Fearless* a romanticization of conflict. If there's one thing we've learnt in telling these stories, it is the silent and humble trust of every soldier that India will not send them into combat unless absolutely necessary. That their heroism comes at an enormous premium. And that the country would rather its soldiers were safe, than forced into a situation where they have to decide between life and death.

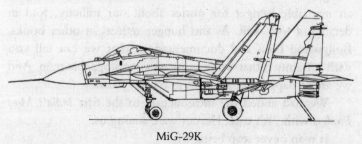

MiG-29K

While the stories in this book seek to keep the spotlight on individual heroism, it doesn't exclude the many hard questions that must rightly be asked about military operations. Questions of leadership and decision-making, of tactics and training, of spirit and initiative, all of which have a bearing on why the heroes needed to face their ultimate dilemma in the first place. Let no one tell you that these questions don't bear asking. If there's one thing our military heroes deserve, it is an unending stream of questions about the circumstances surrounding their operations. The stories that follow answer some of these questions and raise some more. But through them all, as you will see, the core of courage stands unshaken.

If the first book in the series made the front pages of newspapers for the first and only personal account of the 2016 surgical strikes into PoK, the book in your hands features several operations that took place in the aftermath of that momentous mission. Missions that throw important light on India's security after that daring revenge strike by the Indian Army's Special Forces squads, including the 26 February 2019 air strikes in Balakot, Pakistan.

As in the first book, we are also privileged to have been able to feature heroes who went beyond the call of duty to save the lives of others. Stories that still give us sleepless nights, and that we hope will keep you awake too. If there's one thing that *India's Most Fearless* has showed us, it is that there's an insatiable hunger for stories about our military, told in detail and told well. As this hunger reflects in other books, Bollywood films and documentaries, what we can tell you with certainty is that we are now on an unstoppable train. And we are so happy you are with us on this journey.

We had ended the introduction to the first *India's Most Fearless* with, 'It's true. Heroes walk among us.'

It won't ever stop being true.

1

'Killed, Maybe, but Never Caught'

Major Mohit Sharma

Undisclosed location near Shopian, Jammu and Kashmir
March 2004

'Something's not right,' Abu Torara whispered to the man slouched on a cot next to him. A pair of early summer evening sunbeams streamed into the room from a half-open window in their small hideout not far from Shopian, just over 50 km south of Srinagar.

Abu Sabzar drew deeply on a cigarette, exhaled through his nostrils, roughly scratched his beard and turned to look at Torara, who was on his feet, leaning against the wall. A pair of AK-47 assault rifles lay at the foot of the cot. Torara was looking straight ahead of him at the tiny doorway that led to the next room—a small balcony-cum-kitchen that opened out into the woods. Emanating from that direction was the sound of boiling water, the aroma of kahwa, the frothy pour of liquid into glass tumblers and their clink as they were placed on a tray.

'You want to talk to him some more?' Sabzar asked, stubbing out his cigarette on the windowsill next to him. Torara said nothing. A few seconds later, bearing a steel plate with glasses of tea, Iftikhar Bhatt stepped through the tiny doorway and into the room.

Six feet two inches tall, with hair down to his shoulders and most of his face covered with a bushy beard that flowed down his neck, Bhatt wore a stony expression as he stepped forward to offer the other two terrorists their tea. His own rifle was slung from his neck, resting at his side. After they had picked up their glasses, Bhatt picked up his own and sat down at the edge of the cot, silent, staring straight ahead.

Minutes passed as the three men sipped from their steaming glasses. Then, Torara stepped forward and spoke.

'Iftikhar, I'm going to ask you only once,' Torara said, still sipping his tea, placing the other hand on Bhatt's knee. 'Who are you?'

Bhatt said nothing, his face rigid, unmoved, his hand still bringing the tea up to his lips. He had met the two terrorists two weeks earlier in a village near Shopian. They had never seen him before and he said very little apart from telling them the village he was from. A few days later, he opened up a little more, speaking about how his brother had been killed in an encounter three years ago. Another young man, they thought, looking for revenge, looking for work with a militant outfit, both for a livelihood as well as for closure. At the end of a full week, he spoke his first full sentences, telling them he wanted their help with an attack on an Army checkpoint. He showed them hand-drawn maps depicting the movement of Army patrols along a little-known hill trail, research that suggested this young, bearded man of few words had already begun reconnaissance, the most crucial groundwork for a successful attack on security forces.

Torara and Sabzar were moderately impressed. Bhatt, clearly in his twenties, though the beard hid much of his youthfulness, had demonstrated the motivation to take matters into his own hands—half the battle in the process of radicalization. Tall and well-built, there was no doubt he could be useful in the rough, dark life of a militant in Kashmir. Over the following week, the two Hizbul men questioned Bhatt, presenting him with situations and asking him what he would do. Bhatt's answer would remain the same, 'I need your support, I want to learn.'

Torara and Sabzar were no ordinary terrorists. Both had gained a reputation for leading a highly effective recruitment campaign in south Kashmir. If Bhatt wanted to pick up a gun and get started, these were the men to get in touch with. The men weren't surprised that Bhatt knew who they were.

At the end of two weeks, Torara and Sabzar told Bhatt that they would help with his proposed attack on the Army's foot patrol north of Shopian, but that they needed to disappear for a few days, coordinate the logistics and finer points. Bhatt said he would not return to his village without completing his mission, with or without them. So they took him along to their hideout, where they now sat sipping hot tea.

The attack plan had been detailed and fleshed out. A consignment of grenades would arrive that night. Bhatt would be joined by three Hizbul men, who had been summoned from another village and would show up the following morning. They would then proceed in the evening to launch the attack, with the intention of killing as many of the soldiers as possible as they trudged through a short trough in the trail.

But Torara was having second thoughts. Something didn't seem to fit. Squatting before Bhatt, he asked again.

'Who are you?'

Bhatt, who had been circumspect and soft-spoken thus far, placed his tumbler down on the ground with a splash. Rising to his feet, he took the rifle from around his neck and dropped it on the ground with a clatter. Then, looking from Torara to Sabzar, he spoke, his voice quivering. 'If you have any doubts about me, kill me,' he said, his voice raised to its highest. 'You cannot do this if you don't trust me. So you have no choice but to kill me now.'

Torara rose to his feet, looking at Bhatt closely. And then, just as he turned to Sabzar, perhaps to ask what to do next, Bhatt pulled out a concealed 9-mm pistol and shot both the terrorists in the head. Sabzar slouched back into the cot. Torara was thrown against the wall, blood splattering against the white as he crumpled to the ground. Bhatt fired two more bullets, to be sure.

As the swirl of gun smoke cleared, Bhatt sat down on the cot, picked up the tumbler he had set down earlier and drained the tea. Then he waited for the sun to set before he could walk, in the darkness, back to where he had come from. And when he reached there, he would, for the first time in a fortnight, be able to use his real name: Maj. Mohit Sharma, of the Army's 1 Para Special Forces.

* * *

Back at his field base before dawn the following day, another officer in the unit would quip at breakfast, 'You know, Mohit, with that look you've got there, you'll probably end up getting captured or killed by the Army itself while you're on your next covert mission.'

Mohit had replied, 'Killed, maybe. But I'll never get caught.'

Two months later, the twenty-six-year-old officer took leave, his first in over a year since he had joined the elite Special Forces unit, to visit his parents in the sprawling Delhi suburb of Ghaziabad. His brother, Madhur, was at the railway station to receive him, but when the train pulled in, the Major was nowhere to be seen. Perplexed, his brother searched the compartments, wondering if Mohit had missed his train or got off at the wrong station. It was then that he realized that Mohit was standing right in front of him, just a few feet away, silent and completely unrecognizable. He was wearing a Kashmiri phiran, and his long hair and beard now covered everything but his eyes. He had simply stood there, wondering if his brother would recognize him. Madhur was clueless till Mohit finally shouted his name, the beard parting to reveal a toothy grin.

The young officer had just finished twelve months of living his greatest dream—to be a commando in the Special Forces. At the dining table that evening, his mother, Sushila, a Delhi Jal Board employee, anxiously pressed him to describe what his work was like in Kashmir. Maj. Mohit smiled mischievously and said that he had made the right decision to reject the path his parents had chosen for him.

Nine years earlier, in 1995, fresh out of Delhi Public School, Ghaziabad, Mohit had been persuaded by his parents to pursue an engineering degree. Older than Mohit by a year, Madhur had already been admitted to an engineering college. Like many middle-class families, their parents hoped that engineering degrees would allow both to start a manufacturing business of some kind to take care of the family and settle into a 'stable' life near the national capital.

Strangely, though, for a family that couldn't have had less to do with the armed forces, both their sons wanted to join the military. Very eager to become a fighter pilot, Madhur had made three failed attempts at cracking the Services Selection Board examination, finally giving up and deciding to stick with his engineering course. Mohit, who was now at a crossroads, agreed to go with his parents' wishes. As he said goodbye to them and hugged his brother, he whispered something into Madhur's ear.

'Don't worry, I'll serve for both of us.'

Then the seventeen-year-old hopped on to a train that took him to Amravati in Maharashtra, and then on a bus to Shegaon, where he joined the Shri Sant Gajanan Maharaj College of Engineering.

'He took admission, but from the start, it was clear he did not plan to stay,' says Madhur. 'He had taken the NDA (National Defence Academy) entrance exam before leaving.

When the results came, my parents tried to hide them from him, hoping he would just continue with engineering. But Mohit got suspicious and called the UPSC (Union Public Service Commission) himself to find out if his name was on the list. Without telling any of us, he left his hostel keys with his friends and got on a train from Amravati to Bhopal, which was his centre. There, he took the final test, cleared it and was summoned to Delhi for his medical. That's when he called our parents, announcing that he was coming back home, bag and baggage, and that he would not be returning to his college.'

Unnerved by the sudden turn of events, Sushila was comforted by Mohit's father, Rajender Sharma. They decided they would persuade Mohit to see sense, return to college and finish his degree—to forget about the military and focus on his studies instead. What they hadn't accounted for was just how energized and focused the successful crossing of the first few entrance hurdles had made their younger son. When he arrived home, he would respectfully raise his hand and tell his parents to save their breath if they intended to try changing his mind. The Sharmas had never seen their son this way. It worried them, but they quickly realized that any attempt to talk him out of his chosen path was futile.

With a month left for his medical tests, Mohit marshalled his mother's help to surmount a difficult immediate hurdle—he was 6 kg underweight to make the cut. A diet that included litres of milk, high protein foods and a dozen bananas a day was employed to help Mohit pack on a hefty 8 kg in just four weeks.

Clean-shaven and wiry compared to the hairy, hulking man he would become a few years later, Mohit entered the hallowed portals of the NDA in Pune, quickly proving how committed he was to his journey into the Army. Emerging as one of the best all-round cadets with trophies for excellence in boxing, swimming and horse-riding, Mohit finished his three years at the NDA and then graduated from the Indian Military Academy (IMA) in Dehradun in 1999.

While he was at the IMA, India would fight the Kargil War with Pakistan, an intense fifty-day skirmish that put the two countries on edge. Mohit, along with every other cadet at the Academy, would crowd into common rooms to watch the evening news bulletins carrying reports from TV journalists in Kargil and Dras. These reports would shock, depress, but ultimately galvanize the entire batch of cadets, infusing in them an even greater urgency to get out into the field and serve.

Years earlier, when Madhur had asked him which arm of the military he wanted to join, Mohit had fired back without a pause, 'Infantry. What else is there?'

Watching dispatches containing interviews of soldiers and young officers in Kargil, Mohit found the strongest affirmation yet that the path he had chosen was a worthy one, even if it had meant disobeying his parents. Electrified and angry at Pakistan, like each one of his course mates at the time, the young cadet from Ghaziabad awaited his turn.

On 11 December 1999, Lieutenant Mohit Sharma was commissioned into the 5th Battalion of the Madras Regiment, one of the Army's oldest infantry regiments, which dated back to the eighteenth century and which had the famous war cry '*Veera Madrasi, adi kollu, adi kollu* (Brave Madrasi, hit and kill, hit and kill)!'

That war cry couldn't have been more appropriate. During celebrations and revelry on the night of his commissioning, when Mohit was asked by a course mate where he was hoping to be sent, he replied, 'Anywhere I can hit and kill terrorists.'

'Get yourself into the Special Forces, then,' his course mate said. 'If that's what you're looking for, that's the knife-edge.'

Mohit clinked glasses with him and said, 'That's the plan. I'll get there.'

He would need to wait only five months. In mid-2000, Mohit's unit was sent to the Poonch–Rajouri sector of Jammu and Kashmir to operate under the 38 Rashtriya Rifles (RR) counter-insurgency force. Thrown into one of the most challenging sectors along the LoC, he would frequently operate alongside officers and soldiers from the Army's Para Special Forces units. On foot patrols and reconnaissance missions, from high-altitude cordon-and-search missions to full-blown terror hunts, Lt Mohit would take to his duties with great eagerness. That eagerness would see him peel away the layers of counter-insurgency operations to discover the terrifying complexities he was being entrusted with.

Almost exactly two years into the Army, with over half of that time spent in Jammu and Kashmir, a piece of news exploded on the morning of 13 December 2001. Military intelligence reports streamed in from Delhi as five terrorists from the JeM and LeT breached security at India's Parliament House. They were stopped in their tracks only after a tense and extended firefight that killed nine Indians—six Delhi Police personnel, two Parliament Security personnel and a gardener. The terrifying assault, coming as it did just three months after the 11 September attacks in the United States, was the most insidious and shocking provocation from Pakistan's notorious state-sponsored terror instruments. It was, in effect, a call to war.

In Jammu and Kashmir, where Lt Mohit and thousands of Army personnel were deployed, an already volatile situation had just been violently escalated. The attack on Parliament triggered a massive five-month standoff between India and Pakistan, with enormous mobilization of troops, missiles, artillery, tanks and other weaponry to the LoC and the international border, the largest both countries had seen since they had gone nuclear three years earlier. India code-named the mobilization 'Operation Parakram'.

On the threshold of war, Lt Mohit and his unit were compelled to significantly crank up the tempo of their operations. The Poonch–Rajouri area was seeing major exchanges of fire across the LoC. The hostilities were also aiding the movement of terrorist infiltrators across and through these sectors, resulting in a significant increase in the need for patrolling and search operations.

On one such cordon-and-search operation (CASO) on the Poonch–Mendhar road in early 2002, as Mohit and a Special Forces Major took a break, Mohit asked the officer if he had a chance with the Special Forces. The officer's reply was all the validation he needed at the time.

'*Bhai, dekh* (Brother, look), I've seen absolute beasts of men come and fail to make the cut. And I've seen seemingly unimpressive guys come and nail it better than anyone. So what I'm saying is, there is only one way to find out.'

Weeks later, Mohit would receive his first recognition, a Chief of Army Staff commendation from the Army chief, General Sundararajan Padmanabhan, for leading a counter-insurgency operation in the Rajouri area. But the fight against terrorists was hardly being won. For every small victory, there was a body blow waiting around the corner.

A horrific reminder of how the flow of terror across the LoC hadn't been stopped by the massing of forces came on 14 May 2002. Three Pakistani terrorists infiltrated across the LoC, boarded a bus in Jammu's Vijay Pura, then went on to massacre Armymen and their families at their living quarters in Kaluchak. The dead included ten children (the youngest was four) and eight women, with a total of thirty-one killed. The attack would have a devastating effect on Mohit. On a phone call to a course mate in Chandigarh four days after the attack, he would say he had totally lost the ability to sleep, asking how the terrorists could bring themselves to fire at toddlers.

Then Prime Minister Atal Bihari Vajpayee would describe it as 'a most brutal and inhuman carnage'. If bad blood defined relations between India and Pakistan after Kargil and the Parliament attack, the Kaluchak massacre stirred India into a frenzy of disbelief and fury.

Operation Parakram would see military exchanges along the length of the frontier, but enormous restraint from India, diplomacy and a great measure of global pressure helped ease tensions, resulting in a gradual pullback of troops starting June 2002.

A year later, in June 2003, after being rejected in his first attempt due to an illness, Mohit, now promoted to Captain, was welcomed into the 1 Para Special Forces.

Brigadier Vinod Kumar Nambiar, then a younger officer with the unit and later its Commanding Officer (CO), remembers the time clearly.

'Mohit had come for Special Forces probation to 1 Para. He didn't get selected initially because he was unwell. And when we turned him away, he said he would be back. Normally, people give up. Probation *breaks* you. But Mohit recovered his strength and came back to the same unit again. So his feeling for 1 Para was very strong. He had the humility to come back despite being rejected in his first attempt. Any normal person would hesitate a bit about going back to the same unit for a probation attempt. He could have volunteered for another battalion, to avoid being rejected twice by the same people. To me, that was the determination aspect of it. Not afraid of failures and not afraid to come back to the same challenge. It also showed his love and affinity for 1 Para "*ki kuch bhi ho jaaye* (whatever happens), I will come back to the same unit."'

Getting to wear the maroon beret and *balidaan* ('sacrifice') badge for the first time would be a day of solemn reflection for Mohit, once the celebrations at his unit had died down. On a phone call home, his mother, Sushila, who had become used to worrying every day ever since her son was deployed in J&K, would now demand to know why he had felt the need to move into even more dangerous territory with the Special Forces. At that moment, Mohit had news he knew would calm his mother down—he was to report shortly to Chandimandir, the headquarters of the Army's Western Command on the outskirts of Chandigarh, to take charge as a Special Forces team leader. He was right. Sushila Sharma did exhale, but knew it was only a matter of time before he was sent back to Kashmir.

'You have finished your responsibility in Kashmir, Mohit,' his mother said. 'Why don't you seek a posting elsewhere now?'

In Chandimandir, Mohit met and fell in love with Captain Rishma Sareen, an officer with the Army Service Corps (ASC). Months into their relationship, in early 2004, Mohit would be summoned back to Kashmir. It was at this time that he would spend weeks planning a dangerous, deep-cover mission to kill the two dreaded Hizbul Mujahideen recruiters, Abu Torara and Abu Sabzar, near Shopian. The hair-raising mission would win him a Sena Medal, with a deliberately vague citation crafted to mask the true nature of what he had managed to achieve. The mission instantly became legendary.

'He did share that story with me a few weeks later, when he came to see me,' says Rishma, now a Lieutenant Colonel posted with an Army unit in Haryana. 'The story shocked me—it would have scared anyone. I asked him to please be careful. I mean, I knew for sure that he was very good at what he did. I knew he planned everything very well. He was very meticulous by nature. He was professionally very sound. So I didn't panic, but I did ask him to be careful.'

On 19 November 2004, Mohit and Rishma were married in Chandigarh. Two months later, with less than two years of Special Forces experience under his belt, Mohit was dispatched to Belagavi (previously Belgaum) in northern Karnataka for two years to serve as an instructor at the prestigious Commando Training Wing of the Infantry School there, followed by a two-year stint in Nahan in the hills of Himachal Pradesh, home base of the 1 Para unit and the Indian Army's Special Forces Training School (SFTS), the largest elite warfare training institute in the country. While there, he would drive every week to see his wife, who was posted at the Army base in Patiala, a little over two hours away by road. Mohit's parents had welcomed the idea of their son working at the two training schools. He had won two gallantry awards in J&K—surely he had nothing more to prove?

The training in Nahan was pointed in one direction, and one direction only—which his parents knew but dreaded. In October 2008, Mohit, now a Major, was summoned back to Kashmir, arriving on the threshold of one of the fiercest winters in decades.

Over the next five months, through steadily worsening weather, Maj. Mohit and his team of Special Forces men would prowl the countryside in the forbidding snow-blown stretches of northern Kashmir, operating alongside the RR as he had at the start of his career.

In spring 2009, when the snow had reluctantly begun to melt, Maj. Mohit and his team were at their base in Kupwara. It was the afternoon of 20 March. His buddy,[1] Havildar Rajeev Kumar, then twenty-two years old and holding the rank of Paratrooper, remembers it like it was yesterday.

'It's been more than ten years, but there are some things that you can never forget throughout your life,' says Havildar Rajeev. 'I remember the sequence of events very clearly. We were being briefed by our team leader, Maj. Mohit, at our

---

[1] The buddy system, which dates back to World War II, places officers and soldiers into pairs to enhance efficiency, bonding and lethality in combat. The system is based on the theory that camaraderie will amplify safety and combat effectiveness.

base in the Kupwara sector about an anti-terror operation to be conducted in Bangus Valley.[2] Mohit Sir had a solid network of informants and he had received some intelligence about terrorist activity in that area. We were deployed in Kupwara with 7 Sector, RR. While Maj. Sir briefed us, he got a call from the Sector Commander. We knew it was an important call because he cut the briefing short. The Sector Commander told Mohit Sir that a terror squad had crossed the LoC and was hiding in the dense Haphruda forest. Our team leader told us that the Bangus operation was no longer on and we would all be proceeding towards Haphruda instead.'

The team knew immediately that something big was unfolding at Haphruda. Every man in that briefing room was familiar with the tone and tenor of Maj. Mohit's voice. This was clearly something urgent, something that could not wait. The men didn't have all the details yet, but they knew they had been placed on quick reaction alert, which meant they were poised to leave their base within minutes of being asked to do so.

Tavor TAR-21 assault rifle

[2] Bangus Valley in Kupwara district is a stunningly picturesque sub-valley at 10,000 feet, rich in animal and plant life and sprawling sun-kissed meadows in the mountains. But for the security situation, this would count as an effortlessly beautiful tourist destination. Efforts are now on to build more infrastructure there.

'Within a few minutes of that call from the Sector Commander, we left our base at 3 p.m. and headed towards the headquarters of the 6 RR Battalion based at Vilgam,' says Havildar Rajeev. 'We always stay ready for operations and can launch within minutes. It was dinnertime, about 9 p.m., when we reached Vilgam. There were twenty-five of us, including Maj. Mohit.'

After reaching the 6 RR base, Maj. Mohit quickly met the CO of 6 RR, receiving a briefing on the infiltration and the operation he now needed to launch and lead. He then communicated the full picture to his team, including a situation report from the forest. An hour earlier, a team from 6 RR had spotted some terrorists in the Haphruda forest and fired at them—for the second time that day. The terrorists had managed to give their attackers the slip again and had ventured deeper into the darkness of Haphruda.

The reason Maj. Mohit's team had been called in was clear. It was to hunt down the terrorists that had escaped the 6 RR net. It was unclear how many terrorists there were in the group, and details about their movements remained sketchy at that point. The one thing they were told, beyond doubt, was that the terrorists had infiltrated into north Kashmir two days earlier, on 18 March.

A series of briefings followed that night, continuing till very late. Maj. Mohit's team then rolled out from Vilgam at 2.30 a.m., marching on foot towards the 6 RR's Alpha company base on an approach to the Haphruda forest. The men reached before dawn, at around 4 a.m., on 21 March. The RR men there knew that the Special Forces team was coming and were waiting for them. In the shadow of the looming Haphruda forest, Maj. Mohit met the 6 RR Alpha company commander, also an Army Major.

The 6 RR squad that had fired at the terrorists was from the Alpha company. Maj. Mohit and his men asked an officer

and two men from the Alpha company to take the Special
Forces team to the point where they had fired at the terrorists,
which was nearly 700 m inside the forest. He then told the
6 RR men to return to base, saying the operation would be
conducted from that point by the Special Forces team. Maj.
Mohit's team checked their weapons again before trudging
deeper into Haphruda.

Another soldier from Maj. Mohit's team, Naik Hajari Lal
Gurjar, holding the rank of Paratrooper at the time, recalls
how the next few hours played out.

'The sun had risen and was out in the skies, but the
Haphruda forest is so dense that sunlight doesn't reach the
ground in many of its parts,' says Naik Hajari Lal. 'It was a
deviously thick forest, offering a large number of hiding places
to terrorists. It was around 8 a.m. and it seemed like it was
the middle of the night. A few minutes later, we noticed
something. It was our first clue. We could see footmarks in
the snow. It had to be the terrorists. Mohit Sir asked us to be
very careful, watch every step we took, and scan every nook
and cranny around us.'

'*Woh jungle itna bada hai ki kuch pata nahin woh kahan chhupe
ho sakte the* (The forest was so vast that there was no way to tell
where they could have been hiding),' says Havildar Rajeev.
'The ground was covered in a sheet of snow at least two-and-
a-half feet deep. The entire squad halted as soon as we saw the
footprints.'

Maj. Mohit's team had been split into three squads by
this time, with eight men each. One man from the team had
been asked to remain at the 6 RR Alpha company base to
coordinate with the 1 Para Battalion headquarters in Srinagar,
in case additional forces were needed.

One squad was led by Maj. Mohit himself, along with his
buddy, Havildar Rajeev. The second squad was led by Naib

Subedar Uttam Chand with his buddy, Naik Hajari Lal, and the third was led by Havildar Rakesh. The second squad, led by Naib Subedar Uttam Chand, was ordered to deploy along an elevated ridge inside the forest, so it could keep an eye on the other two squads moving forward on lower ground and give them warning or cover, if required. The two squads, led by Maj. Mohit and Havildar Rakesh, followed the footsteps in the snow, moving forward as noiselessly as possible.

'The terrorists were moving very cleverly, most likely in single file,' says Havildar Rajeev. 'It appeared that the terrorists following the lead terrorist were deliberately stepping right into his footmarks and moving forward, so it was difficult to even guess how many terrorists we were hunting that day. A small thing, but a pointer to how well they were trained to evade us.'

Separated by a short distance, the two squads on lower ground trudged forward, crossing a ridge after a few minutes and halting. Maj. Mohit ordered the third squad to move quickly and hold that ridge, and then continued to move forward soundlessly. Every soldier in the forest that day remembers how silent it was that morning.

The men then hit a patch where the snow had melted, washing away further footprints. The trail they had been following ended abruptly. The men stopped, looking carefully in every direction for where the footprints could have moved to next.

'At that point, we got a call over the radio from the three men from 6 RR's Alpha company, who had earlier been asked by Mohit Sir to return before the Special Forces could take over the operation,' remembers Havildar Rajeev. 'All of us had radios, and all of us could listen to the conversation. The Major from 6 RR said that they had spotted footprints in the snow in another location inside Haphruda. So we linked up with the three men from 6 RR. Now we were two squads of sixteen men plus the three RR men, including their company commander. The third squad continued to move on higher ground to cover us. We again started following the footprints. But once again, we hit a dead end. There was no snow there, there was a small *nallah*[3] and the footprints just vanished.'

Just as the squads were deliberating about which direction to head in, there was a breakthrough.

The team's scout, Paratrooper Netra Singh, who was marching ahead of Maj. Mohit's squad, froze in his tracks and relayed a message over the radio that he had spotted two terrorists. He quickly added that the terrorists had spotted him too at virtually the same moment.

And then it began.

'Less than a second after Netra Singh radioed us about the two terrorists, our squad came under heavy automatic fire,' says Havildar Rajeev. 'Netra took a bullet straight to his forehead and collapsed to the ground. He was killed instantly, the first casualty of the operation. Nothing could be done. It was a headshot.'

In seconds, the intensity of the attack escalated, with bullets flying in from multiple directions now.

'It is hard to explain the intensity of that incoming fire,' says Havildar Rajeev. 'Bullets were flying all around us. They seemed to be coming from all directions. We all fell flat on our stomachs and took whatever cover we could. Someone took cover behind a tree, someone took cover behind a boulder. *Jo kuch bhi humein mila, humne ussi ke peeche cover le liya* (We took cover behind whatever we could find).'

---

[3] Nallahs are mini tributaries of rivers, more like small streams, common across Kashmir. They are commonly used by infiltrators as pathways for undetected movement.

It was 11 a.m., and it was clear that the terrorists were spread out ahead of the squads. The bullets were flying in from the front. Maj. Mohit ordered the men to engage the terrorists by approaching them from the right. The moment a pair of soldiers tried to crawl in that direction to take position, they were pushed back with heavy firing from the right. It was now abundantly clear that they weren't up against just one small group of terrorists.

An attempt to engage the terrorists from the left was met with a similar burst of pre-emptive fire. The terrorists knew exactly where the squads were. And the firing was becoming more accurate.

'*Jis tarah se hum par firing ho rahi thi, aisa lag raha tha ki terrorists ne humein gher liya hai* (The way we were coming under heavy fire, it seemed the terrorists had surrounded us),' says Havildar Rajeev, who was, at that time, crouched behind a tree a few metres away from his team leader. 'The pattern of firing made it clear that the terrorists had spread out in a semicircle, in a C-shape, ahead of us and that's why it appeared that bullets were coming in from all sides. They had formed an arc around 50–60 m away and all of them had AK-47s. So their guns were very effective at that range. They were terrorists trained military-style. It was obvious, given the way they brought us under fire.'

Then Maj. Mohit radioed Havildar Rakesh, who was leading the second ground squad, and told him to head left, try to get up on a ridge and engage the terrorists. The moment Havildar Rakesh headed in that direction with his squad, the terrorists started firing at them. His squad split into four buddy pairs and fired back at the terrorists with their Israeli Tavor TAR-21 assault rifles.

'In front of my eyes, Rakesh was hit by a burst of bullets in his thigh,' says Havildar Rajeev. 'His leg seemed to have been split open. He immediately removed his combat patka (the scarf that Special Forces men wear) and administered himself first aid to prevent excessive blood loss. And right through this he kept firing at the terrorists with one hand.'

With one man dead and another badly injured, Maj. Mohit quickly realized that their vulnerability had gone up several notches. Quickly assessing the situation, he decided that the squads needed to retreat a short distance to find protective cover, so they had a moment away from the line of fire to plan their counter-attack.

'The terrorists clearly had the better position,' says Havildar Rajeev. 'I asked Mohit Sir to move back and take cover, but he kept firing and said he would stay right there and engage the terrorists so that other squad members could move back and take cover. I said, "*Sahab, aap pehle cover lo. Main inko sambhalta hoon* (Sahab, you take cover first. I will handle them)." But Mohit Sir said, "*Main nahin, tum jao. Main last mein aaonga* (Not me, you take cover. I'll take cover in the end)."'

Havildar Rakesh's squad continued to return fire from halfway up the ridge. The squad on higher ground, led by Naik Subedar Uttam Chand, hadn't yet linked up with the two ground squads at that point. As Maj. Mohit provided cover fire to the squads pulling back, a bullet tore into his left arm. Havildar Rajeev watched as his team leader quickly tied his patka around the wound to prevent blood loss, and then resumed firing non-stop at the terrorists.

'I called out to him, saying, "Sir, pull back, let me check your wound." He replied, "Nothing has happened to me. I have only been shot in the arm, Rajeev. You keep firing and moving back till you have good cover. Don't worry about me. Don't stop firing."'

The sun was high in the sky by this time, but none of the men could see it.

'The idea was to get in the nallah and get cover as soon as possible,' says Havildar Rajeev. '*Netra Singh shaheed ho gaye the, Rakesh Sir ko kaafi goliyan lagi thi aur Mohit Sir bhi ghayal the* (Netra Singh was dead, Rakesh and Maj. Mohit were injured).'

Still firing from the front, Maj. Mohit ordered a soldier on his squad, Lance Naik Subhash Singh, to fire at the terrorists with his multi-grenade launcher (MGL). But just as the soldier positioned himself to fire the grenades, a bullet tore through his elbow, incapacitating him. There was no way he could effectively operate the weapon.

'Mohit Sir saw Subhash getting hit, ordered him to move back and took his MGL,' says Havildar Rajeev, who, by this time, had taken cover and was still firing at the terrorists. 'Mohit Sir then started firing the MGL at the terrorists. By now, his entire squad had taken cover. Mohit Sir fired six grenades from the MGL in the direction from where the maximum fire was coming at us. After that bombardment, the firing from the terrorists slowed down considerably. *Woh shaant ho gaye the. Firing bahut kamm ho gayi thi.* We didn't know it at the time, but the bombardment had killed four terrorists.'

As the smoke from the grenades cleared, Maj. Mohit crept back towards the rest of his men to finally take cover alongside them. Just as he was about to reach them, a bullet smashed into the left of his chest. His bulletproof vest provided protection in the front and back, but the sides remained vulnerable. The bullet tore right through him. He staggered a little, but stayed on his feet. Havildar Rajeev rushed to his team leader.

'I am fine, Rajeev, these are not serious wounds,' Maj. Mohit told his buddy. 'Keep firing at them. We cannot let them get away today.'

By this time, the squad deployed on higher ground reached the site of the firefight. Naik Hajari Lal, who was on that squad, saw a clearly injured Maj. Mohit leaning against a tree and firing at the terrorists without pause.

'Mohit Sir kept telling my squad *ki terrorists ko bhagne nahi dena. Upar se fire karo inn par* (that don't let the terrorists escape. Fire at them from your height). The only thought in his mind was that the terrorists should not escape. It appeared to us that there were around eight to ten terrorists, given the volume of incoming fire.'

Maj. Mohit had turned visibly pale from blood loss. But he didn't stop firing. And over the roar of the crossfire, the men could hear their team leader on the radio, his voice short of breath now, '*Firing rukni nahi chahiye. Hum issi ke liye SF* [Special Forces] *mein hain aur issi ke liye train karte hain* (Don't stop firing. We joined the SF [Special Forces] for this and this is what we train for day in and day out).'

Havildar Rakesh's squad then got their rocket launchers out and started firing at the terrorists, giving the soldiers a chance to climb higher up and assume what they hoped would be an advantageous position. Maj. Mohit had stopped firing by this time. He was sitting with his back against the tree he had taken cover behind.

'*Buri tarah woh ghayal ho gaye the* (He was grievously injured),' Havildar Rajeev says. '*Poore squad ko unhone wahan se nikala tha* (In that condition, he had helped the entire squad take cover).'

The situation was grim.

'Four commandos in our squad had been hit,' remembers Havildar Rajeev. 'Netra was no more, the man behind him was also injured, Subhash had been hit and Mohit Sir had taken bullets. Despite being so gravely injured, he kept firing for as long as he could, kept telling us not to leave cover, and keep engaging the terrorists. He just refused to stop.'

Minutes later, Havildar Rakesh would be killed in the crossfire. Attempts by the other soldiers to pull him to safety failed, because the terrorists were using his body as a trap—whenever somebody tried to crawl towards him, the terrorists would start firing to cause more casualties.

Maj. Mohit had gone completely still, but his eyes were open. Firing from the terrorists prevented the soldiers from reaching him.

'He kept saying, "*Meri injury normal hai* (My injury is normal)." He was only concerned about two things that day: that we should not take casualties, and that the terrorists should not get away. *Woh akhiri dum tak bas yehi bolte rahe,* "*Main theek hoon. Baakiyon ko dekho*" (He kept saying till the end that he was fine and asked us to take care of the other injured commandos). He ensured that every man on the squad had taken cover before he did.'

At 4 p.m., Havildar Rajeev managed to reach his team leader, still seated with his back to the tree, clutching his weapon. Maj. Mohit had bled out and wasn't breathing any longer. The magazine in his rifle was empty.

Along with Maj. Mohit and three from his squad, a total of eight Special Forces men were killed in the Haphruda operation, which continued for four more days, till 25 March. A total of twelve terrorists would be killed in the operation.

'He kept guiding us throughout that firefight. We didn't even know the exact extent of his injuries. He was just not bothered about his safety,' says Naik Hajari Lal. 'By late night, multiple squads from our unit had come down to Haphruda forest from different locations and cordoned off the entire area. Choppers were flying above us, looking for any patch where they could land to evacuate the injured commandos to hospital. But there was no place for the choppers to land in the dense forest.'

Havildar Rajeev and another soldier carried their team leader's body back to the 6 RR Alpha Company base.

'His body was still warm. I was hoping he would survive,' Havildar Rajeev says. 'It was not possible to think of him as dead. His back was on my back and the other man was holding his legs. There was no time for a stretcher. There was no time to check vital signs. His eyes were closed and he was unconscious. We carried him for over a kilometre. I kept thinking throughout that Mohit Sir had guided and protected us non-stop till he fell unconscious. Even after taking so many bullets, he was only concerned about us. *Unko humari life ki zyada chinta thi* (He was more worried about our lives). When I was carrying him, I just wanted to take him to the chopper as quickly as possible. He was taken straight to 92 Base Hospital in Srinagar. We returned to join our squad in the forest. We learnt only the next morning that Mohit Sir did not make it. Carrying Mohit Sir that day to the helicopter is the heaviest burden I have ever carried.'

Maj. Mohit's CO, Colonel Vinod Kumar Nambiar, had arrived and was monitoring the situation from an adjoining area.

'Mohit laid the foundation for the success of that five-day operation,' says Col. Nambiar. 'He had killed four terrorists himself with the MGL. Two or three more terrorists were also killed by his squad. Because of Mohit, the terrorists were unable to break away and run from the firefight. And by that time, we had positioned multiple teams. It was his decision to stay engaged even after so many injuries, because of which our boys were able to finish them off.'

Naik Hajari Lal says, 'Our squad was more furious than sad. We had to avenge Mohit Sir's death. If we were alive, it was because of him. In an intense firefight, it is difficult to remember or recall every detail, but his last order was that the terrorists should not escape. Those were his last words. And that was our only focus. I was with him till his last moments. He knew, perhaps, that it was his last firefight. But he kept motivating us till the very end. We kept thinking that Sa'ab is OK.'

'Had Mohit Sir not guided us and led us the way he did that day, perhaps I too would have returned home in a coffin,' says Havildar Rajeev, his eyes welling up. 'I was only twenty-two then. *Aakhiri saans tak unhone humein lead kiya ek sherdil commander ki tarah* (He led us till his last breath, just as a braveheart commander should).'

His CO cannot forget the reports he heard from the other soldiers after the operation.

'When three of his boys have died, he has also been hit, and he is sticking around, leading his men from the front and continuing to fight, it means a lot and it raises the morale of others; it motivates them. And him sticking around despite his injuries was precisely what motivated the other squads there.'

All twelve terrorists killed that day were Pakistani nationals from the LeT. The firefight with an elite Indian Army squad proved just how well-trained and armed the terrorists were. They had scale maps of the whole area on them—some better than the ones used by the security forces. They even had route maps.

'We lost eight men that day, some of the best trained men in the Indian Army. That can happen in battle. But how could it happen to someone like us, the 1 Para?' Col. Nambiar remembers wondering at the time. 'We had a sense of professional arrogance. How could we take such casualties? We are good, we are well-trained, we have worked hard, we have prepared for such scenarios, we have conducted some remarkable operations in Kashmir in the past. We knew we were very good. Against that background, when something like this happens, it was like, "How could this happen to us?"

I still think of it. I play it back in my mind very often. The terrorists were on a height. They had some advantage. I think they had a sharpshooter in their squad, someone with the ability of a sniper. That person took accurate shots. While the other terrorists were firing, this person was taking his time and picking his targets. Invariably, most casualties happened when they were trying to retrieve injured commandos. I think it was this guy who caused the maximum damage. I play the whole thing in my head over and over even now.'

When a message was transmitted to the 1 Para base camp informing them that Maj. Mohit had been hit and was sitting motionless, saying nothing, an officer at the camp remembers replying with disbelief.

'It was not possible to imagine him lying motionless,' he says. 'I kept asking the jawan to make sure, and then make doubly sure. How could Mohit be gone? But they replied, he isn't moving and he isn't saying a word. It took us a long time to accept this.'

At 1 a.m., just under 1000 km away in Ghaziabad, the phone rang at the Sharma residence. Maj. Mohit's father answered the call.

'Two officers were at the other end of the line, saying they wanted to visit us,' says Rajender Sharma. 'I woke Mohit's mother and shared this with her. She found it strange that Mohit's friends were coming over this late and that Mohit had not informed us. She felt there was something amiss. Then we called his wife, Rishma, who was in Patiala at the time. His colleague Maj. Bhaskar Tomar took the call, but didn't tell us, despite knowing what had happened. Half an hour later, the two officers arrived at our house. They shared the news with us eventually.'

Sushila Sharma lost consciousness when the two officers finally said the words. In Patiala, Mohit's wife, Maj. Rishma, had also fainted when she was told.

'The news was broken to me on the night of 21 March by his unit officers, accompanied by my formation officers,' says Maj. Rishma. 'They had come to my house. I went blank. I couldn't believe what I had heard. I fell unconscious. I was taken to the intensive care unit at the base hospital and was there all night. I was taken in an ambulance to Ghaziabad the next day, 22 March.'

Every 21 March, Maj. Mohit's unit observes a two-minute silence in his memory and of those who died with him.

'Everyone in the unit knows about that operation,' says Havildar Rajeev. 'He never made us feel he was our senior. He treated us as equals. In fact, that's the culture of 1 Para, officers and soldiers intermingle a lot. Eat together, live together, stay together, fight together.'

A decade since the operation, there isn't a Special Forces soldier who doesn't know about the Haphruda operation or the covert strike by Iftiqar Bhatt.

Lt Col Vikas Dhuria, Second-in-Command of the 1 Para Special Forces, says, 'I first met Mohit Sir when I was doing my probation with 1 Para Special Forces in 2004. People outside the unit may not know about it, but all of us in 1 Para Special Forces had heard about what he had done in Shopian, masquerading as a terrorist and killing two of them. It used to be a dream for us to conduct such an operation. It involved a lot of risk. Few can pull off something like that. I actually cannot think of anyone who could do so except Mohit.'

Maj. Shantanu Sinha, twenty-eight years old and currently adjutant of 1 Para (having joined the unit in 2012, three years after Mohit's death), says, 'The first thing that anyone joining 1 Para learns of is Maj. Mohit's gallant actions. One of the tasks for probationers is to find out about the major operations of the unit. His actions still motivate everyone in the unit.'

'In many incidents, you have a person suddenly becoming brave in the heat of the moment. In Mohit's case, it wasn't in the heat of the moment. It was repeated—he was brave each and every time. I will say it was in his grain,' says his CO at the time, Col. Nambiar. 'His bravery was there for all to see, and not just in the battlefield. It was visible during training and in other aspects also. That moral courage was remarkable and that physical courage was also remarkable.'

Speaking of the Iftikhar Bhatt operation, Naik Hajari Lal says, 'He could have easily died in that operation. We would not have been able to even find his body. But he still went in. *Bahut bada jigra tha unka. Itna dum rakhte the woh* (He had a big heart. He had a lot of courage). Nothing mattered more to Mohit Sir than operations. The moment he would get a lead or an intelligence input, he would be ready to launch an operation. *Sher ki tarah toot kar padte the ki chalo abhi, operation karte hain* (Like a lion, he would pounce at the opportunity and say, let's go, let's launch an operation). He believed in launching operations quickly. He was in Kashmir only to conduct operations. *Operation ke maamle mein shayad koi nahin hoga unke jaisa* (There might not be many like him when it comes to operations). He knew the area very well and had an excellent network of informants. *Agar source ka phone aaya toh Rishma ma'am ka phone woh rakh denge* (He would choose to speak to his source over Rishma ma'am).'

Maj. Mohit's buddy, Havildar Rajeev, says that the officer's story is incomplete without a mention of his guitar. 'Guitar *hamesha saath rakhte the. Unke haath mein ya toh Tavor hoti thi, ya guitar* (He would either be holding a Tavor in his hands or a guitar),' says Havildar Rajeev.

The men of 1 Para Special Forces also remember Maj. Mohit for a particularly morbid sense of humour. Naik Hajari Lal recalls how he had completed a medical course several months before the 2009 operation.

'*Mohit Sa'ab asked me kya grading aayi hai.* I said, *"Sa'ab, grading toh B hai."* He said, *"B toh theek hai par agar mujhe goli lagegi toh mujhe bacha lega na* (B grading is fine, but if I get shot, you will be able to save me, won't you)?"'

At 6.45 a.m. on 23 March, Maj. Mohit's body reached Ghaziabad, where his inconsolable mother, wife and father received him amid crowds from the locality and several more who had arrived to pay their respects. Later that morning, the officer's mortal remains were transported to the Brar Square crematorium in Delhi Cantonment, where, in the presence of senior officers from the Special Forces, his pyre was lit by his brother, Madhur, who had given up his plans to move abroad as a software engineer when Mohit had decided to join the Army.

A decade later, the wounds of their loss are still fresh for Mohit's parents.

'I can't hold back my tears when I talk about my Mohit,' says his mother, Sushila. 'He was such a wonderful and caring son. He left us ten years ago, but we feel his presence in every corner of our home. We have not stopped crying. All parents love their children. But the qualities he had, he was different. I find it very difficult to talk about Mohit even today. We are his parents and you can understand how we feel, having lost our loving boy at such a young age. We have lost everything. He had tremendous respect for us and he would stop associating with anyone if they had a bad word to say about his parents. There can be no one like Mohit. Yes, he made the country proud and served with honour and bravery, but nothing can heal the loss of a child. For a mother, the void left by the death of her child can never be filled. A son gone will never come back.'

Sushila Sharma looks at pictures of Mohit as a boy, and one of how his face had lit up when his parents had brought him a Casio keyboard from Nepal, a gift to encourage his love for music.

Mohit's father, Rajender Sharma, a retired employee of the Punjab National Bank, says, 'Our life has come to a standstill after Mohit left us. Nothing can fill the void he has left behind. We miss our son every moment of our lives. It's a wound that will never heal. My wife and I often talk about his childhood and go through our old photo albums. Mohit would always say that if he lived, he would rise to the rank of General, but if he was killed in action, he would earn the topmost gallantry award.'

On 15 August 2009, Maj. Rishma would receive her husband's posthumous Ashok Chakra, India's highest peacetime gallantry award, from Pratibha Patil, the then President. Rishma had last spoken to her husband the morning he died.

'It was a short call. He never told me about operations,' Maj. Rishma says. 'He would never disclose those things. He only said he would not be available on the phone for some time, and I understood he was out there doing what he liked most—conducting an operation. He was to come home on leave in a week's time, around the end of March. He had delayed his own leave as he wanted his team's officers and men to be able to visit their homes on Holi. He was very concerned about them. He used to consider them at par with family. He postponed his own leave. We had bought a house in Noida and were planning to take possession during Mohit's leave. These ten years have definitely been difficult. And every single day, I have thought of Mohit and missed him. I miss the songs he would sing to me with his guitar. His two favourites to sing to me were "*Pal pal dil ke paas*" and "*Pyar humein kis mod pe le aaya*". The love we had for each other gives me immense strength. He was the best. There can be nobody else like him. When you have been with the best, you just can't think of anything else. I miss him. He was a happy guy. The rage and aggression would surface only when he was conducting operations.'

'"*Pyar humein kis mod pe le aaya*" was Mohit's signature song,' says Maj. Shantanu Sinha of his unit. 'We still play it sometimes in his memory at our parties.'

Col. Nambiar, now a Brigadier and a decorated commando himself, says the Special Forces will never stop talking about Maj. Mohit Sharma.

'Loads of his friends keep meeting up and they come to me. We miss him. It is not about mourning his death, his sacrifice, it's about celebrating his life and his legacy. *Yeh nahin ki aankhon se aansoo nikal rahe hain, inspiration waali baat hai* (It's not that we shed tears, it's more to do with being inspired by his bravery). We stare into the eyes of death every day. It's like, Mohit has done such a great job, so how can we not do better and make him proud?'

Maj. Mohit's name and legacy have been preserved in many ways. Apart from the infinite recounting of his exploits within the Special Forces, a road and a metro station were named after him in Ghaziabad, and his family has established a trust that gives out scholarships and holds medical camps in his name each year.

'We in 1 Para rejoice that he walked this earth and he was one of us,' says Col. Surendra Singh Rajpurohit, current CO of 1 Para. 'Mohit will forever inspire 1 Para and the Indian Army. Men come and men go. Being remembered the way Mohit is is the ultimate honour for a soldier.'

Before he set out for the Shopian operation in March 2004, a soldier remembers hearing another officer call Mohit by his name. Mohit turned around, his bushy beard and hair covered in a checked scarf.

'*Mohit nahin, Sir, Iftikhar.*'

2

'He Avenged Them, Didn't He?'

Corporal Jyoti Prakash Nirala

Manasbal, Jammu and Kashmir
17 November 2017

The familiar tone of an incoming WhatsApp video call interrupted proceedings inside the darkened operations room at a secret Garud Special Forces base in Kashmir's Manasbal. The call was from three-year-old Jigyasa. In one corner of the room, a commando pulled out the phone from his pocket, looked at it furtively for a moment and then cancelled the call. Five hundred kilometres away in Chandigarh, the child would try to reach her father three more times over the next few minutes before giving up. She had to—he had switched his phone off.

There was no way Corporal Jyoti Prakash Nirala could have taken the call. He thanked technology every day for allowing him to video chat with his baby daughter, but that day, on 17 November 2017, Jigyasa had chosen to dial him when he was halfway through the most sensitive mission briefing of his life. The sort of briefing where there was no option to excuse himself even for a moment. He would speak to her later, after the briefing was done.

The dimly lit operations room, like most the Army used, had maps covering nearly all its walls. At one end stood Sqn Ldr Rajiv Chauhan, thirty-six, the oldest man in the room and CO of the IAF Special Forces unit, 617 Garud Flight. Facing him were eighteen commandos, each man listening intently as their boss shared a piece of fresh intelligence with them. Intelligence the unit had been awaiting for weeks.

'I've just received word that Osama Jungi and Mehmud Bhai have been tracked to a house in Chandargeer. It's a reliable input from one of our known guys. He has said we can launch a hunt immediately,' Sqn Ldr Rajiv told the men.

He didn't need to say the names twice. Every man in the room knew that Osama Jungi was special—if the blood that flowed through him was any measure, he was terror royalty. Jungi was closely related to India's most wanted Pakistani terrorist, Hafiz Muhammad Saeed, founder of the LeT and its front organization, the Jamaat-ud-Dawa. Known by the alias 'Ubaid' in Kashmir, Jungi was the son of Hafiz Saeed's brother-in-law, Abdul Rehman Makki, the LeT's second-in-command, and nephew of the LeT commander, Zakiur Rehman Lakhvi, a key Pakistani terror boss who helped organize the 26/11 attacks in Mumbai. Ajmal Amir Kasab, the lone terrorist captured alive in the Mumbai attacks, would later refer to Lakhvi during an interrogation as 'Chacha Zaki', a term of familiarity that established Lakhvi's role in the operation. For Osama Jungi, Lakhvi was an uncle related by blood.

The other man named in the briefing wasn't of high terror pedigree, but no less notorious—Mehmud Bhai was the LeT's north Kashmir commander. In classified lists of wanted terrorists in Kashmir, both names were high up on the first page.

Corporal Jyoti knew what every man in the room was thinking. Actually, for over a month, they had thought of little else.

Only thirty-seven days earlier, two men from their unit, Sergeant Khairnar Milind Kishor and Corporal Nilesh Kumar Nayan, had painstakingly tracked down and killed two senior LeT terrorist commanders in a brutal, brief eight-minute pre-dawn operation at Bandipora's Rakh Hajin village. It was an operation that would have tested the IAF in a never-before role, and its Garud commando force had only recently been deployed in counter-terror operations. At 4.40 a.m. on 11 October 2017, while Sergeant Milind fought and killed one of the surrounded terrorists at close range, even after being shot multiple times, his buddy, Corporal Nilesh, in an act of indescribable courage, took direct fire from the terrorists just so he could provide cover to his track leader. He killed the second terrorist before succumbing to his injuries.

The killing of these terrorists, Abu Bakar and Nassuralla Mir, had come at the heaviest price imaginable for the Garuds—both soldiers returned to their villages the next day in flag-draped coffins. Both would later be posthumously awarded the country's third-highest peacetime gallantry award, the Shaurya Chakra. Milind would be decorated for displaying 'bravery of the highest order in leading the attack', while Nilesh would be commended for having displayed 'extreme valour and the highest order of camaraderie with total disregard to personal safety'. Their partnership and sacrifice would serve as a reminder of what it meant to be 'blood brothers', a phrase that's just a cliche outside the military.

Since then, not a moment had passed when the men of 617 Garud Flight hadn't wanted revenge on the LeT.

'The operation that we are about to launch could be one of the biggest we Garuds have undertaken in Kashmir,' the CO told his men. 'Milind and Nilesh are gone because of these people. It's time to make them fear the Garuds and show them what we are capable of.'

No detail was spared during that hour-long briefing. Every patch of the layout of Chandargeer, the village the two terrorists were said to be in—the number of houses, count of inhabitants and the approach that the squad would take—were all laid out on a series of projected images on a screen. Not that the commandos were not familiar with Chandargeer— it had been on their radar since the 11 October operation, which involved not just the Garuds, but also the Army's 9 Para Special Forces and two units of the counter-insurgency force, the RR.

The unit had actually been on the hunt for Osama Jungi and Mehmud Bhai long before the fatal Rakh Hajin operation. Both terrorists had managed to give the Garuds and their counterparts in the Army's Special Forces units the slip on a number of occasions, reinforcing the superiority of the LeT's formidable on-ground intelligence and its local network, enforced as much with ideology and radicalization as with threats of violence to families. The deaths of their two comrades had energized the Air Force unit's hunt. When their CO revealed that the terrorists' locations had finally been reliably tracked to Chandargeer, every man in that room was thinking of payback.

Corporal Jyoti certainly was. A week after the loss of Milind and Nilesh, he would proceed on leave for Diwali to see his family in Chandigarh. Over three days, he spoke of virtually nothing else, remembers his wife, Sushma Nand.

'Jyoti surprised us by landing up at home on Diwali, 19 October,' says Sushma. 'I immediately sensed that he was a changed man, shaken by the loss. He showed us pictures of Milind and Nilesh and talked endlessly about them. He was in a very emotional state and couldn't hold back his tears. He wanted to get even, but he was just in deep mourning. They lived and worked like brothers.'

Nudged by his wife, Corporal Jyoti would change the subject and put on a happy face when Jigyasa accosted him for stories, always with an endless barrage of questions about his work. They had named her prophetically—'Jigyasa' means curiosity, inquisitiveness.

'I could tell that it was very difficult for him to come to terms with the loss,' says Sushma. 'It was Diwali and we were spending happy times with our extended family. But Jyoti was a broken man. I would find him awake in the middle of the night, in tears. He would tell me that nothing was going to console him except getting even. What could I say to that?'

A month later, Jigyasa would wonder why her father wasn't accepting her incessant WhatsApp video calls. Her mother assured her that her father was probably busy and would probably call later that evening.

Walking back to his barracks from the operations room, Corporal Jyoti switched his phone back on, immediately tapping WhatsApp open and placing a video call to his wife's phone. Jigyasa answered in a second.

'*Papa, aap ghar kab aaoge? Mujhe nayi kahani kab sunaoge* (Papa, when will you come home? When will you tell me a new story)?' the little girl asked straightaway.

'*Main jaldi aaonga, beta. Mujhe subah chaar baje uthna hai. Aap ko bhi ab so jaana chahiye* (I will come soon. I have to wake up at 4 a.m. It's your bedtime too),' said Corporal Jyoti, convincing his daughter after several minutes to hand the phone to her mother.

'He sounded tired but alert,' says Sushma. 'He said he had an early start. We spoke for barely two minutes and then said goodnight.'

Corporal Jyoti and the eighteen men of 617 Garud Flight barely managed three hours of sleep that night. Before first light the following day, they were at the high-security base of 13 RR.

Attached to the Indian Army's 13 RR, the Garuds had arrived in Kashmir three months earlier for a six-month tour of duty, the first such IAF ground deployment in a counter-terror role in the Kashmir Valley in more than a decade. Corporal Jyoti had volunteered to join the Garud Commando Force in 2006 when he was twenty years old and just a year into service in the Air Force, enlisting from his village of Badladih in Bihar's Rohtas district.

The Garuds had been raised in 2004 as a specialized force to protect airfields, IAF bases and sensitive establishments, though their role and spectrum of responsibilities has widened and evolved since then. Garud units have begun training for offensive strikes, much like the Army's Para Special Forces, been deployed on UN Peacekeeping missions abroad, assisted in humanitarian operations and, as of 2017, with the unit in question, been inserted into the Kashmir Valley for counter-terror operations. Corporal Jyoti had been handpicked by Squadron Leader Chauhan.

More detailed briefings followed at the 13 RR base in Manasbal, and it was decided that two combat teams would take part in the daytime operation to hunt down Osama Jungi and Mehmud Bhai. An eleven-man Garud squad was formed to be led by Sqn Ldr Rajiv, and another eleven-member 13 RR team was to be commanded by an Army Major.

As it happened, the 18 November operation that was about to unfold had tangible links to the previous month's encounter in Rakh Hajin, in which Milind and Nilesh had died after killing Abu Bakar and Nassuralla Mir. Seized mobile phones, documents and intercepted phone calls of terrorists injured in that firefight had all pointed in one direction—Chandargeer in Bandipora.

Two rickety civilian trucks trundled out of the 13 RR base that afternoon, moving at an unhurried pace towards Chandargeer. The first truck, covered with yellow tarpaulin, carried the eleven Garud commandos. Their CO sat in the front passenger seat wearing a phiran, a traditional loose Kashmiri garment, to conceal his camouflage battle fatigues. All the men sported beards of varying thickness.

Corporal Jyoti had been quietly pensive since the day began. In the truck, he spoke, '*Aaj Milind aur Nilesh ka badla lena hai* (We have to avenge the deaths of Milind and Nilesh today),' he whispered to Sergeant Sandeep Kumar, the commando sitting next to him. '*Bahut intezaar kiya hai. Jitne zyada terrorists milen, utna hi accha hai* (We have waited too long for this. The more terrorists we find, the better).'

Sergeant Sandeep nodded, the barrel of his fully-loaded, standard issue, Israel-made Tavor TAR-21 assault rifle pointing towards the truck's floor. Corporal Jyoti was holding the deadliest weapon the squad was carrying that day, an Israel-made Negev light machine gun (LMG), with an attached ammunition belt that held 150 rounds.

In the second truck was the RR squad. The two trucks kept a distance of 100 m between them on the 30-minute drive to Chandargeer. It was crucial that they maintained some distance between them because the village sat on a knoll, and any movement could be spotted from 2 km away. The trucks were handpicked to minimize suspicion, since such vehicles regularly plied the roads in the area, including in Chandargeer, hauling timber from sawmills.

The Garud squad had done its homework well before their CO had received the intelligence input that had set them on course for Chandargeer. A few houses in the village had been under surveillance by the Garuds for several days, with reconnaissance patrols sent out regularly to collect information about terrorist movement. The patrolling teams had taken photographs and videos to acquaint the squad with the likely target area.

'Dressed in civvies, my men had managed to gather intelligence both from vehicles and on foot,' says Sqn Ldr Rajiv. 'The last recce was on 14 November. My men had walked the nooks and crannies of Chandargeer, which has around 200 houses and 1500-odd inhabitants. When our ground contact phoned me with intelligence of the whereabouts of Osama Jungi and Mehmud Bhai, it basically confirmed what we had suspected.'

Not for a second doubting the reliability and trustworthiness of his source, Sqn Ldr Rajiv still decided to corroborate the information he had received. Counter-terrorism specialists in the Kashmir Valley know that nothing is of greater significance than accurate and detailed intelligence. And given that the input was coincidentally about the very terrorists the unit had been hunting, the CO needed to be absolutely sure that he wasn't leading his men into a death trap.

The effort to cross-check the intelligence input paid off in a critical way. Shortly before the squads left the base in their trucks, a fresh intelligence input landed, indicating that Osama Jungi and Mehmud Bhai were not alone in the target area— at least four other LeT terrorists had joined them there. The encounter would now be against six highly trained terrorists, instead of two. While the intelligence was useful in confirming the presence of the two senior LeT commanders, it also made the men realize that the operation ahead would be dramatically more difficult than they had anticipated.

When the Garud squad had piled into their truck, their CO had exhorted them with, 'We have a chance to eliminate the top LeT leadership in one go. It doesn't get better than this. And this time, we are doing this without taking any casualties. *Hum badhiya operation karenge* (We will conduct a good operation).'

The teams were to be launched from the base at 1 p.m., but their departure was rescheduled as the squad leaders factored in the possibility of the terrorists going to the village mosque for afternoon prayers.

'We thought, let the afternoon prayers be done, let them have their lunch and allow them some rest. That's when we will strike,' says Sqn Ldr Rajiv.

The trucks rumbled past a gently rising and falling landscape studded with poplar trees, the serene Bandipora countryside belying the dangerous work on the path ahead. A commando in the truck quipped, 'Bandipora is famous for its three As—*a'lim* (knowledge), *adab* (good habits) and *aab* (water). But we are more interested in a different 'A' today—Category A++ terrorists!'

Conversation remained sparse on the 30-minute drive to Chandargeer. If any man spoke, it was about the mission that was about to begin.

'*Jitne zyada terrorists milein, utna hi accha hai* (The more terrorists, the better),' said another commando in the truck, Corporal Devendra Mehta, echoing his buddy Corporal Jyoti's words.

Arriving at Chandargeer at 3.27 p.m., the trucks rumbled slowly past a few houses in the village before rolling to a halt a short distance from where the terrorists were believed to be hiding. The two teams quietly climbed out of their trucks and approached a cluster of six houses that had to be cordoned off to prevent anyone inside from getting away.

Sqn Ldr Rajiv and the 13 RR Army Major quickly organized their twenty-two men into a wide cordon around the cluster of homes. Corporal Jyoti and Corporal Devendra were positioned at a spot that their CO felt would be the route most likely to be used by any terrorist looking to escape. Just how many terrorists were hiding in that cluster would be revealed minutes later, but with the cordon, all escape routes were now effectively blocked.

'We wasted no time and immediately took our positions,' says Sqn Ldr Rajiv. 'These positions concealed us from the terrorists' possible line of sight and provided us cover from any incoming fire. The chances of getting hit are the highest when a cordon is being laid. But once you have settled into your positions, you are likely to be relatively safe.'

The CO had scanned the target site as best he could before the cordon was laid. An effective cordon demands that soldiers have the best possible view of what they've cordoned off, with as much of the target area visible as possible, while still providing protection from outbound fire. It's a delicate, difficult balance that goes way beyond simply surrounding a house. A cordon that relies too much on providing cover to the troops deprives them of a view of the target, and exponentially increases the chances of the target's escape. Too little cover makes troops vulnerable to terrorists, who get to fire accurately from the protected confines of a house.

'It was critical for me to make sure that my Garuds could acquire targets with ease,' says Sqn Ldr Rajiv. 'I wanted my men to have the best field of fire to take the terrorists out quickly. If the terrorists were to take the escape route I thought they would, they would most certainly run into Nirala and Mehta.'

The cordon established, the men lay in wait. The two squads had moved stealthily to take position around the cluster of homes, but none of the men was depending very much on the element of surprise. It was almost certain that if the terrorists were indeed inside one of the houses, they were likely to have been tipped off by their contacts in the village. The LeT's human intelligence network remains without par among foreign terrorist organizations operating in Kashmir.

The men didn't have to wait long. The first rounds were fired less than sixty seconds after the cordon was laid. And they came from an AK-47 inside one of the houses. As those first bullets came flying, an ironic sigh of relief passed through the cordon. It was confirmed now that the intelligence they had received was accurate. The terrorists knew they had been surrounded and, as expected, had decided to put up a fight.

The 13 RR team was tightening its cordon at around 3.40 p.m. when a figure emerged in a flash from the rear door of one of the houses, lunged towards the soldiers with his assault rifle and directed a fully automatic spray of ammunition at them. In seconds, a Garud commando cut him down with a hail of return fire. He crumpled to the ground, motionless. How many more terrorists were holed up in the cluster was still unclear at this point. But if their intelligence was 100 per cent accurate, there were at least five more inside. The cordon slowly tightened.

Ninety seconds after the first terrorist was gunned down, five men leapt out of the same house, each one of them firing their weapons at the Garud and RR men, who were barely 20 m away. Two of the terrorists were also firing from under-barrel grenade launchers (UBGLs) attached to their rifles. So in addition to the spray of bullets came the deadly explosion of grenades, with shrapnel flying in every direction.

The bullets flew inches above their heads, making a distinct *crack* sound. Corporal Jyoti and his buddy had a split-second to dive for cover as one of the grenades exploded dangerously close to them. The sound of gunfire now filled the air in Chandargeer.

Negev light machine gun

The five terrorists quickly grouped together and began moving in a single file towards the position held by Corporal Jyoti, their fire focused in every direction so they could approach unchallenged. Jyoti and Corporal Devendra were the first commandos to engage the advancing terrorists in close-range combat because of where they were stationed. Their CO had been right—the terrorists had chosen precisely the path he thought they would to make a break and escape.

From his position, Corporal Jyoti watched the terrorists, now just over 10 m away and advancing. In moments, they would be within breathing distance. How many times had he heard of situations like these, when small groups of terrorists had used heavy and indiscriminate fire to fight their way out of a cordon and escape? Milind and Nilesh flashed through his mind as he wondered if the opportunity for revenge was seconds away from slipping out of his hands. He turned to look at his buddy Garud. Their eyes met for a moment. And then, Corporal Devendra watched as his fellow Garud did something entirely unexpected.

Corporal Jyoti suddenly sprang up, abandoning the safety of his cover. He had decided to head straight into the advancing line of terrorists.

'I remember Jyoti's eyes just before he stepped forward,' says Corporal Devendra. 'They were blazing with fury. He had made up his mind. Nobody could have stopped him.'

Corporal Jyoti charged at the terrorists with his LMG. This was a weapon capable of firing a stunning 150 rounds per minute. Expending the 150 rounds the belt was holding that Saturday afternoon would take mere seconds once the trigger was pulled.

'What are you doing, Jyoti?' Corporal Devendra screamed. 'Don't lose your cover! Come back!'

But, as his buddy had correctly observed, Corporal Jyoti had made up his mind. With the terrorists in his direct line of sight and a perfect field of fire, the commando tightened his hold on the handle of his machine gun and rained down multiple 5.56 mm rounds at them with a single trigger squeeze. A few metres to his right was his CO.

'Tck tck tck tck tck tck—all I could hear was the rat-a-tat of his LMG fire,' says Sqn Ldr Rajiv. '*Woh fire karta jaa raha tha. Bas karta jaa raha tha. Woh nazara kuch aur tha* (He just kept firing non-stop. That sight was something else).'

The nearest terrorist in the advancing group was unmistakably Osama Jungi. The men had seen his picture in a woollen cap and sleeveless olive-green T-shirt, smiling at the camera. Now, he wore a dark grey phiran over an olive-green garment. Wrapped around his neck was a checked black and grey scarf. The nephew of the 26/11 mastermind, Zakiur Rehman Lakhvi, was firing in short bursts from his AK-47 as he stepped towards Corporal Jyoti.

Refusing to move from the line of fire, fearing he would lose his chance to cut them down, Corporal Jyoti returned fire, pumping a hail of shots directly into Jungi's chest, sending him crashing to the ground. It was the sixth minute of the firefight, and the Garuds had got the man who had given the security forces the slip at least a dozen times before.

Watching Jungi collapse, the four other terrorists stopped in their tracks, now vulnerable and exposed. Corporal Jyoti could have retreated at this point to his position of cover. He decided not to, most likely because he believed that if he stepped away now, the remaining terrorists would find an opportunity to escape.

Corporal Jyoti had expended half his ammunition in the initial burst, but he still had enough left. Corporal Devendra watched in silence as he saw his buddy step towards the remaining terrorists.

'Cover me,' he shouted, advancing to close the few metres that separated him from the terrorists. As the crossfire erupted again, he got a fleeting glimpse of one of the terrorists. Once again, a flash of familiarity—it was Mehmud Bhai. Unlike Jungi, though, the LeT's north Kashmir commander was in Army-like battle fatigues, a common ruse used by terrorists to evade capture.

Stumbling over Jungi's bullet-ridden body lying in front of him, Mehmud opened fire at Corporal Jyoti, his bullets missing their target by bare inches. Before the terrorist could regain his balance and fire another burst, the Garud commando let loose a spray of machine gun rounds straight into him, throwing him off his feet.

Less than three minutes apart, the names of two of the most wanted terrorists in Kashmir had just been struck off the hit list at Chandargeer. But the operation was far from over.

Half of the six-man terror squad had been eliminated. Two of the remaining three terrorists behind Mehmud Bhai had suffered grave injuries in Corporal Jyoti's relentless machine gunfire. Unable to hold out against the advancing commandos and running out of ammunition, the three scampered for cover into a ditch a few metres to their right. They were now out of sight.

Once again, Corporal Devendra called out, pleading with Corporal Jyoti to wait until his buddy could reach him. It was clear that there was no stopping Corporal Jyoti, though. He turned around momentarily, the faintest smile on his face, which was glistening with sweat.

'He said nothing, he just looked at me. And I understood. He had avenged Milind and Nilesh. Jyoti had made his peace even before it happened,' says Corporal Devendra.

Sqn Ldr Rajiv screamed from the right, asking Corporal Jyoti to slow down, to wait until his buddy could reach him. The commando stepped forward towards the ditch, his machine gun blazing. It was then that one of the terrorists popped up for a fleeting second to fire a burst straight at the advancing Garud.

One of the bullets hit Corporal Jyoti in the head. As he fell to the ground, the machine gun in his arms kept firing, his finger still squeezed around the trigger.

'I remember the moment so clearly,' says Corporal Devendra. 'The LMG was still firing when Jyoti fell. I can never forget that.'

On that grassy patch under a winter sun, Corporal Jyoti breathed his last.

'I saw it with my own eyes,' says Sqn Ldr Rajiv, who, by this time, had advanced and called for Corporal Jyoti's buddy to join him in the front. 'That sort of courage is almost impossible. I had never seen anything like that in my life. And perhaps, I never will. Few men can match that kind of grit. I am not exaggerating when I say it was an honour for every man in my squad to fight alongside Jyoti that day.'

'*Pata nahin uske dimaag mein kya chal raha tha us din* (I don't know what was going on in his head that day),' says Sqn Ldr Rajiv. 'The mission had become an obsession for him. He was completely transformed in those minutes. He didn't feel the need for self-preservation. He had heard a call from above, maybe for Milind and Nilesh.'

The operation was not over. The three terrorists in the ditch were still firing at the Garuds, emboldened now after felling the machine-gunner who had torn Osama Jungi and Mehmud Bhai to shreds. Their ammunition running out, they were now desperate to take out a few more soldiers before the inevitable.

Dodging direct fire, Corporal Devendra dashed forward from his position to drag away Corporal Jyoti. As he moved, he remembers hoping his buddy was somehow still alive. Corporal Jyoti's eyes were still open, still blazing, he remembers. Dragging him to a point outside the arc of the terrorists' fire, Corporal Devendra looked down at his buddy, reaching down to close his eyes. He set down his TAR-21 rifle next to Corporal Jyoti's body and grabbed his buddy's machine gun. There were no more than ten rounds left, a single brief burst of ammunition. The weapon pointed, Corporal Devendra rushed towards the ditch at high speed, spraying the last remaining bullets in the ammunition belt straight at the terrorists with a scream.

At that same moment, Sqn Ldr Rajiv aimed heavy fire at the terrorists and lobbed hand grenades into the ditch. There was no way the three could have survived that final onslaught. Twelve minutes after the first shots were fired by Osama Jungi, the encounter was over.

Twelve minutes.

In the two-hour mopping-up operation that followed, the Garuds followed standard operating procedure, taking headshots of each of the fallen terrorists from close range to make sure they were dead. Two of the three dead men in the ditch were LeT commanders Abu Qital and Abu Zargam.

'I keep thinking what could have happened had the encounter stretched on,' says Sqn Ldr Rajiv. 'It was because of Nirala's otherworldly courage that we were able to finish off the terror squad. He saved many lives by refusing to back down. I watched him throughout that operation. There was a total absence of fear. He was fully at peace with what he was doing.'

With the encounter complete, the men loaded Corporal Jyoti's body into one of the trucks and returned to base. Six senior terrorists, including a family member of the LeT's leadership, had been eliminated that afternoon, a stupendous feat for a unit so new to counter-terror operations. But there would be no celebration. The men were in mourning. The CO of 617 Garud Flight knew the loss would never leave his mind. It was the second big blow to the Garuds in just over a month.

'An operation is good if you don't suffer any casualties. We killed six terrorists, but the bottom line is we lost Jyoti. I will have to live with it. It wasn't a victory for us. A man I had trained for years was lost on my watch,' he says.

The 18 November operation will go down in the Garuds' short history as their finest hour yet. A little over two months later, the government announced India's highest peacetime gallantry award posthumously for thirty-one-year-old Corporal Jyoti, the IAF's first Ashok Chakra in combat. Only two other IAF men had been decorated with the top honour before him: transport pilot Flt Lt Suhas Biswas in 1952 and Sqn Ldr Rakesh Sharma (later Wing Commander) in 1984. Biswas was decorated with the Ashok Chakra for averting a mid-air disaster by belly-landing his burning de Havilland Devon aircraft, which had the Indian Army's top leadership on board, while Rakesh was awarded for being the first Indian in space on board the Russian spacecraft Soyuz T-11.

When Sqn Ldr Rajiv made the dreaded phone call to Corporal Jyoti's wife, Sushma paused for a few moments. Then, faltering, she spoke, 'He avenged Milind and Nilesh, didn't he? Then Jyoti has gone happy,' she said, before breaking down.

The commando's flag-draped casket would be flown that evening to Chandigarh, where a weeping but calm Sushma would salute his remains. Jigyasa would be kept away from the airfield. The next morning, she and her mother would board a flight with Corporal Jyoti's coffin to Bihar, where the commando's inconsolable mother and silent, stoic father waited with crowds of mourners.

On Republic Day 2018, in a pink fur-lined jacket, Jigyasa would be held aloft by her two grandfathers as Corporal Jyoti's wife and mother, Malti Devi, were escorted to the central dais to receive Corporal Jyoti's posthumous Ashok Chakra from President Ram Nath Kovind. As the two women were escorted away, cameras would zoom in to find that the President had broken down, wiping away tears with a handkerchief.

Sushma, now thirty-four, will never forget a moment of that cold January morning. 'I was trying hard to hold back my tears, but eventually broke down,' she says. 'I kept thinking that Jyoti should have been there on the dais to receive his medal. The country is proud of him, but imagine our joy had he been alive to receive the medal himself,' says Sushma, herself the daughter of a retired Army Subedar.

Married for six years, she remembers how life had changed completely in the month after Sergeant Milind and Corporal Nilesh were lost in combat.

'He would always tell me to be independent, but after Milind and Nilesh were killed, something just snapped in Jyoti,' says Sushma. 'He was permanently distracted and restless. He loved us and gave us time every single day. But I could tell that his mind was constantly troubled by their deaths. He was looking for peace. Even in that state he would reassure me that things were not as bad as I was imagining.'

Sushma remembers the day the two commandos were killed in October. Hours later, her husband had video-called her, fully aware that the news on television would have terrified the families of Garuds spread across the country.

'We were all panic-stricken as we didn't know what was going on in Kashmir,' says Sushma. 'The Garuds were launching operations every day. I received a video call from him on the night Milind and Nilesh died. He said, "Look at me. I am absolutely fine. Stop panicking unnecessarily." But he was saying that only to calm us down. He himself was shattered, though he had no choice but to be strong.'

If there was one thing that Sushma and Jigyasa looked forward to, it was those video calls. The WhatsApp video call tone became the sweetest sound in a barracks room in Manasbal and in a small Air Force quarter in Chandigarh.

Corporal Jyoti's call on the night of 17 November was his last. Rebuffing his daughter's incessant calls earlier, he had remembered to call back before turning in.

'How was I to know that I would never hear his voice again?' says Sushma. 'I so wish we had spoken a bit longer that night. He said his Kashmir deployment would end on 17 January 2018 and he would be back with us. *Main bahut khush thi ki bas doh mahine ki baat hai* (I was very happy that it was a matter of only two months).'

Sushma remembers how ecstatic her husband had been when he was deployed to Kashmir for the first time early in 2017. His dream to do something real for the country had come true, she says. In their final call, Corporal Jyoti made no mention of the big operation planned for the next day at Chandargeer.

Hours after the Republic Day ceremony, Sushma and Corporal Jyoti's father, Tej Narayan Nirala, would remember him live on a television news channel.

'*Itihas racha hai mere pati ne. Mujhe aur desh ko garv hai in par. Woh hamesha mujhe bolte the ki desh ke liye kuchh karna hai. Bahut bahadur the mere pati* (My husband made history. The country and I are proud of him. He always told me he wanted to do something for India. He was incredibly courageous),' Sushma would tell the channel, fighting back tears.

'Nobody can alleviate our pain. But we are immeasurably proud of Jyoti. He truly believed in country above all else,' the commando's father had said.

Corporal Jyoti's Ashok Chakra citation says he demonstrated 'exceptional battle craft' as he positioned himself near the terrorist hideout, cutting off all possible escape routes. Laying such an ambush at close quarters, the citation says, demanded exceptional courage and professional acumen.

It added: 'While the detachment was lying in wait, six terrorists rushed out, shooting and lobbing grenades at the Garuds. Corporal Jyoti, disregarding personal safety and displaying indomitable courage, retaliated with lethal fire and gunned down two Category "A" terrorists and injured two others. In this violent exchange of fire, Corporal Jyoti was hit by a volley of small arms fire. Despite being critically injured, the Corporal continued retaliatory fire. Subsequently, he succumbed to fatal gunshot wounds received in the fierce encounter, which resulted in the killing of all six dreaded terrorists.'

The commando's buddy, Corporal Devendra, and CO, Sqn Ldr Rajiv, would also be decorated with gallantry awards for their actions during the Chandargeer firefight, receiving the country's third-highest peacetime gallantry award, the Shaurya Chakra, and a Vayu Sena Medal for gallantry, respectively.

The Shaurya Chakra for Corporal Devendra recognized his fearless role in the operation, his choosing to disregard his own safety to remove the body of his fallen buddy. Terrorist Abu Qital had fallen to a bullet fired by Corporal Devendra during the firefight. 'To counter other advancing terrorists, he readjusted his arc of fire and provided cover to the LMG man, fully aware of the risk of being exposed to automatic gunfire. Disregarding personal safety, he displayed indomitable courage while assisting in the evacuation of his buddy, Corporal Jyoti, who was critically injured in the gunfight,' reads Corporal Devendra's citation. It also mentions the heroic final act, when the Corporal picked up his fallen comrade's machine gun and charged at the remaining terrorists.

Sqn Ldr Rajiv's citation credits him for being directly responsible for the killing of Abu Zargam, a Category 'A' terrorist and a key Lashkar frontman in north Kashmir. It says the officer exhibited 'indomitable courage and admirable leadership' during the 'intensely fought close quarter battle.'

On Air Force Day on 8 October 2018, the 617 Garud Flight was awarded the Air Chief's citation for outstanding performance in counter-terrorism operations in Kashmir.

'I am the Jyoti Prakash of the family now,' says Sushma, who lives with Corporal Jyoti's parents and sisters in the IAF quarters allotted to them in Chandigarh. 'I have to take care of everyone the way he would have.'

It was Corporal Jyoti's dream to see Jigyasa join the IAF, perhaps as a doctor. He would fondly address her as 'Dr Jigyasa Kumari', hoping to instil ambition in the little girl.

'*Jigyasa ko doctor banna padega har keemat par,*' says Sushma, smiling. '*Unka yeh sapna toh poora karna hai* (Jigyasa will have to become a doctor at any cost. This dream of his has to be fulfilled).'

Sushma herself aspires to join the IAF as a short-service commissioned officer. She is above the age one needs to be to pursue a career in the service, but the military is known to relax rules for widows of men killed in the line of duty.

Jigyasa, fortunately too young to fully understand where her father is, often tells her friends that he has taken his trolley bag and gone away on duty for a long time.

'She is the spitting image of him,' Sushma says. 'She knows the truth, but she's too young to process it. I will tell her everything when she's older and has her father's strength. She already does, in many ways. I pray that no one has to face such a situation. It is very difficult to live without him. We miss him every second of our lives. He surprised us by coming home on Diwali in 2017. Even on Diwali in 2018, I was hoping he might surprise us again by some miracle. It's that hard to believe that he's gone.'

'*Agar kissi baat ki khushi hai toh bas yeh ki unhone badla le liya* (If I am happy about one thing, it's that he avenged the death of his comrades). I know Jyoti must be smiling from above hearing me say this,' she says.

Hoping to ease her daughter into the truth, Sushma has begun telling Jigyasa a tale of how her father left the world to meet his two close friends, Milind and Nilesh. Jigyasa listens rapt, with her usual barrage of questions.

Sushma doesn't know yet how to finish the story.

3

'Fire when You Can See Their Faces'

Lieutenant Navdeep Singh

Gurez, Jammu and Kashmir
18 August 2011

'*Woh kya kar rahe hain? Dikhai de raha hai?* (What are they doing? Can you see anything?)'

Fifteen minutes before midnight, on 19 August 2011, the soldier focused his night-vision device, the circular view it captured glowing a techno-green, his hushed whisper sharp with disbelief, '*Kuchh inflate kar rahe hain* (They're inflating something)!'

Standing on the west bank of a bend in the Kishenganga River, barely a kilometre from the LoC in north Kashmir's Gurez sector, both men were looking in precisely the same direction, their battery-charged monoculars whining softly as the lenses shifted in the tube to focus on a point across the river.

'Is this possible? Are you able to see clearly?'

'Zooming now. Looks like a boat. A dinghy.'

The picture was as sharp as it could possibly be. A dozen men stood huddled around an inflatable boat on the Kishenganga's east bank. Two of the men had just pushed the dinghy into the river. In pairs, they began to clamber aboard.

'That's definitely a boat,' said the first soldier, lowering the night-vision device and staring straight out into the darkness across the 80-m-wide swell of the river.

'Call Rana. *Now!*'

Rana, about 800 m away, was the operational headquarters of the 15 Maratha Light Infantry and sat in a small clearing alongside the tiny Kanzalwan village. In the small mess on site, two officers—the senior-most and the junior-most in the unit—had just finished dinner and were going over the following day's patrolling plan when the surveillance unit deployed on the Kishenganga's west bank called in to raise the alarm.

Thirty minutes earlier, Lt Navdeep Singh, twenty-six years old and barely five months into the Army—the baby of the unit, really—had grumbled to his CO, Col. Girish Upadhya.

'Sir, what is the point of going on ambushes every day when we are unable to make contact?' Lt Navdeep asked gloomily, spooning the mess staple of chicken curry and rice into his mouth. 'I'll tell you frankly, Sir, I can't wait for some big group of infiltrators to show up.'

Col. Girish had chosen to keep Lt Navdeep with him at the tactical headquarters, keen that the 'baby' learn the ropes while also learning how to keep his emotions in check. That March, Lt Navdeep had graduated from the Officers Training Academy in Chennai and been commissioned into the Army Ordnance Corps, a combat logistics arm that supplies the Army with weapons, ammunition and clothes. He had been posted with the 15 Maratha Light Infantry for his mandatory three-year tenure with an infantry fighting unit, a regimen that gives officers of every arm an initial burst of ground experience that stays with them, no matter where they go. Deploying an officer fresh out of the academy in the Gurez sector along the LoC, an infiltration hotspot, was the very definition of dropping a man in the deep end.

Col. Girish knew he needed to employ a careful mix of indulgence and firmness to handle the young officer who was hunched over his food.

'Navdeep, wait, relax,' said the CO. 'Don't worry. You will get your chance. *Yeh Gurez sector hai* (This is the Gurez sector). It's only a matter of time.'

Returning to his barracks at 11.15 p.m., Lt Navdeep dialled his girlfriend back home in Gurdaspur, Punjab, a town just 10 km from the international border with Pakistan. He was on the phone for only a few minutes when the first call from the surveillance team came in.

The 11.45 p.m. call from the surveillance unit was actually the second call that night. It had first raised the alarm 15 minutes before, at 11.30 p.m. Lt Navdeep quickly ended the call with his girlfriend and ran out of his barracks, back to the operations room.

In Gurdaspur, Lt Navdeep's girlfriend sighed and put her phone away. She couldn't really complain—he had told her that if he ever disconnected abruptly, it meant that the boss was calling him. Lt Navdeep had gone a step further with his mother, telling her that if he was unreachable for four or five days or more, she needn't worry, since his missions normally lasted that long. Her husband a thirty-year Army veteran, Jagtinder Kaur would wonder *when* the endless anxiety would finally end. Lt Navdeep's father, Subedar Joginder Singh, would calm her by gently admonishing her, telling her that the worry in her voice shouldn't distract their son from his work.

In the operations room, the CO was waiting for Lt Navdeep.

'In that first call, the surveillance boys had reported some suspicious movement near the Kishenganga River,' says Col. Girish. 'The team reported seeing three or four infiltrators. This was not uncommon, since we had already anticipated the route any Pakistani infiltrators were likely to take. But crossing the river is not easy. It has a very fast current.'

Only the previous day, a team from Rana had tried to cross the river using ropes, but had to give up halfway and return because of how cold the water was and how aggressive the current. So when the second call from the surveillance unit came in, informing Rana about the inflatable boat launched into the water, there was disbelief.

Lt Navdeep wasted no time, asking to be sent out immediately to lead an ambush team.

'At 11.30 p.m., our guy confirmed movement,' says Col. Girish. 'I immediately told him to keep the infiltrators in his sights using night-vision and his hand-held thermal imager (HHTI). We already had a few ambush parties, with eight men each, scattered in that area as part of our regular anti-infiltration deployment. And within minutes of receiving the input, we sent out more ambush parties to cover the likely infiltration routes. I asked Navdeep to lead one of these ambush teams.'

The gloom dissipated in seconds. Lt Navdeep quickly gathered his team of seven soldiers, picked up his AK-47 assault rifle and departed from the Rana headquarters.

'Navdeep had sensed that this was his operation,' says Col. Girish. 'All that sulking about having to wait endlessly for an encounter was washed away in seconds. I had never seen him so electrified as he left the base with his team.'

Lt Navdeep's ambush team positioned itself near a bend in the river, about 500 m upstream from the surveillance unit that had detected the infiltrators. There were three more ambush parties along that section of the river, scattered between Lt Navdeep and the surveillance unit. The ambush party next to Lt Navdeep's was led by Naib Subedar Mengare Shankar Ganpati, and sat across a small nallah that branched off from the Kishenganga River to run through Kanzalwan town. Two other ambush parties closed in to cover every patch of vulnerable ground between Lt Navdeep's position and the surveillance team downstream.

Once they were deployed and ready, the radios of the ambush teams crackled, delivering another message from the surveillance team.

'Counting fourteen or fifteen men with weapons and backpacks,' came the alert.

'I received the message in the Rana operations room too, as I was monitoring every move,' says Col. Girish. 'This was a big number being reported. The surveillance unit requested permission to fire at the infiltrators using their LMG. Their targets were across the river diagonally, and about 700 m distant.'

The team was denied permission to use the LMG.

'*Aur paas aane do unko. Jitna paas aa sakte hain utna aane do. Jab unki aankhon mein dekh sakte ho, tab hi engage karna* (Let them come closer. As close as they possibly can. When you can look in their eyes, then you open fire),' Col. Girish said over the radio to the surveillance team.

He had asked the team not to use the LMG because he knew that the chances of hitting the infiltrators at that distance in the dark were low.

'At best, the team would have managed to bring down only one or two guys, and the rest might have escaped and gone back. Even if you engage at 100 m at night, it is very difficult to get kills,' he says.

The call that came at 11.45 p.m. about the boats suddenly changed everything. Never before had infiltrators tried to cross the river in a boat. There was a bridge less than 100 m upstream, which was used by locals to cross the river to cut wood or graze their animals. But the bridge was manned by Army soldiers. So it was impossible for infiltrators to use it without a fierce firefight first.

Around midnight, the infiltrators had begun crossing the Kishenganga in their dinghy. The surveillance team watched as, repeatedly, teams of four men would climb into the boat, with two of them at the oars. The boat would drop two terrorists to the west bank of the river before returning to collect the next batch. This continued until a dozen infiltrators had been transported to the side of the river where the Army ambush teams lay in wait.

A soldier in one of the ambush parties remembers the scene that played out over the next few minutes, starlight painting the darkness with a faint milkiness, made possible by how high above sea level Gurez sector is—*8000 feet.*

'As we were watching, within a few minutes, they all crossed the river and started moving in the direction of Lt Navdeep and Naib Subedar Ganpati's ambush parties,' the soldier says. 'They were slowly approaching the nallah where these two ambush teams were stationed. Naib Subedar Ganpati's team was one side of the nallah, and 25 m away was Lt Navdeep's party on the other side, closer to Rana. There was a small nallah behind Lt Navdeep's position too, so his party was sandwiched between two nallahs.'

From the Rana base operations room, where he was receiving a stream of real-time inputs from the surveillance team, Col. Girish got on the radio with Lt Navdeep and Naib Subedar Ganpati, who were leading the two ambush parties closest to the unit base, a distance of about 500 m.

'Navdeep, Ganpati, here is what you will do—try and engage the infiltrators when they reach a point between both your parties along the riverbank,' Col. Girish said over the radio. 'From there, both of your positions can bring the group under combined fire from two directions and ensure sure-shot kills.'

The CO needed to stay at the base to provide crucial command and control to the unfolding operation.

'Navdeep, stay calm and wait till they are between your two parties,' Col. Girish called in. 'Once trapped there, there will be no escape for them. But wait till they get there. Under no circumstances should you fire early.'

The two ambush parties were positioned behind sangars,[1] their weapons ready and waiting. Their CO at Rana, half a kilometre away, had given them broad guidance on what to do next, but he knew that the final call could only really be taken by his men on the ground.

'I was depending on the surveillance guy for the latest inputs,' says Col. Girish. 'He allowed them to come as close to the Navdeep–Ganpati point as possible. The standing order was to wait till they were very close, then take the call and open fire.'

Seconds later, the group of terrorist infiltrators appeared in front of Naib Subedar Ganpati's ambush party. By this time, Lt Navdeep could see the group too.

The infiltrators were walking in a tactical single file, their weapons raised and ready. They were taking no chances either. The high-altitude Gurez sector comprises a scattering of villages that are largely friendly to the Army, and therefore provide no safe havens or stop-over points for terrorists crossing the LoC and making their way into the Kashmir Valley. There is a steady flow of infiltrators in this sector, but those who manage to sneak in successfully never stay too long in Gurez, using it only as a transit route before disappearing into the hinterlands of Bandipora and onward to the Kashmir Valley.

'Ganpati, hold fire,' Lt Navdeep called into his radio. '*Koi fire nahi karega* until my orders.'

From behind his sangar, Lt Navdeep counted each terrorist as they all stepped into the range of his weapon just 10 m in front

---

[1] A temporary breast-high fortification constructed with stones and sandbags. The term is understood to have been used first by the British Indian Army in the nineteenth century.

of him. The number of terrorists on foot was now clear—there were nine of them. Some of them had scarves wrapped around their heads. Others didn't. All of them had rucksacks and assault rifles. Finger on trigger, every man in the two ambush parties held his breath.

Eight metres.

'This young officer was demonstrating an amazing measure of resolve in allowing the terrorists to come close enough to finish them,' says a soldier from Naib Subedar Ganpati's ambush party. 'It was hard to imagine he had joined the Army just five months before. Every word he spoke was with confidence. He was sure of the order he was giving. There was no hesitation in his voice.'

'*Sa'ab, ab fire karte hain* (Let's fire now),' came a whisper from Lt Navdeep's left. It was his buddy soldier, Sepoy Vijay Gajre, a jawan who had joined the Army only the year before. He was, in effect, the other baby of the unit.

Lt Navdeep signalled to him to wait.

'*Aur paas aane do, Vijay. Aur thoda paas. Unke chehre dikhne chahiye* (Let them come closer, Vijay. A little closer. We should be able to see their faces),' Lt Navdeep said.

Five metres.

Lt Navdeep looked to his buddy for a moment, nodding. Every one of the infiltrators had stopped at a position between the two ambush parties and they were now just 5 m away. A few minutes past midnight, the young officer gave the order to open fire.

The sequence was thus: the infiltrators had been spotted at 11.30 p.m. The ambush teams had been deployed by 11.45 p.m. And at 12.03 a.m., the first bullets flew.

'The terrorists were barely 5 m from Navdeep when he ordered the men to open up their weapons at them,' says Col. Girish, who heard the first shots fired over the radio, but could also hear them echo from the site half a kilometre away. 'The terrorists were around 20 m from Naib Subedar Ganpati's ambush team. Once Navdeep opened fire, everyone began firing simultaneously.'

The decision to wait till the last moment had paid off. The first hail of bullets from the two ambush parties instantly killed eight of the infiltrators. A sniper from an ambush party further downstream shot and killed three more terrorists who were still in the dinghy that had brought them. Across the river, the surveillance team spotted three more infiltrators break into a run back to the LoC once the firing began.

Of the nine terrorists ambushed by Lt Navdeep and Naib Subedar Ganpati's men, one had sustained a gunshot wound but was still alive. He picked himself up and crouched between two small boulders on the riverbank. From that position, he began to fire at Lt Navdeep's team.

'He had taken such a position that our team could not fire directly at him; only Navdeep's could,' says the soldier on Naib Subedar Ganpati's team.

Lt Navdeep kept his squad's fire focused on the space around and between the boulders, pinning down the last terrorist. As the firing continued, the terrorist lobbed a grenade from behind his cover towards Lt Navdeep's position.

The grenade smashed into the sangar Lt Navdeep and his team were using for cover and exploded, sending shrapnel flying everywhere. The men dived for cover, but a splinter hit Lt Navdeep's buddy soldier, Sepoy Vijay, throwing him off his feet, a wound torn into his shoulder.

'*Vijay, tum theek ho* (Are you okay)?' Lt Navdeep screamed over the gunfire, crawling up to his buddy as the six other men in the ambush party continued to fire at the last terrorist behind the boulders.

'*Sa'ab, laga hai par chhota ghaav hai* (I'm hurt, but not badly),' Sepoy Vijay said. '*Main theek hoon* (I'm fine).'

'*Tum neeche raho, Vijay, main sambhal loonga* (Stay down, Vijay, I'll take care of this),' Lt Navdeep said, as he pulled his buddy soldier closer to the sangar. Sepoy Vijay slouched, with his back against the fortification, bleeding profusely. He looked up at the young officer, who had got to his knees and begun firing again.

'*Sa'ab, sambhal ke* (Be careful),' Sepoy Vijay said. 'Give me a few minutes, I will pick up my weapon again.'

'*Neeche raho* (Stay where you are),' Lt Navdeep said. '*Yeh khatam hone wala hai* (This is about to end).'

Lt Navdeep raised his head a few inches to get a better look at precisely where the last terrorist was—whether he had changed his position from behind the boulders while still firing. At that precise moment, one bullet came flying in, grazed the edge of Lt Navdeep's bulletproof patka and went straight through his head. Just as he was hit, Lt Navdeep squeezed the trigger of his own AK-47, sending a burst of ammunition straight into the face of the last terrorist. Five metres apart, both fell in their positions at the same time.

A few seconds passed and the guns fell silent. It had been just 5 minutes since the first bullets were fired. Back at Rana, Col. Girish received a radio message from a Havildar in Lt Navdeep's squad.

'*Navdeep sa'ab ko goli lagi hai* (Navdeep Sir has been hit),' he told the CO.

'*Goli kahan lagi hai* (Where has he been hit)?'

'*Sa'ab, sar par* (In the head, Sir).'

Col. Girish told the Havildar not to worry, and immediately sent a column of troops from Rana to remove Lt Navdeep and his buddy from the encounter site. Naib Subedar Ganpati had also suffered a splinter injury in the grenade attack. An ambulance was summoned. Fifteen minutes later, at Rana, a doctor examined Lt Navdeep. He still had a pulse when he was moved from the banks of the Kishenganga.

At 12.30 a.m., a doctor at the base pronounced him dead.

All the ambush squads remained in their positions till sunrise, as the surveillance team had alerted them to the possibility of more infiltrators lurking in the vicinity. In the clean-up operation that morning, the bodies of twelve terrorists were recovered from two different sites—the banks of the Kishenganga near Lt Navdeep's post, and the dinghy on the banks of the river about 200 m downstream, where they had crossed.

At 9 a.m. on 20 August, one of the search parties reported seeing a trail of blood leading into a large meadow to the west of Kanzalwan village. This suggested that a certain number of terrorists had survived the ambush and escaped with their lives. The meadow led to a hilly, forested stretch and on to two more small villages, Bagtore and Taarbal, the final settlements before the LoC.

'We launched a search operation again but couldn't find anyone,' says Col. Girish. 'But I didn't move the boys from the ambush sites for the next two days. They were being fed on site. My gut feeling was that if there were some injured terrorists, they would try to return to the other side of the LoC rather than try to go deeper into our area. The area had to be sanitized.'

His suspicions proved correct. Two days later, on 22 August, one of the ambush parties that was patrolling near the LoC fence spotted a terrorist crouched behind a pine tree. In a brief firefight, the thirteenth terrorist was shot in the head by Havildar Zore Bapu Bhagoji. The terrorist had a gunshot wound on his hand from the firefight two days ago.

'The terrorist had torn off a piece of his shirt and tied it around his hand to prevent blood loss. His hand was swollen.

He was firing with one hand,' says a soldier who was part of that search team.

Lt Navdeep had fallen after killing four terrorists that night, his decision to wait until the final moment ensuring that most of the infiltration group was eliminated in the first few seconds—crucial to the success of the operation.

The dead terrorists had plenty in their rucksacks to sustain them for a long and potentially damaging operation. They were carrying a large load of paranthas, dates, anti-venom ampoules and morphine, with each man also hauling ten ammunition magazines, grenades and military-grade night sights. It was enough material to last them a full week without having to seek local shelter or support of any kind.

Hours after he was pronounced dead, Lt Navdeep's body was flown 500 km to his home in Gurdaspur, accompanied by another officer of the unit and a senior soldier.

As the flag-draped casket arrived at the family home, Lt Navdeep's father, Subedar Joginder Singh, stepped out, his eyes dry.

'*Mera beta lada na? Achhe se lada! Kitne aatankwadi maare usne?* (My boy fought, didn't he? He fought well! How many terrorists did he kill)?' he asked the Army personnel who had accompanied the body.

Subedar Joginder Singh, who retired as an Honorary Captain from the Army's Corps of Engineers, was overjoyed when his son, unenthused by life after a hotel management degree and an MBA, had decided to join the Army. He would be the third generation from the family to put on the olive-greens.

'*Main toh kehta hoon ki Navdeep ne apni duty bahut hi acchi tarah nibhayi hai* (Navdeep performed his duty very well),' says the officer's father. 'But as parents, we are completely shattered. When you lose your twenty-six-year-old son, your world comes to an end. Nothing can be more painful than the loss of a child. *Sab kucch khatam ho jaata hai. Duniya ujjad jaati hai* (Everything ends. One's world becomes barren).'

Subedar Joginder Singh and Jagtinder Kaur have two other children, a son who works in Chandigarh, and a daughter who recently got married to an Army Major. Lt Navdeep's mother has only recently managed to compose herself. Her last conversation with him was days before his operation.

'I spoke to Navdeep for the last time three days before we lost him,' his mother says. 'He told me that the phone network in that area was bad, and that if he was out of reach, we should not worry. We had plans to get him married. He was supposed to come home on leave in November 2011 and we were hoping to get him engaged then. But he said he wanted to be in the field for at least two or three years before marriage. He said he would marry when his wife could join him where he was posted. All those plans were wiped out in a second.'

Lt Navdeep was commissioned into the Army in March 2011.

'He completed other courses, but his real dream was always to become an Army officer,' says Subedar Joginder. 'Had Navdeep been alive, he would have been a Major now. His course-mates are Majors. They meet us. And we think *aaj agar humara beta zinda hota toh woh bhi Major hota* (if our son were alive today, he too would have been a Major). Going by what he achieved in just five months in uniform, I feel he had the capability to rise to the rank of General. The Army has thousands of officers, but Navdeep *jaise kam hote hain* (there are few like Navdeep). I am not saying this because he was my son. Ask anyone in the Army who knew him. *Yeh hamara loss toh hai hi par Army ke liye bhi ek bada loss hai* (Navdeep's death is not only our personal loss but also the Army's).'

Thirteen years his senior at the time of the operation, Col. Girish says he still finds it difficult to think of Lt Navdeep without his heart swelling, both with sorrow and with pride.

'I used to consider Navdeep a kid brother,' says Col. Girish, posted to the Integrated Defence Staff in Delhi at the time of writing this. 'He was a good, solid boy. Losing him is a deep personal loss. I am forty-six now. The kind of *josh* (enthusiasm) he had is hard to describe. He used to go out for ambush missions and return very late at night. Sometimes, if I wanted to leave the base early, I would wait, thinking, let Navdeep sleep a bit longer. And if I left early without telling him, he would somehow find out and catch up with me as early as possible. He was a tough-as-nails soldier.'

Before their final dinner together, the CO teased Lt Navdeep, asking him of what use his hotel management degree was if he couldn't cook them a delicious snack. Lt Navdeep had disappeared into the mess kitchen and rustled up a few plates of paneer tikka.

'He was talking to his girlfriend on the phone when I summoned him for the ambush,' Col. Girish says. 'Who knows how many things were left unsaid? This always plays on my mind. And his parents' too. When I met Navdeep for the first time, I had a hunch that this kid would do something big.'

Col. Girish would know. A two-time recipient of the Sena Medal for gallantry, he would be decorated with a Vishisht Seva Medal for his command and control leadership during the Gurez encounter.

Naib Subedar Ganpati would receive a Shaurya Chakra, while Havildar Bhagoji, who killed the last terrorist, would receive a Sena Medal for gallantry.

Given his youth and astonishing grit and leadership on the ground, the Army had no hesitation in recommending Lt Navdeep for the Ashok Chakra, India's highest peacetime award for gallantry.

On Republic Day 2012, as tears streamed down Jagtinder Kaur's face on the pavilion, Lt Navdeep's father was escorted to the President's dais to receive his son's posthumous Ashok Chakra.

'His father is a brave man, he didn't break down, and accepted the award like a soldier,' remembers Col. Girish. 'It was my life's proudest moment, but I kept thinking Navdeep should have been there to receive this honour. He would have been amused by all the attention. He had a very strong mind, but he was also a kid.'

'His mother and I miss him a great deal,' says Subedar Joginder. 'There's pride and there's sorrow, both, in equal measure. I can't say that there's more pride and less sorrow. *Navdeep ka khayal dil mein hamesha rehta hai* (We constantly think of Navdeep). One room in our home is dedicated to Navdeep, his Ashok Chakra, the citation, his uniform, his boots, his photographs. We often sit in that room and talk about our boy and his short life.'

In Gurdaspur, a ceremonial gate was constructed in his memory, and a local college stadium renamed in his honour. His birthday, 8 June, is celebrated every year at the gate, where his parents set up a *chabeel* and a langar, ceremonial stands with food and sweetened water. On his death anniversary, 20 August, his parents organize a memorial function at the college stadium.

'There's no better life than life in the Army,' says Subedar Joginder. 'If I were to be born again, I would like to join the Army again. And I am sure Navdeep would have said the same had you asked him that question.'

In mid-2011, two months after he was commissioned into the Army, Lt Navdeep and the 15 Maratha Light Infantry moved from Kanpur to Khrew, in Jammu and Kashmir's Pulwama, for pre-induction training at the 15 Corps Battle

School, a curriculum designed to toughen up troops before the demanding nature of high-altitude operations at the LoC. It was the first time Col. Girish saw Lt Navdeep come into his own.

'We had five or six young officers and Navdeep was the youngest,' says Col. Girish. 'Seeing his physical fitness, agility and level of motivation, I put him in charge of a Ghatak platoon. Navdeep was brilliant during the training phase in Khrew. Other battalions were also there for training, and some competitions were held. Navdeep's Ghatak platoon stood first in many. He demonstrated excellent soldierly and leadership qualities in Khrew. He was gelling very well with the troops. They had also started liking him. He came across as a tough guy who understood the nuances of operations very quickly. He could take crucial decisions swiftly. He would demonstrate these qualities just three months later, in a life-and-death situation. Try and think about that for a moment.'

At Khrew, Lt Navdeep would be restless to be deployed at Gurez, calling his girlfriend and parents frequently to tell them how much he was longing to be at the LoC.

'Once he was posted in Gurez, Navdeep didn't waste a single moment; he simply hit the ground running,' remembers another officer from the 15 Maratha Light Infantry. 'He quickly dived into a routine of extensive area familiarization. He became obsessed with understanding every inch of the area, every peak, every nallah, every patch of jungle. By August, he had analysed all previous operations in that area, the likeliest infiltration routes, how better to plan the next mission. The CO would take him around to all the places, and it became clear that Navdeep was picking up the basics very quickly. In his final moments, he showed just what could be done with training and dedication.'

A few months after the August operation, the CO of 15 Maratha Light Infantry invited Lt Navdeep's father to visit the unit in Gurez, to see for himself the place where his son had fallen fighting.

'When Subedar Joginder arrived, I took him to the sangar from where Navdeep fired his last bullet,' says Col. Girish. 'It was a very emotional moment for both me and Navdeep's father. He bent down, dug his hand into the earth and grabbed a fistful of soil from the place where his son had fallen. I can't describe how moving that sight was. There are absolutely no words. It can only be experienced. I think he could feel Navdeep's presence there. I saw that look on his face. *Unhone uss mitti ko maathe se lagaya* (He touched the soil to his forehead).'

Lt Navdeep's father had looked up at his son's CO, a fist filled with the soil stretched out in front of him.

'*Mere bete ka khoon iss mitti par gira tha* (My son's blood fell on this soil),' he said. '*Main ek muthi uss mitti ki Gurez se laya. Uss muthi bhar mitti ki koi keemat nahi hai. Woh mitti mere liye Waheguru se kam nahin hai* (I brought a fistful of that soil from Gurez. It is priceless for me; It is no less than god for me).'

The soil sits in a bottle now in Lt Navdeep's room.

4

'I've Been Ready since the Day I Was Born'

Major David Manlun

Greater Noida
January 2009

Nobody had seen David Manlun dance the way he did that night. Channelling his inner Salman Khan, the young Manipuri ripped off his T-shirt to bounce to the blaring beat of *Oh Oh Jaane Jaana*, mouthing the lyrics almost completely wrong, but with euphoric abandon. Plastic glasses filled with Old Monk rum were passed around the crowd of friends, suffusing one end of the hostel block in Delhi's outskirts with its unmistakable aroma. They wouldn't miss this for the world. They had all agreed that if there was one night they needed to be together, this was it.

Twenty-four years old, bare-chested and playing an air guitar with his eyes scrunched shut, the young man at the centre of the revelry had just achieved something he had failed at twice before and had dreamed about since his days as an NCC cadet. David Manlun had made it to the Indian Army.

He had been biding his time for a year at the Army Institute of Management and Technology in the sprawling Greater Noida suburb of Delhi, filling his days with football, friends and all the heady amusement afforded by student life in India's capital. But with the weekly partying, few of his friends ever got to see David's other side. His, always-on cheery manner concealed a simmering frustration, an unremitting yearning to join the military.

His father, Manlun Khamzalam, had been a junior commissioned officer in the Army, a Subedar. In 2008, through phone calls and text messages from Shillong, 2000 km away, he and David's mother, Mannuamniang Manlun, had kept tabs, with a mixture of pride and parental concern, as David seemed unwilling to let go of the Army dream. They hoped that two failed attempts hadn't broken their son's confidence and spirit. They had really only seen the cheerful, mild-mannered boy they had raised, and prayed that he stayed strong. But far from Shillong, fuelled by the turbulent freedom of life away from home, David's determination had only intensified with each letter of rejection he received.

'I'll never forget the party that night he made it to the Army,' says Rajni Rangra, a classmate and friend of David. 'Every one of us there was very happy for him. None of us had seen him as full of joy as he was that night. And for a guy like David, that's saying something.'

Days later, when he packed his bags to leave for the Officers Training Academy (OTA) on the outskirts of Chennai, Rajni knew she would miss him deeply.

'David knew I loved bike rides in the winter,' she says. 'He would borrow someone else's motorcycle and take me for a ride at 8.45 p.m. at 100 kmph, delivering me back to the hostel in 10 minutes, right before the gates shut. He found joy in taking pains to make his friends happy.'

When they had celebrated his admission to the Army, the alcohol-fuelled Salman-style air guitar had given way to David's real one—a black acoustic guitar. He had acquired it in Delhi and propped it up in his room. It quickly became one of the many things David was popular on campus for. He made sure the guitar followed him wherever he went thereafter.

Sad to be leaving his friends but ecstatic at the prospect of what lay ahead, David began life at the OTA, which trains officers for the Army's short-service commission. A year later, in March 2010, his parents travelled to Chennai to watch their son complete his training and get commissioned into the 1st Battalion of the Naga Regiment, a unit that had cut its teeth in the 1971 war just a year after it was raised.

'All through his training, David was restless,' a course-mate who was commissioned alongside him at the academy, and is still serving, remembers. 'David wanted just one thing—to put on fatigues and get out there. He was hungry for that life. And he could not have got a better first posting.'

That first posting, with 1 Naga, was in Naugam in north Kashmir. Receiving orders to move to the location, which is not far from India's LoC with PoK, David had called his father to give him the news.

'God bless you, be careful,' Khamzalam told him. 'Give it your best and make us all proud, son. But be careful.'

In Naugam, Lt David Manlun threw himself into the daily whirlwind of counter-insurgency and counter-terror operations. Throwing himself into the role that had played out in his mind for years, the young officer would volunteer to lead a non-stop series of operations. He would give up opportunities for leave so he wouldn't miss the chance to be part of missions. In the words of another officer in the unit at the time, young Lt David was now fully in combat mode. When he phoned home every few days, he was aware his father was intimately familiar with the trails and forests where he now stalked militants—Khamzalam had served in Naugam years ago with 35 RR,[1] a unit affiliated with the Army's Assam Regiment, of which he was a member.

---

[1] For a counter-terror operation in Naugam in 2016, Havildar Hangpan Dada of 35 RR would be posthumously decorated with the country's highest peacetime award, the Ashok Chakra. An account of his mission is in *India's Most Fearless 1*.

After nearly five years in Naugam and in regimental training centres in Bakloh in Himachal Pradesh, David received word that he would be heading closer home—a posting to the 164 Infantry Battalion of the Territorial Army[2] in Nagaland.

On his way to the North-east, he stopped at home in Shillong for a quick break. His mother had insisted, since David had postponed leave several times earlier to stay with his unit in north Kashmir. Khamzalam and Mannuamniang Manlun spent those days with a young man who had been transformed by his five years in the Army. More serious and disciplined than before, his grimness lifted only in the company of loved ones.

'He was very satisfied with Army life,' says Khamzalam. 'After Kashmir, he was headed to Nagaland, which is another extremely challenging place to operate against outfits like ULFA (United Liberation Front of Assam) and NSCN(K).[3] I advised David again, stay strong, but please be careful.'

---

[2] Part of the Indian Army, the Territorial Army serves as a second line of defence, drawing its stock from civilians with elements from the regular Army. The 164 Infantry Battalion draws troops and officers from the Naga Regiment and is headquartered in Zakhama, Nagaland. As a 'home and hearth' battalion, it is intended to keep local youth from joining separatist terror outfits, while also directly operating against those outfits.

[3] The S.S. Khaplang faction of the National Socialist Council of Nagaland (NSCN[K]) is a banned terror outfit operating across states in the North-east. In 2015, the group unilaterally abrogated a fourteen-year ceasefire, going on to mount major attacks across Nagaland and Manipur. A June 2015 cross-border operation by the Indian Army Special Forces to destroy NSCN(K) camps, as revenge for an ambush a few days before in Manipur, is detailed in *India's Most Fearless 1*.

The ULFA, a separatist terror outfit founded in 1979, has been banned by the Indian government since 1990, and has mounted attacks, big and small, nearly non-stop, since the eighties. With training camps in the border forests of Myanmar and with proven support from China, the terror group has managed to remain a violent presence in the North-east's turbulent narrative since its inception. A common cause had led the ULFA to forge ties with the NSCN(K), with intelligence pointing to a long list of coordinated logistics that help both organizations. The ULFA has recently re-energized itself, riding on an exploding controversy over India's Citizenship (Amendment) Bill, which it sees as a threat to the indigenous people of Assam. The place that David was headed to was the backyard of both terror groups.

Mokokchung district has a long border with Assam to the east and north. On 5 December 2014, bags and guitar in hand, David reported to the headquarters at Zakhama. With a glowing record of leading counter-insurgency operations in Naugam, the unit's CO, Col. K.V.K. Prakash, immediately dispatched David out into the field to command a company of infantry soldiers at Mokokchung.

'This man had two distinct sides to him,' remembers the young officer quoted above, who served with him in Naugam and was also posted to Nagaland. 'In leisure, he was all about fun and frolic with his music and guitar. But during the lead-up to operations, you could not meet a more serious and focused guy than David.'

A common refrain directed at David by his comrades was to 'grow up', an affirmation of his boundless energy. But fuelled by it, over the next two years, during which he was promoted to the rank of Major, David would lead a series of crucial operations against terrorists in the troubled area that was now his responsibility.

These included two frenetic chases in the River Belt Colony and Dhobinala areas of Nagaland's Dimapur, where three NSCN(K) and two NSCN(R) terrorists were captured alive with a large quantity of arms and ammunition. Another NSCN(K) terrorist was intercepted with bomb-making equipment in Zunheboto, while a foreign terrorist was arrested with a bunch of extortion notes in Namsa village in Tizit, David's backyard.

'He was a Manipuri from Meghalaya operating in Nagaland,' says the officer who served with him. 'And in the North-east, where state and tribe affiliations are sometimes drawn in blood, David was operating at the intersection of all these fault lines. It was infinitely more challenging than his stint in Naugam. Here, terrorists believe in hit-and-run tactics, and operate large-scale extortion rackets to terrorize local communities. So David's own identity was very much in the mix.'

In June 2015, David, like the rest of the Army, had been emotionally shaken by the NSCN(K) ambush of an Army convoy in his native Manipur's Chandel district, in which eighteen soldiers were massacred. Those serving with him remember David wishing that he could participate in the cross-border strike that a unit of the Para Special Forces mounted deep inside Myanmar as an act of revenge on 4 June. Except, David and his unit had their hands full in their own area—they knew there would be an escalation in NSCN(K) and ULFA activity following the raid inside Myanmar.

After ten months spent in operations, David took a few days off to see his parents in Shillong. During that visit, he would take one of his happiest photographs, one that would be splashed across the media less than two years later. Standing on the terrace of a house, the photograph showed David and his two brothers, Jimmy and Siampu, captured while jumping in the air in total glee. 'Three *paagal* brothers,' a friend would comment when David made the photograph his profile picture on Facebook—one that remains till today.

But David knew that visits home were going to increasingly become a luxury on the path he had chosen. Back from leave, he wasted no time in jumping right back into work. There was never a shortage of intelligence inputs about the movement of militants and terrorists—the real work was to judge which of those alerts would actually lead to results. Separatist groups had learnt the fine art of jamming intelligence networks with false alarms in an effort to fatigue the alertness and energy of units like David's. But he knew that even a single show of weakness would embolden groups like NSCN(K) and ULFA to step up the audacity of their operations. And that meant a direct threat to the youth in the area, the fodder needed by these groups to fuel their activities.

Apart from institutionalized outreach methods that included medical camps, vocational training and career counselling sessions, David tried to use football to win over local youth and divert their minds from the lure of militancy. It wasn't difficult for David—if there was one thing he prized nearly as much as Army life, it was the beautiful game. All through his time at the Army Public School and St Anthony's College in Shillong, David had been obsessed with football. When he moved to Delhi, football followed him.

'I can't forget the way David would guide the whole team and take full responsibility,' says Sagar Pande, David's classmate at the management institute. 'He was an amazing centre forward and used to make some of the best passes I've ever seen on the ground. He made sure that every player on the ground was contributing to the game as per his potential.'

A major fan of international football, but even more obsessively, a follower of the North-east's football clubs, David's

Facebook page stands testimony to just how closely he tracked even the smallest games. Only weeks after he took position as company commander in Tizit, he began organizing football tournaments, drawing local youth from surrounding villages. The games would be fiercely competitive and sometimes even turn violent. But David didn't mind. He wanted the youth to be emotionally invested in anything but militancy.

His CO, Col. Prakash, had known immediately that David was special. Unusually motivated and with an action-oriented ethic, he had proven, in just two years of operations in Nagaland, how young officers with comparatively little experience in the area could lead with both lethality and empathy. As the arrests of NSCN terrorists piled up, David's energy levels seemed to permeate his company, transforming it into a highly energized unit in one of the most challenging conflict-ridden areas in the country. In August 2016, the results delivered by a troop team under his leadership in Dimapur won David the Chief of Army Staff's commendation from the Army Chief at the time, Gen. Dalbir Singh, a man who had served as Eastern Commander and personally recognized the worth of the young officer's difficult work.

The operation itself had become legendary in the unit. David and an officer from the Army's Para Special Forces had chased a highly prized commander of the NSCN(K) in broad daylight in Dimapur, overpowering him and capturing him alive. The captive turned out to be a major source of intelligence on the location and movement of terrorist logistics from Myanmar, across Nagaland and into Assam.

In Shillong, David's parents were proud of the award. And Khamzalam knew that it meant his son had truly thrown himself into his work. He sent David a text message that evening: 'Keep making us and your unit proud, son, but take care of yourself and get enough rest.'

The award scarcely interrupted David's work, coming as it did in the middle of an operation near the Myanmar border. He had been moved from Mokokchung to Mon district, at Nagaland's northern tip, with Assam to the west and north, Arunachal Pradesh to the north-east and, most significantly, an international border with Myanmar to the east.

David was excited about the move—a patch of international border in his area of responsibility provided an even greater canvas for combat. But for the young officer, the move up the chain of responsibility also served as a reminder that he had less than a year to go with the 164 Infantry Battalion. And given that he had served back-to-back in two operational areas, it was almost certain he would be sent next to a peace posting, effectively a desk job, for a few years before he could be circled back into active missions. The prospect disturbed him greatly.

'He was simply unwilling to accept a staff posting,' says the officer who served with him. 'He had got it in his head that he needed to stay in active operations at all costs. One of the avenues available to him was the National Security Guard (NSG).[4] So he put up his name. I remember him telling me, "Bro, no way I can do staff posting, too boring."'

Four months after the award, leadership changed at the unit and a new CO, Col. K.K. Mishra, replaced Col. Prakash.

'The moment I met David, I knew he was a maverick,' says Col. Mishra. 'I was impressed by his energy and focus, but was also concerned, right from the start, that these high

---

[4] The NSG is a Special Forces unit under India's Home Ministry. The Special Action Group of the NSG draws its forces from the Army, and is primarily a counter-terrorist force with specialization in counter-terror operations in built-up areas, anti-hijack operations, hostage rescue and bomb disposal missions.

motivation levels should not lead him to harm. I always had this at the back of my mind. *Always*. I needed to make sure that I could harness that energy, but without endangering him and the other boys.'

Embracing the challenge of his new position near Mon district's Tizit village, David set about cultivating new sources of intelligence in the ever-shifting landscape. His fears proved to be true—both the NSCN(K) and the ULFA(I) stepped up activities to recuperate and re-arm following the blistering Myanmar raid of 2015, and clearly had a point to prove. Challenged at nearly every step, they were increasingly desperate to score a major attack on the Army and other security forces deployed against them.

On 4 June 2017, David had picked up the buzz that a group of ULFA(I) terrorists had infiltrated from Myanmar, and were likely to move towards Assam with a large quantity of weapons and ammunition. The buzz was typically vague, with no actionable information. As he always did, David tried to build on the intelligence and flesh out an action plan.

On the evening of 6 June 2017, David was at his base, WhatsApping friends and family. He sent a message to his friend, Richa, in Shillong, telling her he would be back home in a week for a break. To his father, Khamzalam, he asked that he pray that the NSG plan worked out.

'I told him, everything will work out,' Khamzalam says. 'You just focus on your work and stay alert.'

At 8.30 p.m., David's phone buzzed. It was a local contact he had cultivated near the Assam border who was calling with information about the movement of suspected ULFA(I) terrorists in the hilly Lapa Lempong area of Mon. Unlike the many vague inputs that came in daily, this particular piece of intelligence was more specific than anything David had heard before. It not only specified the number of terrorists, but also where they could be intercepted and the direction they were heading in.

'David had been doggedly pursuing that input for three days,' says Col. Mishra. 'It was clear to him that the terror cadres were attempting to cross into Assam. The exact time when they would cross Tizit was not known. That's when he got that call, informing him that the terrorists had commandeered two autorickshaws and were moving towards Tizit to cross over to Lapa Lempong. He was sitting with Para officers. His men were already on standby when he got the call.'

David assembled two groups of men in two Gypsies, one with his own company and another with men from the 12 Para Special Forces. At 9.05 p.m., the two vehicles crept out of Tizit base and sped towards a suspension bridge near Lapa Lempong to establish a mobile check post (MCP). The function of the MCP was to intercept and challenge the two autorickshaws that were expected to pass that way on the Lapa Lempong-Lunglam-Oting road.

Three minutes after 10 p.m., with the MCP established and the men waiting, the two autorickshaws emerged through the darkness from Lapa Lempong village, moving in the direction of Oting. On being signalled to stop, the two autos swerved away and accelerated up a nearby hill, a highly suspicious action that confirmed, if nothing else, that those in the autos were up to no good. Given the intelligence, it was all that David needed to drop everything and give chase.

'Move! Move! Move!' David screamed, diving back into the front passenger seat of his Gypsy, AK-47 armed and ready, bursting out of the location in pursuit of the two autos up the winding hill road.

The second Gypsy with the Para unit followed 200 m behind. He knew he could have fired at the autos, but the smallest chance that those in the autos weren't terrorists stopped him from doing so. Killing civilians accidentally would have destroyed over two years of painstaking work and the many hearts won. And as a non-Naga in Nagaland, he knew such an incident had the potential to spiral into a nightmare for the Army and the people. His weapon aimed and ready, David leaned forward in his seat, watching the two autos race through the darkness.

'This is a very narrow mountain road, so there's no question of overtaking,' says Col. Mishra. 'They could not open fire either, because the last thing David would have wanted was a case of mistaken identity. So he kept pursuing the autos at a distance of 25 m. Then, at one of the blind turns up the hill, the trailing auto halted while the one ahead sped away. Through the darkness, David and his team saw at least three people jump out of the auto and run to the right, up the hill behind some rocks. And almost immediately, these men began firing at David's Gypsy.'

Immediately jumping out of the moving vehicle from the left, David ordered the driver to duck and crawl out of the vehicle, screaming to the six soldiers in the passenger benches to get out and take cover behind the vehicle. Kneeling on the ground with the passenger door as a shield, David fired back at the three terrorists.

'With fire coming from the darkness, David could have gone down the hill to protect himself, but he did not,' says Col. Mishra. 'He ordered his men to a safe spot behind the vehicle and away from the line of fire, while he stood at the door returning fire. It was a very fierce firefight.'

The second Gypsy, carrying the Para Special Forces men led by their commander, Capt. Nitesh Kumar, had pulled up seconds later straight in the line of fire, with bullets flying through the vehicle. The Para soldiers immediately emerged from their vehicle to join the firefight, but a hail of bullets hit three soldiers just as they jumped out of their Gypsy, critically injuring them. A fourth man, Paratrooper Manchu, crawled towards the three injured men in an attempt to pull them to safety.

David screamed again at the soldiers to get out of the vehicle and take cover as quickly as possible. As he did so, a bullet from one of the terrorists tore through the car door and went straight through David's chest. The terrorists followed this quickly with a grenade hurled between the two Gypsies, the shrapnel hitting David in the head and grievously injuring Paratrooper Manchu in both the eyes and his shoulder. Blinded by the injuries, Paratrooper Manchu still pushed himself forward to pull his three injured comrades to safety behind the vehicle. Shaken by the head injury but standing his ground, David turned back to scream once again, telling the soldiers in both Gypsies not to emerge from behind the vehicles, and to stay away from the line of fire.

'If David had not fired back at the terrorists and instructed his men to take cover, the entire party would have been eliminated in seconds,' says Col. Mishra. 'A grenade splinter hit his head, and it was followed by another bullet hitting him in the arm, but he remained standing and firing. He was bleeding out, but he kept firing at the terrorists.'

After minutes of non-stop firing, David realized the engagement was useless unless he got a clear shot of the terrorists. The three men on the hill had every advantage. They were standing on higher ground, had rocks to hide behind, and were raining their bullets down from three weapons, as against David's solo counter-fire from below. Looking back at the three injured Para Special Forces men, David looked down at the wound in his chest. He knew the blood loss meant he might pass out at any moment, so if there was anything he could do, it needed to be right then.

'David signalled to us to provide him covering fire, but we did not understand why,' says a soldier from the second Gypsy.

As the soldiers emerged from their positions to fire back at the terrorists, David got on to his stomach and slowly crawled out from behind his Gypsy, and in the darkness, snaked his way, bleeding, towards the terrorists still firing from the hill. Reaching a spot 10 m from the terrorists, David then used the last of his energy to explode out from in front of the rocks and kill the three terrorists at point-blank range. Then, with a roar that echoed down the hill, he collapsed there, unconscious from blood loss.

'The entire operation took just 5 minutes from start to finish,' says one of the soldiers who provided covering fire to David as he crawled towards the terrorists for the final attack. 'The entire party was saved by this act by David. Initially, it was only David who could fire, because there was nobody else in a position to fire back.'

At 11 p.m., Col. Mishra got a call informing him about the operation that had just taken place and that Maj. David had been injured in the chase.

'David did the very best he could have in the circumstances. My priority at midnight was to send a backup party to the hill and bring down David and the other injured men.'

When the truck arrived at the encounter site, three men from David's unit carried him back to the Gypsies, administering emergency aid. The young officer was unconscious, but he still had a pulse.

'Initially, we were told that the first bullet on the chest is fatal, but after some time, we came to know that David had a pulse. But the damage was severe. It was futile,' says Col. Mishra.

On the way down the hill in the truck, Maj. David succumbed to his three injuries.

His men, still on the hill, secured the position, confirming by dawn that the three men David had killed were indeed ULFA(I) terrorists. The terror group itself would confirm that their names were Bipul Asom, Santosh Asom and Phanindra Asom. The leader of the group was found to be a notorious cadre who was wanted for causing serial blasts in Assam on Republic Day six months earlier. The autorickshaw they were in carried a large quantity of bomb-making material and weapons, along with documents that indicated a widespread network of extortion. The men David had crawled bleeding towards, and eliminated, were part of the cutting edge of ULFA(I)'s terrorist operations.

At 5 a.m. the following morning, Col. Mishra made the dreaded phone call to David's father in Shillong.

'I woke up to the call telling me my son was no more,' says Khamzalam. 'He said, "*Bahut sorry, sa'ab*, but this is the news I have to bring to you." What could I say? When a man does his work honestly to protect his country, this can happen.'

'David may have been impulsive, but he took the correct decision, and acted in the best way he could to save his team and finish the operation. Even in his final mission, his act of total selflessness saved over a dozen men,' says Col. Mishra, who would go on to recommend the young officer for a posthumous Kirti Chakra, the country's second-highest peacetime gallantry award. 'It was a very well-planned operation but it happened quite suddenly. There was no other way of doing it. Some people may say that chasing two autorickshaws in Gypsies and having a firefight like this within a space of 25 m seems more like a police operation than an Army one. But I visited the site and saw how things played out. There was no other way it could have been done.'

After the men under his charge had had a chance to say goodbye, David's body was airlifted to Shillong the following morning. In a truck, accompanied by a full ceremonial guard, the flag-draped coffin would snake its way through Shillong's roads to the Happy Valley area where his parents lived, where a wailing Mannuamniang, helped up by two relatives, would welcome her son home for the last time. Her husband, in contrast, would be unshakeably stoic, calm, even smiling, as friends, family and a stream of officers lined up to offer their condolences.

'I was proud, but I also felt guilty when he died,' says Khamzalam. 'The Army was his duty and it was a dangerous life. It is my good fortune that God gave me a son for good work, and then God took him back. My son fought very bravely. If more men are like him, this country will have peace.'

'My son has passed away, but I'm with my son always, and he is with me,' says Mannuamniang. 'I'm proud of my son. He died a hero.'

Holding herself together with enormous strength under the hot sun, David's mother would take the microphone and tell the crowd, 'I know it is quite warm today for all of you sitting outside like this. But for David's sake and ours, I would request you all to bear it for a while since it is my son's last journey.'

David's sister, Melody, married to an Army officer and settled in Delhi, would be unable to arrive home in time for David's last rites at the Assam Regimental Centre and his burial in the cemetery there. Posting a picture of him that day on Facebook, she would write, 'My hero. You made us proud. You are coming home with the highest honour, wrapped in the tricolour.'

A large number of friends, including those he had spoken to the previous night, would show up for his funeral. The roads leading up to Happy Valley would be lined with mourners that morning, with Armymen and friends taking the microphone to pay rich tributes to David for hours.

'We miss him, but what can we do? He has gone for our country. Gave his life for India,' says Khamzalam. 'Rest in peace, David. I will also be gone some day. But going like this is very good. Such people are good. He is accepted by God. I am happy and peaceful in my mind. I don't worry about his soul. I appreciate his bravery. And I am proud of the son God has given me, and then taken away from me. I don't worry, I am happy. I would like to congratulate my son for completing his duty. I would like to think that God believed my son was too fine a person to be kept on this earth and therefore took him back.'

In Delhi, a group of David's classmates from the management institute received the news with disbelief. They would spend an evening recounting their favourite memories of the young upstart from Manipur who wouldn't sit down for a moment.

'He's generally unforgettable, but there's one small thing I will remember him for, above all else,' says his classmate Sagar Pande. 'Some guys and I would get late getting back to the hostel and would miss dinner. David would always make sure to keep a few extra plates of food in his room. So after 10 p.m., when we returned, we would go straight to his room. And we never once asked him to do this for us. He just did it.'

Another classmate, Parneet Hira, a public relations expert in Delhi, says, 'I couldn't believe he was no more. It's hard to think of him as anything but a bundle of joy. He was never gloomy. I remember how he was on top of the world when he made it to the Army. It was all he ever wanted. His life was the Army, apart from his football obsession, dancing with his shirt off and those secret drinking sessions. Women loved him. Everyone loved him.'

Col. Mishra would travel to Shillong with his wife a few days later to meet David's family, a customary visit for every CO. Condoling the loss of a son and an officer together is a bond few outside the Army can fully appreciate.

'With the heaviest of hearts, I shared with his parents that David had made it to the NSG, and I was to share the news with him just two days after his final operation,' Col. Mishra says. 'Had he not made this sacrifice, by that time, he would have been on his way to Manesar near Delhi to begin his training and probation with the NSG. He was moving out.'

Khamzalam had smiled at the news.

'David would have been very happy to hear he had made it to the NSG,' his father says. 'The last thing he wanted was to sit at a desk in his unit. He would have had his fill of operations with the NSG. He could talk of nothing else in his last six months.'

David leaves behind a legacy of loyal sources that continue to help his unit hunt terrorists in Nagaland. His football-driven connect with civilians in the area is being carried forward despite his loss. Four days after his death, the North East United Football Club (NEUFC) paid tribute to David, hailing his 'outstanding act of bravery'.

'No doubt, football was in his blood, and he had a large female fan following too,' remembers Col. Mishra. 'When he was company commander in Mokokchung, he cultivated many sources who were women. He had this idea that women are the most reliable sources of intelligence. It helped that he was a charmer and they loved him. I know David did not like to be bound by rules and regulations and methods.'

During his final days, David had experimented with a new haircut, shaving one full side of his head. His CO had laughed, asking what he was hoping to achieve with the new look. 'It may give the impression that I'm not serious, Sir,' he said with a wink. 'It will be good if others think that.'

In the months after his passing, David's identity would cause complications in the family's wish to build a house. As Manipuris—and not Khasis—the law forbids them from buying land in Meghalaya despite having lived there for decades. The Army unveiled a memorial bust of David in Shillong, but his parents were prohibited from owning land on account of ethno-political fault lines.

'For all practical purposes, David was from Shillong, and he was a local hero,' says Col. Mishra. 'But instead of accepting him fully as a hero, the community fault lines come into play. The Army tried to help the family get clearance to buy land either in Meghalaya or Manipur. After hitting many walls, the family has now purchased a plot of land in Guwahati, where they are building a house.'

On 27 March 2018, Khamzalam and Mannuamniang travelled to Delhi to receive their son's posthumous Kirti Chakra from the President of India. His citation would declare that the young officer had displayed 'conspicuous personal bravery and leadership of the highest order' in his final mission.

On his final night in Delhi before leaving to join the Army, David had been drinking with a friend, who asked him, 'So you think you're ready for this? It's not fun and games, mate.'

David bottoms-upped his drink, narrowed his eyes into a grinning grimace and replied, 'I've been ready since the day I was born.'

5

'Get to the Upper Decks, Don't Come Back'

Lieutenant Commander Kapish Muwal and
Lieutenant Manoranjan Kumar

Mumbai
14 August 2013

The explosion lit up the sky over Colaba in south Mumbai. Those who didn't hear the sickening blast saw it from miles away. A massive ball of angry flames rose into the air, followed by a fountain of projectile explosions that could be mistaken for celebratory fireworks by those observing it from far away. The blast settled into a roaring blaze that would send up an ominous cone of orange light into the sky, as if a portal to hell had opened up on the ground. Not until later that night of 14 August 2013 would Mumbai know what that blast really was.

It was the *INS Sindhurakshak*.

The Indian Navy attack submarine had suffered a terrifying accident in its berth at the naval dockyard, which opened out into the Arabian Sea. As the minutes passed, horrific details of the disaster began to emerge. Eighteen personnel were inside the submarine at the time of the catastrophic blast, which mutilated its double hull and sent out a thudding shockwave that shook the other ships in the cramped dockyard that night. Forty-eight hours would pass before rescue personnel could enter the carcass of the *Sindhurakshak*. As the Navy had feared, none of the eighteen men on board survived. Most had perished in the blast, which was later found to have been caused by a mishandled torpedo and a series of tragic lapses.

For the Indian Navy, the tragedy reverberated in many directions. With eighteen personnel gone, it was the single biggest peacetime loss in its history, an unspeakable tragedy above all else. The eighteen personnel were all submariners, some of the hardiest and best qualified men in service, trained to function in the most difficult and dangerous conditions imaginable. The destruction of a submarine that wasn't at war was a crushing blow—the Indian Navy had already been wrestling with a drastic depletion in its submarine fleet, and was desperate to keep the small number in service as functional as possible for the enormous responsibility that rested on its shoulders in the Indian Ocean.

Preparing to conduct the most difficult accident investigation in its history, a shaken Navy ordered a safety stand-down, a short period of pause where all non-essential sailing would cease and the entire gamut of service safety procedures would be revised across naval bases, air stations, ships and, especially, submarines. It was to serve as a powerful refresher and reminder of just why those rules had been written in the first place, and how horribly wrong things could go if even a single rule was given a pass.

Marine commando divers would inspect the shattered *Sindhurakshak* in its berth, using it for months as a training wreck for salvage operations. The submarine had returned only the previous year after a twenty-four-month overhaul and upgrade at western Russia's Zvezdochka shipyard on the White Sea, where it had been fitted with new sensor systems, communications gear, safety rigs and modern Klub-S anti-ship and land attack cruise missiles. To the commandos swimming among the wreck, the sight below the waterline was devastating. A mangled, twisted hull breached at several points, a far cry from the silent, deadly hunter of the deep it was built to be.

That August night in 2013, two young Navy officers had heard the explosion from their quarters in the Colaba naval area. Word quickly spread about what had happened. Lt Cdr Kapish Muwal and Lt Manoranjan Kumar, both submariners themselves, made for the naval dockyard—they personally knew most of those who were on board the *Sindhurakshak*— but found that the area had been cordoned off and secured for safety reasons. There was every chance that there would be more explosions, since there was no guarantee that all the armament and ordnance on board the submarine had detonated. Hurriedly heading to the naval mess, they found a large group of officers glued to a television screen. News channels had begun beaming live footage of the smouldering orange blaze over the naval dockyard and amateur mobile phone footage of the explosions from earlier.

Nobody said a word as the TV anchor described the hellish images. As he watched, Lt Cdr Kapish's mobile phone rang. It was his father, a retired naval officer, calling from Delhi. Over the next 15 minutes, every submariner in the officers' mess would receive a phone call from a loved one. Lt Manoranjan's father, a retired Subedar from the Army, called from Jamshedpur. Every one of the callers would thank their gods when their son or brother or father picked up the phone.

'I'm okay, Dad, but they are saying eighteen people were inside *Sindhurakshak*,' Lt Cdr Kapish told his father. 'There is no information yet. We are waiting. We can't go anywhere near that place.'

As Lt Manoranjan's mother, Rukmani Devi, came on the line, he asked her not to worry, promising he would keep them posted.

For eighteen other families spread across the country, phone calls to loved ones would go unanswered. Not until the next day would a full list of those who were inside the

Sindhurakshak become available. And it would take another day for the Navy to announce that its worst fears were true. The *Sindhurakshak* had entombed a part of her crew—there were no survivors.

For the two young officers, the tragedy hit even closer home. They were both crew on another submarine, the *INS Sindhuratna*, a sister vessel to the ill-fated *Sindhurakshak*. The two vessels were among ten Kilo-class attack submarines built by Russia's Sevmash shipyard and delivered to India between 1986 and 2000. The *Sindhuratna* was nearly a decade older than the *Sindhurakshak*, and it wasn't sailing for the time being— it had been dry-docked in Mumbai for crucial maintenance procedures and wouldn't be ready to sail for at least another six months.

Lt Cdr Kapish had joined the crew of *Sindhuratna* in August 2011, with Lt Manoranjan joining five months later, in January 2012. Both were electrical officers tasked with overseeing the huge quantity of electrical equipment on board—notably, the large battery pits that provide part of a diesel-electric submarine's propulsion.

With their submarine out of action, the two young officers would be consumed by the storm of intrigue erupting over what could have caused the *Sindhurakshak* disaster.

It was all that submariners would talk about for months. And since the Navy operated ten submarines of the *Sindhurakshak*'s kind, crew members of the other nine submarines—including the two young officers from *Sindhuratna*—were drawn, at some level or the other, into the investigation and its implications. Was there something wrong with the submarine? Could something similar happen to its sister submarines? Were standard operating procedures on the Kilo-class vessels faulty? Were maintenance procedures introducing new, undiscovered risks? Did the new systems added during extensive overhauls in Russia hamper the safety regime on board? These and countless more questions would overwhelm the daily lives of the Navy's small submarine arm in the aftermath of the *Sindhurakshak* catastrophe.

In the military, there is barely any time or luxury to mourn lost comrades. But if the comfort of routine served as a salve to the wounded submarine arm, it would, at the time, be unaware that the next tragedy was only six months away.

In January 2014, Lt Cdr Kapish visited his parents in Delhi to celebrate his twenty-eighth birthday. A day before, on 18 January, the Navy's Kilo-class submarine fleet would have a major scare. The lead submarine of the pack, *INS Sindhughosh*, touched the seabed while entering the naval dockyard in Mumbai, stranded by a combination of low tide and lack of desilting and dredging work in the harbour approach. While the incident was a serious lapse that sent alarm bells ringing, the submarine itself suffered no damage and nobody on board was hurt. What the incident did was remind the submarine arm again how delicate their operations were.

'Why do you need to work on these submarines?' Lt Cdr Kapish's younger brother, Ashish, would ask him during that break.

'Somebody has to do it, and I enjoy it,' Lt Cdr Kapish had said. 'It's difficult, but I've chosen this.'

His mother, Dayawati Singh, who tried not to let her worry show, put all her energy into trying to persuade her son to think about getting married. Before his birthday on 19 January, she had even managed to get him to meet prospective brides.

The officer remained non-committal, playing along for his parents' sake and hoping it would at least alleviate some of their worry. He knew there was little he could really say to take their minds off the horrors of *Sindhurakshak*, but he did have news he felt would comfort them. His three-year tenure with the *Sindhuratna* would, after all, end in August that year, and he had been told that he would be sent by the Navy to the Indian Institute of Technology (IIT), Bombay, to do an MTech degree in electrical engineering. His parents were exultant. His father, Cdr Ishwar Singh, a naval veteran himself, knew this meant the Indian Navy had seen promise in their son, and was investing in upgrading his skills with a prestigious degree.

It was gratifying for his parents for another reason. Kapish, a high-ranking student in school, had got admission to Delhi's prestigious St Stephen's College for physics, but had chosen to leave after only six months to take up an engineering degree, since his real intention was to join the Navy. He had worked very hard to get into one of India's finest colleges, so his parents wondered if he was certain about the path he was choosing. Kapish would prove just how committed he was when he was adjudged best cadet at the Naval Academy, and awarded the Sword of Honour by the Chief of Naval Staff. Backing him for an MTech degree now was an enormous show of faith by the Navy.

Feeling recharged after a week with his family, Lt Cdr Kapish returned to Mumbai, ready to dive back into his work.

The *Sindhuratna* was nearing the end of her refit and would be ready to sail by mid-February. With sailing duties back on the horizon, Lt Manoranjan also took a short break to visit his parents in Jamshedpur.

As an electrical watchkeeping officer on the submarine, Lt Manoranjan was living a childhood dream. In class V at the Army Public School in Bareilly, where his Armyman father was posted at the time, Manoranjan had come home after watching a military demonstration on his campus on the occasion of Republic Day. He had told his parents that there was nothing he wanted more than to wear a uniform. His father, Subedar

Navin Kumar, had given the usual advice: study hard, pay attention in school, do well, and you can choose whatever you want to be. Manoranjan would top his class in senior school, train with the Navy's engineering and electrical establishments and join the Indian Navy in 2009. Three years later, he would join the crew of the *Sindhuratna*.

Back in Mumbai, the two young officers, along with over ninety other men who comprised the *Sindhuratna*'s complement, waited for their submarine to be lowered back into the water. The 2300-ton hunk of metal had been out of action for months, and the crew couldn't wait to get back inside and stretch its legs out in the Arabian Sea.

When the day finally arrived for *Sindhuratna* to be put back into the sea from her dry dock, the anxious crew assembled at Mumbai's naval dockyard. One thousand four hundred kilometres away, another submariner, an alumnus of the *Sindhuratna*, was also closely tracking the events as they unfolded.

Commodore Ravi Dhingra had begun his underwater career on the *Sindhuratna*, doing his entire initial training on it. Many of the younger officers who were part of the crew in February 2014 were personnel he had trained. And since his duties at the Naval Headquarters were directly related to the submarine fleet, he was keeping daily tabs on what was going on.

'*Sindhuratna* had been in refit for some time and when the submarine comes out of refit, officers and sailors have not bonded for months as a full sailing unit,' says Commodore Ravi. 'To get back into action mode, to be able to handle any kind of requirement or emergency, the crew goes through something called a "work-up". It begins with a harbour phase and then out at sea. The crew essentially carries out various drills involving simulated emergencies like a fire or smoke in a compartment. They practise safety procedures like de-energizing compartments and restoring the delicate balance to the submarine so all the other functions work fine.'

On 19 February, with Capt. Sandip Sinha in command, Lt Cdr Kapish and Lt Manoranjan embarked the *Sindhuratna* with the rest of her crew for its first sail out to sea since the refit. For the next five days, the submarine would conduct a series of manoeuvres and trials, returning to its dock on 24 February. According to established procedure, the crew of the *Sindhuratna* needed to demonstrate that the post-refit 'work-up' had been satisfactorily completed. For this, the Western Naval Command's senior-most submariner, the Commodore Commanding Submarines (COMCOS), Commodore S.R. Kapoor, would embark and sail with them for what the Navy calls a Task-II examination,[1] a crucial step before the submarine is cleared for operations.

At 7.30 p.m. on 25 February, before setting sail, Lt Cdr Kapish called his parents. They didn't pick up. He called again. Maybe they were busy, he thought. So he sent them a text message saying he would be out at sea and unreachable for the next few days, and they should not worry.

The crew of the *Sindhuratna* was upbeat that evening. They were finally ready to prove they had held together professionally and were ready to handle the submarine in all respects.

---

[1] The layers of 'work-up' are indicative of how delicate and difficult submarine operations are. The myriad procedures that must align for successful and safe operations require constant checks and balances, since even small deviations or violations can mean disaster in the deep sea. In December 2018, the Indian Navy commissioned its first deep-submergence rescue vehicle (DSRV), a mini submarine designed to rescue the crew of submarines in distress.

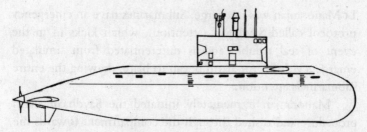

Kilo-class attack submarine

'The purpose of the Task-II was to practically demonstrate what kind of training level the crew had achieved,' says Commodore Ravi. 'So on the evening of 25 February, with the COMCOS on board, the *Sindhuratna* sailed out. During the evening, when they were leaving Mumbai harbour, and also that night, simulated emergencies were being given to the submarine's crew. That's how it works.'

In submarines, the crews work in shifts, since the vessel's stations can never be left unmanned. The night passed as *Sindhuratna* sailed, at a depth of 40 m, 110 km out into the Arabian Sea. As one part of the crew climbed into their 'slot in the wall' cabins—a signature of the highly cramped interiors of the Kilo-class design—the other part manned the submarine, sailing it further out for what would be a long day of tests the following day.

'Everything was calm that night,' remembers a sailor who was in Compartment 3 of the *Sindhuratna*. 'Lt Manoranjan was on duty as the electrical officer-in-charge in Compartment 3, and Lt Cdr Kapish, the deputy electrical officer (DLO), was at his post in Compartment 5.'

The quiet hum of the submarine, as it coursed through the water 40 m deep, was about to be dramatically interrupted.

At 5.30 the following morning, as examination drills began again, smoke was reported from Compartment 3 where

Lt Manoranjan was in charge. Submarines have an emergency protocol called Savdhaan (attention), which kicks in in the event of real trouble and is differentiated from simulated emergency drills. An alarm began to blare, drawing the entire submarine's attention.

'Manoranjan immediately initiated the Savdhaan alarm procedure and rushed through the compartment towards the source of the smoke,' says a sailor who was present at the time. 'Compartment 3 has a lot of electrical equipment, so he knew he had to move quickly before things got worse. Compartments in a Kilo are very cramped, so a fire can quickly spiral out of control. Manoranjan wasted no time.'

Within minutes, Lt Cdr Kapish had jogged through the narrow corridor of the submarine, arriving in Compartment 3 as the smoke was getting thicker.

'The smoke that was coming out had possibly heated some of the panelling running behind the equipment, and there was a short circuit in the cables, which began to burn, leading to even denser black smoke emanating in Compartment 3,' says Commodore Ravi.

Finding his way through the smoke, Lt Cdr Kapish found Lt Manoranjan hunting for the source of the smoke and fire so he could try and contain it as quickly as possible. The first thing both officers did was get the other men in Compartment 3 out, just as the smoke became unbearably thick.

'They forced us to leave the compartment, so we moved to an upper deck,' says the sailor who was in Compartment 3. 'As I exited, I could see them through the smoke. Manoranjan was using the communication console to speak to the CO to tell him that the situation was very serious.'

It was critical, actually. Compartment 3 housed a portion of *Sindhuratna*'s electric batteries and sat on top of another compartment that contained more batteries. A fire in a compartment with batteries could be catastrophic.

'The presence of batteries in that compartment made this a very tricky situation,' says Commodore Ravi. 'When the batteries charge, they give out hydrogen gas in small quantities, which usually get burned off. But if its quantity is not controlled, hydrogen is a highly explosive gas, and with a fire nearby, it could lead to a catastrophic situation. By virtue of being electrical officers, Kapish and Manoranjan would have known that, and therefore were trying to identify the seat of the fire, while at the same time getting everyone else out of the compartment.'

Receiving another call from Manoranjan about the worsening situation, CO Capt. Sinha took a call to take *Sindhuratna* to the surface.

'There was a major advantage in breaking the surface at that point,' says Commodore Ravi. 'With the submarine stationary and above water, there was a better chance of the smoke escaping from open hatches.'

Lt Cdr Kapish and Lt Manoranjan pushed eleven sailors out of Compartment 3, despite every one of them volunteering to stay and help. The sailors remember that Compartment III was nearly impossible to be in when they were pushed out by the two young officers, who refused to leave.

'*Sambhaal lenge* (We will manage), just get to the upper deck and wait for us,' Lt Cdr Kapish told the sailors as he and Lt Manoranjan got them out of Compartment 3.

'There is a certain sense of responsibility that officers have, and being officers, I guess they felt they were duty-bound to remain within the compartment and fix the problem, while getting everyone else out,' says Commodore Ravi.

Both the officers battled the smoke and continued to try locating the source of the fire, seemingly unconcerned about the harm the smoke was doing to them with each breath. As the minutes passed, the deadly smoke got thicker.

'The last anyone saw them, Kapish and Manoranjan were valiantly fighting the fire and smoke,' says Commodore Ravi. 'At some point, they may have possibly lost consciousness and by that time, Compartment 3 had already been sealed from the other side. Communication from the compartment had also stopped. The two boys had ensured that everything flammable that could allow the fire to spread had been removed from the compartment along with the eleven sailors.'

For all their efforts, the two officers couldn't put out the fire—the material that was burning was more smouldering than fully ablaze—but by removing other equipment, they had ensured that the fire didn't spread.

Just before the *Sindhuratna* surfaced, the CO descended the decks of his submarine for a first-hand inspection of the situation, but was forced to return to the upper decks after inhaling the dangerous smoke. Once the submarine surfaced, he got some of the crew members to put on breathing apparatuses so they could go back down to check on the two officers who were no longer answering calls on the submarine communication system.

Four separate rescue parties were sent down to Compartment 3, but were forced to retreat. The approach to the compartment had become extremely hot, and it was no longer possible for the sailors to go anywhere near it. And with the submarine's electrical mains turned off as a precautionary measure at the surface, the rescue teams were walking in total darkness with thick black smoke engulfing them.

'We couldn't see our hands if we held them out in front of our faces,' says a sailor who was sent down with one of the rescue parties. 'Kapish and Manoranjan had pushed us out of that compartment and had refused to allow us to stay. And they refused to come out till the job was done. If you had seen and felt that smoke, you would not have believed that someone had voluntarily remained in that compartment to fight it.'

With repeated attempts to reach Compartment 3 proving dangerous and futile, and the heat and smoke only increasing, the CO of *Sindhuratna* was faced with a terrible dilemma.

'It had now come to a point where the CO had to look to the safety of the rest of the men on board and the submarine itself,' says Commodore Ravi. 'It must have been the most difficult decision to make, since the two young officers were not accounted for, and there was no absolute clarity on their condition. It must have been a very distressing and difficult decision.'

As a last resort, 4 hours after the smoke was first detected, Capt. Sinha ordered the freon gas fire suppression system to be activated. The action would completely seal the submarine's compartments, suck out all the oxygen and pump freon gas at high pressure to quell the smouldering fire. After the freon gas was administered, Compartment 3 remained sealed as a precaution.

The *Sindhuratna* had surfaced, but it was in distress. The CO authorized a message to be sent out to the Western Naval Command headquarters, requesting emergency assistance. Within the hour, a Sea King helicopter arrived over the submarine, flying back with seven sailors who had taken seriously ill after inhaling the noxious fumes of Compartment 3. The helicopter would fly them straight to the INS Asvini naval hospital on Mumbai's southern tip. A naval fast attack craft (FAC) was also diverted towards *Sindhuratna*, picking up more of those affected by the smoke.

The submarine was now practically a floating shell, all its systems powered down as a safety precaution. A naval Sukanya–class patrol vessel arrived on the scene to tow the

submarine back to Mumbai. In Delhi, the *Sindhuratna* incident
would shake the highest levels of the Indian Navy. Taking
moral responsibility for the incident, coming as it did just six
months after the *Sindhurakshak* tragedy, then Chief of Naval
Staff, an anti-submarine warfare specialist, Admiral Devendra
Kumar Joshi, resigned, becoming the first Indian Navy chief to
do so. The Navy's vice chief at the time, Vice Admiral Robin
Dhowan, would take charge as interim chief with immediate
effect, becoming Chief of Naval Staff two months later.

Limping home with its compartments still sealed, the
Sindhuratna would be back at the Mumbai naval dockyard the
following day, on 27 February.

Once docked, the submarine was evacuated. The
compartments were then unsealed and ventilated with high-
pressure systems to drive out any residual gas or smoke. Later
that evening, a team of naval personnel finally descended the
decks to Compartment 3.

'The team opened Compartment 3 and immediately
saw both their bodies,' says Commodore Ravi. 'Kapish was
found near the electrical equipment. Manoranjan was found
near the possible source of the fire. It looked like they had
been fighting to remedy the situation to the point when
they passed out. We will never get to know their side of the
story. What we do know is they fought till the end, not for
a moment thinking of giving up. They pushed eleven sailors
out from that compartment, but by securing that area and
ensuring the fire did not reach the battery pits, they essentially
saved all ninety-two people on board that day. They saved the
submarine.'

Thirty-six hours after the probable time of their deaths,
the families of both the officers in Delhi and Jamshedpur were
notified. Still in profound shock, an Indian Navy board of
inquiry would immediately begin investigations. To lead the

difficult probe, the Navy would hand-pick an officer, Rear Admiral Soonil Bhokare, who, in 1988, was part of the first crew of the *Sindhuratna*, and the senior-most officer to have served on board.

In the national media, a controversy would explode over suggestions that the *Sindhuratna*'s batteries were dangerously old, and that government red tape had slowed the replacement of critical safety equipment. With a national election around the corner, the tragedy would briefly showcase the political animosities between the government of the day and the opposition, which had reached fever pitch. Within the military, there would be a call for accountability all the way up to the Ministry of Defence.

As it turned out, the batteries on board *Sindhuratna* were not to blame for the fire, but a failure in a regeneration unit in Compartment 3.

'The batteries being old was certainly an issue, but this particular fire wasn't because of the batteries,' says Commodore Ravi. 'What happens is when a submarine is submerged, there is a steady build-up of carbon dioxide (CO_2) inside it. Now, if you're in a situation where you cannot surface for operational reasons, the regeneration compound (RC) essentially absorbs the CO_2. This process gives out heat and also smoke if it comes in contact with seawater. It's possible that some seawater entered the submarine, causing the smoke and heat. These RC boxes are fitted very close to submarine cables. One of the boxes may have caught fire or the heat might have been so great that the cables associated with it gave way, leading to a short circuit.'

By 4 March, the Navy would release information through a press release to battle allegations about expired batteries, saying, 'The batteries presently installed on *Sindhuratna* have till date completed about 113 cycles, as against 200 cycles available for exploitation. The batteries which were being exploited by *Sindhuratna* at the time of the incident were [therefore] operationally in-date.'[2]

Commodore Ravi, who has commanded the *INS Sindhughosh*, says, 'While the batteries were not the culprit, there was always a threat. The older the battery, the higher the percentage of hydrogen discharge. That's a real threat that Kapish and Manoranjan were aware of.'

The *Sindhuratna* remained in harbour for two months, and an extensive exercise was conducted to re-cable and rebuild many of the interiors that had been destroyed by smoke and flame. The submarine remains in service.

On 15 August 2014, the *Sindhuratna*'s two young electrical officers were decorated with a posthumous Shaurya Chakra, India's third-highest peacetime gallantry award. Their citations would acknowledge what they had truly done.

Lt Cdr Kapish's Shaurya Chakra citation concludes with, 'The officer sacrificed his life keeping the safety of the submarine and personnel above his own. His act of courage and bravery was beyond the call of duty and thus in keeping with the highest traditions of the Indian Navy and the time-honoured military adage "Service before Self".'

Lt Manoranjan's citation says, 'The officer laid down his life keeping with his responsibility as the compartment officer, safety of the submarine and personnel above his own. His singular act of courage and bravery resulted in the damage being contained, casualties being minimized and extensive structural damage to the submarine being averted. His valour and dedication is in keeping with the highest traditions of the Indian Navy and ethos of the officer corp.'

---

[2] https://www.indiannavy.nic.in/content/accident-onboard-ins-sindhuratna

For the two families, though, life stands terribly still.

'I cannot imagine what it must have been like inside the submarine, and I am haunted by it,' says Lt Cdr Kapish's father, naval veteran Cdr Ishwar Singh. 'He was a great boy and made us proud at every stage of his life. Wherever he has gone, whatever he has done. He fought till the very end like a true soldier. He did whatever he could to save the lives of his fellow sailors, the men under his charge. Everybody doesn't get a chance like this—to face such a threat and prove their valour. And when he confronted that situation, he faced it with immense courage and died a brave man. He was a true hero.'

Hours after the gallantry award was announced, Lt Manoranjan's mother, Rukmani Devi, would speak to journalists through tears of sorrow and rage.

'What is the use of this award if the submarine wasn't safe to be in?' she would ask. 'If the government wants to know what I want, then let me say I want my boy back. Can they give me my boy back?'

Time barely heals such wounds. Today, Lt Manoranjan's father, Subedar Navin Kumar Chaudhary, says, '*Jab tak saans chalegi, woh ghaav toh rahega humare dil mein* (As long as we are alive, the wounds will remain fresh). But our heart swells with pride knowing he saved so many lives. We miss him every day and we are sure that the men whose lives he saved that day also think about our boy and miss him.'

Lt Manoranjan's younger brother, Sumant, was also headed into the armed forces. He had cleared the written examination for NDA and was to appear for the Service Selection Board (SSB) interview when the tragedy on board the *Sindhuratna* occurred. His shattered parents barred him from going for that interview, refusing to allow him to join the Army.

Lt Manoranjan had been cleared for a promotion to the rank of Lieutenant Commander at the time of his death.

In the most terrible twist of fate, tragedy would return to Lt Cdr Kapish's family four months after they lost their son. They would lose their second son, Ashish, to a heart attack. Their third son, Manish, is twenty-six.

'Kapish was a very precious child,' says his father. 'He was born in 1986, seven years after we lost two infant sons. Kapish was very special and we had taken good care of him. Whatever he has done, he has brought glory to us. Life has been very hard. Now I am left with only one child. We can't do anything. We have to bear it.'

On 26 February every year, as two families hold small memorial events for their sons, the crew of the *Sindhuratna* doesn't forget either. Over the course of the day, when their duties allow them a spare moment, every man descends in turns to Compartment 3.

There, they stand for a minute before two tiny framed pictures of two officers, who saved an entire crew while sacrificing their own lives.

6

'There Are More Terrorists Inside, Sir!'

Captain Pawan Kumar

Shopian, Jammu and Kashmir
20 February 2016

At 2.20 in the afternoon of 20 February 2016, Capt. Pawan Kumar sat back in a metal chair at a secret temporary base in the freezing wilderness outside Shopian in south Kashmir. He had arrived an hour before in a jeep with five men from his unit of ten months, the Army's 10 Para Special Forces. Dressed in a black hoodie, black combat trousers and an olive bomber jacket, he was thoughtful.

He had turned twenty-three a month ago, but his dishevelled beard and exhaustion made him look older. As he sat there awaiting orders for a new mission, he pulled out his iPhone from the pocket of his trousers and began scrolling through a news feed he had made it a habit to glance through at least once a day. That afternoon, his phone's screen threw up picture after picture from two places that meant something to him.

The first were images of groups of angry men setting fire to vehicles and smashing property near Capt. Pawan's home in Haryana's Jind district. The violence was part of a protest by Haryana's dominant Jat community, which had mobilized aggressively and with increasing violence to demand reservation in government jobs. Capt. Pawan squinted at the images—many of the places looked familiar. He had grown up there, but had left home to join the military after school.

The second set of images were from Delhi's Jawaharlal Nehru University (JNU), where the student protests that had begun ten days earlier had intensified into a high-pitched controversy. Some students had held a high-decibel protest to mark the third death anniversary of Mohammed Afzal Guru, an Indian teacher from Kashmir who had been convicted and hanged for aiding a Pakistani terror attack on India's Parliament in 2001. The protests had exploded into a national controversy in the media and the political arena after some among the protesters seemed to call for 'freedom' from India and a 'breakup' of the country. The campus looked familiar, though Capt. Pawan had only been there twice. As a graduate of NDA, he had received a degree from JNU like all cadets who become commissioned officers. It was therefore, in effect, his alma mater.

He clicked the phone shut and glanced at his watch, looking out through the small window to the left of where he sat. A slow breeze rustled a row of chinar trees near the perimeter of the camp. Then, he tapped his phone on again, raised his right arm and took a selfie. But he wasn't looking into the camera. His head bent, his expression was of bored gloominess, staring at the floor.

He looked at the picture for a moment, then posted it to his Facebook profile. When the app prompted him for a caption, Capt. Pawan thought for a moment. Then he keyed in:

> *'Kisi ko reservation chahiye toh kisi ko azadi,*
> *Bhai humme kuchh nahi chahiye bhai,*
> *Bas apni razai'*
> (Some want reservation, some want freedom,
> Man, I want nothing,
> But for my blanket)

He looked at the post for a moment, smiled to himself and clicked the phone off. Sitting back in the chair, he closed his eyes for the first time that day. An afternoon siesta was the furthest thing from his mind, but a few minutes of stillness were welcome. When they arrived at Shopian earlier that day, he and his men knew they had essentially been placed on hunting duty. The villages that dotted the landscape beyond the forest that hid his temporary base were an uninterrupted hotbed of local militancy, armed and funded from across the LoC by terror groups based in Pakistan. Any moment, Capt. Pawan expected to hear either from the superiors in his unit or from the J&K Police Special Operations Group (SOG), teams of which prowled the villages of the area sniffing out terror hideouts and weapon dumps.

The wave of tiredness that swept over Capt. Pawan on that cold afternoon was hardly surprising. He had been deployed in Jammu and Kashmir barely six months earlier, in August 2015, and had been on his feet nearly the entire time. In that chair, lulled by the stillness of his camp, Capt. Pawan slipped into a deep sleep, the kind afforded by Kashmir's unmistakably pristine air.

Two hours later, at the 10 Para Special Force main base in Awantipora 40 km away, Capt. Pawan's team leader, Maj. Tushar Singh Tomar, received a call from the Army's 15 Corps Headquarters in Srinagar. Maj. Tushar was used to receiving calls summoning him at short notice for anti-terror operations—it was his bread and butter, after all. But the brief he received over the phone from Srinagar made it clear that this was going to be a nightmarish mission even by Special Forces standards.

At 4.20 p.m., a convoy of buses transporting over 500 CRPF personnel from Jammu had been ambushed by a small group of terrorists in Pampore, a suburb of Srinagar on River

Jhelum's east bank that was famous for its saffron fields. The number of terrorists was unknown at the time, but three of them had taken position outside the main gate of the state government's Entrepreneurship Development Institute (JKEDI), a plush four-storeyed building that stood out for its modern construction and carefully manicured lawns. Two CRPF men, Head Constable Bhola Prasad Singh and Constable R.K. Raina, had been killed and several injured in the initial ambush. But when soldiers who formed part of the convoy's armed escort spilled out of their buses to return fire, the terrorists rapidly shifted position. All the while firing, the three men scaled the compound wall, dashed across the wide lawn and disappeared into the JKEDI building.

It was a Saturday. As the CRPF soldiers took defensive positions, they hoped the building would be shut for the weekend. But it soon became clear that the institute had over 100 Kashmiri civilians inside, attending special weekend lectures on entrepreneurship. And three terrorists had just entered the building.

'Bloody nightmare,' Maj. Tushar found himself whispering to himself as he disconnected the call. Gathering his thoughts, a few moments later he dialled Capt. Pawan in Shopian, asking him and his squad to drop everything and move immediately towards Pampore.

'We got the information that the JKEDI building was surrounded, but that the forces on the ground had no way in,' says Tushar, who is now a Lieutenant Colonel and second-in-command of the 10 Para Special Forces.

As Team Leader, Maj. Tushar's 'boys' were split into squads deployed across the Kashmir valley. He chose to summon two squads immediately to Pampore—Capt. Pawan's from Shopian, and the squad under another young officer deployed near Kulgam further to the south.

Capt. Pawan and his Team Leader agreed to rendezvous at a common meeting point near Pampore before heading into the encounter area. A cold late winter rain had begun to fall as Maj. Tushar left his unit base in Awantipora, the kind that soldiers in the Valley know well. A steady, unrelenting drizzle that drives the cold into your bones.

'When I departed from Awantipora, Pawan called me saying he was stuck—it had been raining hard in his area, and his Gypsy had got stranded in a nallah that had overflowed on to the road,' says Tushar.

Cancelling the rendezvous, Maj. Tushar headed straight to where Capt. Pawan was stuck.

'When I reached, I see this guy had taken off his shoes, rolled up his pants, and with his feet submerged in freezing sub-zero temperature water, he was pushing the Gypsy with all his strength,' says Tushar.

The Major got down from his jeep and helped the squad push the Gypsy out of the slush and back on to the road. Capt. Pawan was soaked to the skin. His Team Leader suggested they head to the nearest temporary camp so the young officer could change and catch a breath before they moved towards Pampore. But Capt. Pawan refused.

'We'll lose time if we don't move now, Sir,' he told his superior officer. 'Let's move immediately.'

It wasn't the first time Capt. Pawan had demonstrated an unusual youthful keenness to be deployed in an operation. Originally commissioned into 7 Dogra, the new officer yearned to be part of the Special Forces. In April 2015, he successfully made the switch and was inducted into the 10 Para unit. With his maroon beret and *balidaan* badge in place, he immediately requested his CO to send him to Kashmir. He wanted to waste no time getting into the thick of action.

Arriving in Kashmir four months after he joined the 10 Para, he was sent on his first mission on 3 October in Pulwama, an operation in which two terrorists were killed. It would be the first of a nearly uninterrupted series of missions the young officer would throw himself into.

'He would be the first to volunteer for every operation,' says Tushar. 'He was doing a lot of operations—almost every single day he was out on an op.'

As the rain showed no signs of stopping, the two officers and their men got back into their vehicles and made for Pampore, arriving just as the sun was setting.

'We arrived in Pampore and had to dodge a crowd of stone-pelters near the encounter site,' says Tushar. Stone-pelting crowds had become par for the course during anti-terror operations in the Kashmir Valley, and this was no surprise.

A month earlier, Capt. Pawan had been struck in the face by a stone following an encounter in Pulwama. A knot of stone-pelters had attacked the Special Forces men as they embarked on a combing operation looking for additional terrorists. The incident had revealed much about Capt. Pawan to his superiors.

'Pawan had taken three days' leave on his birthday (15 January, which happens to also be Army Day) to go to Ferozepur to participate in a reunion of his original unit, the 7 Dogra,' says Tushar. 'Thereafter, he reported to the Valley on 18 January and was deployed the very next day on another encounter, once again in Pulwama. On the way back, there was a lot of stone-pelting. He was hit by a stone on his face and broke three front teeth. I was with him, but he never told me. And he kept on walking. Later, I found out through another boy, who informed me that Pawan was bleeding. We gave him some first aid, which he accepted reluctantly. He was totally calm about his broken three teeth, with the nerves exposed. He refused an injection. We had to force him to see a doctor in Awantipora and then later send him for a check-up to the base hospital in Srinagar. When he was there, they recommended that he take sick leave and rest for a few days. He agreed to visit the doctor once a week, but refused outright to take leave.'

Carefully navigating through the crowd of stone-pelters near Pampore, Maj. Tushar and Capt. Pawan arrived on the scene to the intermittent sound of assault rifle fire and grenade blasts. Tushar had been right about this being a nightmare.

Stepping out of their vehicles, the two officers quickly found the immediate responders at the site. Apart from the CRPF, an RR unit had been deployed around the JKEDI building, cutting off any chance of escape for the three terrorists who were now confirmed to be inside the building. A team from the J&K Police SOG was also present.

The men quickly assessed what was becoming a devastatingly difficult situation. With information confirming that over 100 civilians were inside, soldiers on the outside couldn't fire indiscriminately at the building for fear of casualties. And grenades were out of the question. The three terrorists, who had made their way into the building from the main entrance on the ground floor, had no such constraints. Switching among themselves and moving cunningly between rooms on the top floor that provided them the perfect vantage point, they fired intermittently at the forces below, keeping them on the defensive and effectively pinning them down.

During a brief lull in the firing, one team of CRPF men managed to approach and enter the building. What they didn't know was that the terrorists had seen them and quietly crept to the ground floor to stop them. Watching their every move, the terrorists flung a grenade at the CRPF men as soon as they entered the lobby, injuring four and triggering the first heavy firefight indoors. One terrorist was hit in the leg in the exchange, forcing him and his partners to return to their positions in the rooms on the top floor. The injured CRPF men were carefully extracted from the building. With the terrorists now effectively restricted to the top floor, they resumed firing at the forces below, even as the injured men were being pulled out on stretchers. The situation had got worse.

What this exchange had done, however, was provide a diversion so that additional CRPF units could approach other entrances of the building and extract the civilians. Throughout that night, civilians would be pulled out in small numbers, often two or three at a time, to ensure the terrorists didn't blow the whole building up.

Capt. Pawan observed the building carefully. Smoke rose from a blaze at the lobby level, and a facade of glass panes on the building's front was completely shattered. The darkness was lit up periodically by flashes of gunfire from the top floors. It was clear to him that the terrorists had the advantage. And with some civilians still inside the building, there was every possibility that the encounter could turn into a hostage situation.

It had been decided that the next offensive action would be at first light the following morning. But Capt. Pawan hated the idea. He took Maj. Tushar aside.

'We can't let the night go, Sir,' Capt. Pawan told him. 'I'm proceeding for a recce of the building. We can finish this.'

Maj. Tushar considered it for a moment. It was a highly dangerous proposition. Approaching the building unseen was virtually impossible.

'Every minute we give them, they can plant more traps and extend the stand-off. There will be more casualties. Let

me go in now and do a recce. What else are we here for, Sir?'
Capt. Pawan insisted.

The young Captain had a point. The Special Forces had
been summoned specifically because of the high possibility of a
night fight in an enclosed space. If approaching the building was
difficult under the cover of darkness, it would be impossible in
daylight. And Capt. Pawan was right—the terrorists appeared
well-trained and armed to stretch the encounter out as long as
possible. It was important to do some damage, any damage,
while it was still dark. Maj. Tushar relented.

Capt. Pawan gathered the five men of his squad and held
a quick briefing in the cover provided by a large armoured
vehicle, with bullets raining down from the top floors of the
building. As they spoke, the men began to dress themselves
with the equipment they would need for the recce. First, they
put on their ballistic vests and gloves. Each man then strapped
an American-built AN/PVS-14 night vision device to his
helmet using a harness—a crucial piece of optical gear that
would allow them to hunt in pitch darkness. Finally, each man
checked his main weapon—a Colt M4A1 carbine along with
its ammunition magazines.

The plan was shared with the CRPF, RR and SOG.
With backup forces in position around the perimeter of the
compound, Capt. Pawan and his men crept over a low wall
and headed towards the building. Through his night vision
device, Capt. Pawan could make out the building clearly,
along with the fire still burning in the lobby area that appeared
to him as a bright green blaze.

At the perimeter, Maj. Tushar had put on his battle gear
too, ready to rush in as part of a second wave. In touch with
Capt. Pawan through a combat communications earpiece, he
watched through his own night vision device as the young
officer's squad made its way carefully around the building.

'There was speculative firing from many of the windows on the top floor. But I could tell Pawan was very calm,' says Tushar. 'He took his time. He walked around the entire building, carefully studying the situation. Then we worked out a plan. He informed me that he planned to take it floor by floor, starting with the top.'

Entering the building from the front lobby was out of the question. The wide atrium would give the terrorists an easy vantage point to pick out the approaching commandos and fire straight at them. Capt. Pawan had found a better approach—through an emergency fire staircase at the back of the building.

Calling for cover fire on the front of the building to keep the terrorists focused on that area, Capt. Pawan and his men carefully slipped to the back and began ascending the stairway to the fourth floor. With reconnaissance complete, the plan was a standard drill—to clear the building floor by floor from the top downward. Every few seconds, Capt. Pawan would whisper into his mouthpiece to tell Maj. Tushar what he saw and what the status of his approach was.

'He sounded very confident as he and his five boys went up the stairs,' says Tushar. 'There was a restaurant on the rooftop. Adjoining it were a number of rooms that had to be cleared. Pawan kept me informed at every step.'

When Capt. Pawan's squad was halfway up the stairs, the firing from the top floors stopped. He quickly received word from Maj. Tushar to proceed with caution as there was no way to confirm that the attention of the terrorists remained diverted to the front. Capt. Pawan noted the warning and proceeded up the stairs even more slowly, listening at every step for any audio clues that might give away the location of the terrorists.

Ascending the final set of stairs, the six commandos emerged onto a small landing with a door that led to the top floor. Capt. Pawan waited, straining his ears to check if he could hear anything at all from beyond the door. There was silence. It was totally dark by this time, but Capt. Pawan and his squad trudged forward through the door, seeing a world painted shades of green by their night vision devices, their weapons at shoulder height and ready. They knew they were a whisper away from a firefight.

Beretta pistol

'Entering floor now,' Capt. Pawan whispered, as the scout from his squad opened the door and the six men entered the floor into a narrow passageway. At the end of the passage were a pair of doors to rooms that looked out over the side of the building. The men would no longer have the luxury of silence, as they now needed to begin clearing the rooms one by one. With the element of stealth gone, they would be infinitely more vulnerable. There was no other way to get the operation going.

In silence, Capt. Pawan signalled to his scout to break down the door.

'The scout tried to break open the door but couldn't, so Capt. Pawan rushed forward and kicked down the door quickly. As soon as he broke the door down, there was a burst of fire from inside the room,' says Tushar, who could hear the firing through his earpiece in real time. Waiting anxiously for an update, Maj. Tushar gathered his men and asked them to prepare to approach the building for backup.

Capt. Pawan did not have the time to report his every move any longer. He had just broken down the door to the room in which the terrorists had taken refuge. The only audio from his feed now was an uninterrupted exchange of fire. Maj. Tushar listened carefully as he signalled to his squad to follow him towards the building.

'The first burst of fire from inside the room missed Pawan, so he immediately charged inside,' says Tushar. 'He was now standing just 2 m from the terrorist who had fired. The second burst hit him in the shoulder and chest.' Shaken but still standing, Capt. Pawan edged a metre closer to the terrorist before opening fire and dropping him in his tracks.

'Pawan's voice came through to me. He said, "*Lagi hai* (I've been hit)," but continued,' Tushar says.

What the men didn't know was that one of the bullets had pierced through Capt. Pawan's chest and ripped away a piece of his heart. Bleeding profusely, he continued to edge forward as he had seen the other two terrorists retreat into another room.

'Two other boys from the squad continued to fire alongside Pawan—they knew they had only one opening to fire through,' says Tushar. 'For the first time, it became clear what the number of terrorists was. Pawan had dropped one. There were two more.'

Maj. Tushar asked the young officer to move back and let the other squad members go forward, but Capt. Pawan said he now had a vantage point from which to proceed. As he edged forward, a third hail of fire came out of the dark recesses of the room, hitting him again. This time, the two lead scouts of the team, Sabarmal Baji and Nayak Singh, quickly pulled him out of the room. As two members of the squad stood in the passageway firing into the room, Capt. Pawan was carried carefully down the stairs by three men, even as he protested weakly.

As they reached the ground floor, Maj. Tushar's team was preparing to ascend the stairs.

'He was bleeding heavily. Pawan was tall and very well-built for his age. It took three of his men to carry him down the stairs,' Tushar says. 'I couldn't believe it, seeing Pawan like that. He had incredible physical strength.'

As Cadet Sergeant Major of his squadron at NDA, Pawan had displayed unusual endurance and might—course-mates remember him carrying other cadets during cross country training and never betraying more than passing tiredness.

Now dizzy from blood loss, Capt. Pawan stammered to his team leader, '*Bande hain andar, Sir, aur bande hain* (There are more inside, Sir, there are more).'

Capt. Pawan slipped in and out of consciousness as Maj. Tushar quickly took a briefing from the other two men of the squad about the situation on the top floor.

'The terrorist had missed him with the first burst of fire, so this guy had charged inside,' says Tushar. 'It was an intensely close combat engagement. Just about 2 m. He was hit but he continued. It was just an unfortunate moment when he was shot—the range was too close; otherwise, Pawan could have dodged it. There was no room, it was impossible. What he did was beyond brave.'

Apart from his bravery, Capt. Pawan had also given the operation its first foothold into the building, a crucial tactical step upon which the remainder of the operation could be planned and executed. The foothold drastically reduced the advantage held thus far by the terrorists by virtue of their position, and effectively began a countdown to their end. For the first time since the encounter began, the terrorists were on the defensive.

'Any average guy would have died on the spot, or wouldn't have been able to stay awake,' says Tushar. 'Pawan wanted to continue even in that state, but his body wasn't allowing it. I could see it was very difficult for him to realize he could not continue the fight, even as he oozed blood.'

An ambulance was summoned to take Capt. Pawan to the 92 Base Hospital a few kilometres away in Srinagar city. When he was stretchered off the encounter site, he was still conscious, still stammering to his Team Leader.

'*Chaloo kar do, Sir, bande andar hain. Ek-do aur hain andar. Pehla banda iss side par hai aur do bande andar nikal gaye hain* (Start the operation, Sir. There are a couple more inside. The first is on this side and two more have escaped within),' Capt. Pawan said before being loaded into the ambulance and driven away.

'One bullet wouldn't have pulled him down. Even two or three rounds wouldn't have stopped him. Unfortunately, one of those bullets ripped off a part of his heart. It was a very bad hit. If it hadn't hit his heart, he would have continued fighting,' says Tushar. 'He was unbelievably strong.'

An hour later, just before dawn on 21 February, Capt. Pawan, twenty-three years old, succumbed to his injuries at the Srinagar base hospital.

Back in Pampore, the foothold he provided into the besieged building would be crucial to an operation that stretched over 48 hours. A terrible reminder of the deadly difficulty of the operation would come the following day, when two more Special Forces men—Capt. Tushar Mahajan and Lance Naik Om Prakash from the 9 Para Special Forces unit—would lose their lives in gun battles within the shattered, blazing building. In the days that followed, questions would explode over whether tactics had failed, or whether the men had taken unnecessary risks in their pursuit of the terrorists. But leaders in the unit would vouch for their men—they had been in the best possible position to take the decisions they did. And what Capt. Pawan had done was, quite literally, open the door to the end of the operation.

'Traditionally, building interventions are done in the daytime. In Pawan's case, they stormed the building at 2 a.m.,' says Tushar. 'He was extremely calm and confident. Try and picture operating in pitch-black darkness.'

The second thing Capt. Pawan had done was cross what is known as the 'fatal funnel'. In close quarter combat, the fatal funnel is described as the cone-shaped path leading from the entry where the assaulter (Capt. Pawan) is most vulnerable to the defenders (the terrorists) inside the room. Once an assaulter enters, defenders inside the room do everything they can to keep the assaulter inside the fatal funnel, where bullets are most likely to find him. It was in the fatal funnel that Capt. Pawan had killed the first terrorist. And it was here that bullets had found him.

'Pawan had conquered the fatal funnel with his life,' says Tushar. 'The first door you enter leaves you with the maximum probability of being hit. After that, you are inside. The terrorists know it. You know it. Earlier, there was concrete between you. Now there's nothing. They no longer have an advantage. It's only a matter of time.'

'We've lost Pawan,' a voice at the other end of the line from Srinagar said. Maj. Tushar had been ready for the news, but somewhere, he had still believed the young officer would pull through. It was then that Maj. Tushar was informed that Capt. Pawan had been shot through the heart. Anything less, and he would have survived.

'I spent that night in disbelief, more than anything else,' Tushar says. 'It wasn't believable that Pawan was gone. He was a supremely strong, intelligent soldier. He had gone through heavy stone pelting and calmly walked away. He took a leadership call to break down a door, knowing those first bullets could have his name on them. He held his nerve no matter what. And he was an incredibly disciplined fighter.'

Tomar refers to how Capt. Pawan unfailingly carried two weapons into operation—his M4A1 carbine, of course, but always backed up by a Beretta pistol.

'This is basic protocol for us in the Special Forces, but people tend to forget during operations,' says Tushar. 'Pawan also made it a point to keep two ammunition magazines strapped together. And he always changed magazines before the first one was empty. These are basic techniques, but people forget. Pawan didn't. He never made those mistakes.'

Nearly 48 hours after the stand-off began, the operation was finally brought to a close on 22 February with the confirmed killing of all three Pakistani terrorists. Intelligence agencies would later reveal that the three men likely infiltrated weeks before across the LoC in Handwara in north Kashmir, before slipping into the Valley along the Jhelum.

On 22 February, wreaths would be laid on a wooden casket containing Capt. Pawan's body at the Army's Badami Bagh Cantonment in Srinagar. Maj. Tushar and the other men from 10 Para Special Forces would be unable to attend, because they were still deployed at the Pampore encounter site.

With the Jat quota agitations still raging across Haryana, including in areas surrounding Capt. Pawan's native Jind district, it became clear to the Army that transporting the young officer's remains by road from anywhere could meet with roadblocks and unexpected trouble. In a rare appeal, the Army officially called for the people of Haryana to extend their full support in ensuring that the body of the soldier could be sent back to his village. To play it safe, however, the casket containing Capt. Pawan's body was flown from Srinagar to Pathankot in an Army Dhruv helicopter. At the base, the Army held another farewell ceremony for the young officer. From Pathankot, the helicopter airlifted the casket straight to his native Badhana village in Jind. From the air, the crew of that helicopter would have glimpsed any crowds that had gathered.

By this time, Capt. Pawan's Facebook post from two days earlier had been discovered by journalists, his words amplifying the irony of the situation to the fullest. On social media, he may have playfully dismissed the agitation by members of his community. His antipathy towards the mobilization actually ran deeper.

'He loved his iPhone and MacBook. Remember how young he was,' says Tushar. 'These gadgets were his steady connection to the world. He wasn't just active on social media, but was also very vocal about his views. He would openly say Haryanvis don't require reservations, and that this was all politics. He hailed the people of Haryana as brave, strong, as winners in sports arenas and beyond. He was like, "*Yeh sab bakwaas hai, Sir* (This is all rubbish, Sir)."

'I couldn't reach [Jind] for the last rites because of operational duties. Most of our unit did go from wherever they were. Our CO was there. The Jat agitation was quite bad, and tempers were on edge. But news had also spread by this time about Pawan, especially in and around Jind. Many of the road blockades simply disappeared when they heard about Pawan. I hear there was a 3-km long line of people leading into his village, wailing and crying. In Haryana, people do care about their soldiers. Crowds arrived from all over for the funeral in his village.'

As deafening chants of '*Pawan Kumar amar rahe* (Long live Pawan Kumar)' broke through the sounds of mourning, marigold petals came showering down as the casket was carried by four Special Forces men into the forecourt of the officer's small home. Stoic and solemn amid the wailing and the slogans, Capt. Pawan's father knelt next to the casket, while relatives pulled the cover off.

Inside, wrapped in white, was Rajbir Singh's only child. His eyes were closed and his face wore a gentle calm. His dishevelled hair and beard were hidden by the folds of the cloth that now draped him. His mother would be brought out of the house to see him one last time. Inconsolable and reluctant, she would touch Pawan's cheek before collapsing near the casket.

'I had one child. I gave him to the Army. To the nation. No father could be prouder,' Rajbir Singh would tell the journalists who waited to hear from Capt. Pawan's father. The comment, made with unusual composure, would stun the country and echo across the media through that day.

'He was an only child. He spoke to his parents once every few days. He knew they worried about him, but they would never let him know that,' Tushar says. 'He always wanted to be in the Army, but wasn't sure which area. He went through NDA and IMA. Initially, he wanted to join the Ordnance Corps. Then he decided to join the Infantry. One of his instructors was from the Dogra regiment, so he was commissioned into 7 Dogra in December 2013. Later, he learnt about the Special Forces.'

Unable to extricate himself from operations at Pampore and another anti-terror operation a few days later in Pulwama, Maj. Tushar would finally get the time to visit Jind on 4 March, two weeks after Capt. Pawan's death.

'I have never seen a braver family. Their pride is not an act. His father isn't lying about the pride he feels,' says Tushar. 'Their sorrow runs perfectly parallel to how proud they are of their son's sacrifice. It is hard to describe.'

'We had many plans for Pawan,' says his father. 'He was in love with a girl whom we had met and liked. We were looking at a possible marriage in 2017. Had Pawan been around, I would have perhaps become a grandfather by now. *Par zindagi ki raftaar mein sab sapne peeche reh gaye* (But the pace of life overtook all our dreams). He had plans for us too. Pawan would often say that we will sell off the Jind house and buy one in Panchkula. That's a far better place, he would say. *Hum baap–beta ne bahut planning ki thi. Par kismet ne apni planning ki thi* (We father–son had planned a lot of things. But destiny had its own plans).'

Six months after his death, a day before the Independence Day in 2016, the government announced that Capt. Pawan would be decorated with the Shaurya Chakra by the Indian President. Capt. Tushar and Lance Naik Om Prakash too were decorated with the Shaurya Chakra for their sacrifice.

Capt. Pawan's parents speak about him every day, to each other and to anyone who visits them.

'We will miss him till our deaths,' says his father. 'He was our only child. We rummage through old photo albums to revisit the happier times of our lives. We have a cupboard in the house and all of Pawan's stuff is in it. His Shaurya Chakra, his uniform and his boots—everything. Sometimes we just take his clothes out of the cupboard and hold them.'

A year into the Army, Capt. Pawan had chosen to use his first spell of leave not to go home, but to bike up on his Bullet motorcycle to Khardung La in Ladakh, the world's highest motorable pass.

Tushar, now second-in-command of the 10 Para Special Forces, says he will never forget the young commando, but believes he will hang on to one story more than any other to remember Capt. Pawan. It was late one night in December 2015, in a snow-blown patch of wilderness south of Srinagar.

'We had been deployed there for an operation. But the intelligence turned out to be faulty, so there was no encounter and no sign of any terrorists,' says Tushar. 'The weather was very bad, and it was snowing very heavily. My legs were nearly frozen and I suggested we return to base. But Pawan had a smile on his face. He said, "*Sir, thodi der baithte hain, aayenge aayenge* (Sir, let's sit here a while, they'll come)." He persuaded me to sit there the whole night in the snow and brutal cold. My brain knew that no terrorists would come. But Pawan insisted we wait. I don't think he expected any terrorists either. I think he just liked being out there.'

7

'I Rust when I Rest'

Major Satish Dahiya

'*Aap ghar se bahar mat jana, aaj kucch aane wala hai* (Don't leave home, something is going to arrive today).'

Sujata Chowdhry wondered for a moment why her husband was speaking in an unusually hushed voice. He was calling from the headquarters of his Army counter-insurgency unit in north Kashmir's Kupwara, where voices were kept low as a rule. But it was clear he was making an extra effort to be discreet.

Sujata understood. Maybe Maj. Satish Dahiya's men were within earshot and he was embarrassed to be speaking to his wife on Valentine's Day. Yes, that must be it.

She had taunted him the day before, after he had had a package of children's towels delivered to their home in Jaipur for Priyasha, their daughter who would turn two in a few months. The towels were better suited for an infant, but Sujata had smiled and kept them, despite her husband's repeated pleas that she have them exchanged. Later that night, she sent him a message on WhatsApp: 'You know what day it is tomorrow? You've sent presents for your daughter. What about your wife?'

Sujata didn't receive a reply that night, but was woken early the next morning by her husband's hushed instructions not to leave home.

'After that, he disconnected the phone,' says Sujata. 'I began the day, got our daughter ready for school, dropped her off and returned home to get ready for the day. That's when Satish called again, asking where I was. He again asked me to stay home and to expect a parcel at noon. Like his first call in the morning, he talked for barely 30 seconds before hanging up. He kept saying, '*Bahar hoon kaam pe* (I'm out on duty).'

Shortly before noon, Sujata drove to Priyasha's nursery school near their home. On their way back, Maj. Satish called for the third time.

'He asked me why I'd left the house, and what if the parcel arrived while I was gone,' says Sujata. 'After reminding him that there was nobody else to collect our child from school, I teased him, saying I hoped the parcel was in fact for me, and not for someone else. Satish was anxious but taunted me back, saying it looked like he would be doing nothing else that day but coordinating this parcel business. He hung up again quickly.'

After Priyasha had been fed and put down for an afternoon nap, Sujata settled down to wait for the parcel, half expecting her husband to call back every hour for updates.

But Maj. Satish would call next only at 5.22 p.m. This time, it wasn't from his own mobile phone, but a number she recognized as being from his unit. And this time, he didn't ask about the parcel. He quickly informed her that he was leaving for an operation, before hanging up abruptly.

This wasn't unusual. Maj. Satish was an officer with the RR, the chief counter-insurgency and anti-terror force in Jammu and Kashmir. The 30th Battalion of the RR, which the thirty-two-year-old officer was a part of, operated in Handwara, one of the most militant-infested zones near the LoC in north Kashmir. This was a restive militancy hotspot that was regularly fed by a stream of Pakistan-trained terrorist infiltrators who stole across the frontier fence to launch attacks.

Far from unusual, dropping everything to dash to an operation was, in fact, part of the day's work for the RR. But it had taken Sujata a while to get used to it.

Maj. Satish was already on the road when he had called Sujata. He was headed with his company of soldiers to a tiny village called Hajin Kralgund, not far from Handwara town and only a few kilometres from a vast swathe of some of the thickest forests in Kashmir, west of the Jhelum. The officer had barely been able to call his wife as he and his men rumbled down the highway towards their destination.

For the previous five hours, from his position on the fringes of Kupwara, about 40 km away from the battalion headquarters, Maj. Satish had been in constant touch with Col. Rajiv Saharan, the CO of 30 RR.

'Satish was absolutely clear when he called me,' says Col. Rajiv. 'He had cultivated a very good source in the local community since he had come to us in 2015. That source turned out to be highly reliable and had tremendous faith in Satish. Generally, people are not open to providing information because they fear that sooner or later, their identity will be revealed and it will be game over for them at the hands of the terrorists. But this particular source had tremendous faith in Satish and said, "*Sahab, main aapke liye karoonga* (I will do it for you)". Finding such a source is difficult and dangerous. We have a large number of sources that are not reliable because they might be double agents. But Satish had 100 per cent faith in this guy. On 14 February, the source had confirmed to Satish the whereabouts of certain hardcore Pakistani terrorists whom we, along with several other units, had been hunting for weeks, but without success. Finally, there was specific information about their location. And there was no doubt in Satish's mind that it was reliable information about the group's movements and location.'

The group, as it turned out, was from one of the most specialized terrorist units that Pakistan had sent into India that year—the so-called 'Afzal Guru Squad' of the JeM. These weren't ragtag infiltrators, but men with fearsome commando-style training that armed them with both physical endurance and the sort of tactical combat training required to engage ably with any military force hunting them. Making the fight even more complicated, the terror squad was believed to be using YSMS—a crafty trick in which smartphones were paired with high frequency radio sets to send out SMS text messages that were nearly impossible to intercept. Terror groups had begun using this technology in early 2015, but there was still no credible way of tapping these conversations.

These were men, in other words, who could put up a real fight in total stealth. If no terrorists were to be taken lightly, the men of the Afzal Guru Squad were to be taken least lightly of all. And it was a group of these men that Maj. Satish's source confirmed was hiding in Hajin Kralgund.

'Satish vouched for the tip-off, and requested permission to proceed towards Hajin Kralgund,' says Col. Rajiv. 'The input was very specific. Three to four terrorists were hiding in two separate houses, one on the fringe of the village and the other somewhere in the centre.'

With Maj. Satish and his men on the way, Col. Rajiv phoned Ghulam Jeelani, Handwara's Senior Superintendent of Police (SSP), an officer well-regarded for his commitment to going after terrorists. Militants had flung a grenade at Jeelani's Srinagar home late at night only two months earlier, though neither he nor his family were at home at the time.

Col. Rajiv's calls to Jeelani went unanswered. He gathered from sources that the Jammu and Kashmir police was inaugurating a women's cell in Handwara on Valentine's

Day, and the SSP was probably busy at the function. Twenty minutes later, though, Jeelani returned the Army officer's call.

'Jeelani finally called me back to confirm that he had also received an identical input about the same terrorists,' says Col. Rajiv. 'I told him my men were already on their way to Hajin Kralgund and requested him to join the operation with his SOG. Jeelani was very enterprising and committed. He sent a huge contingent of his men to join the operation.'

In his Maruti Gypsy, Maj. Satish went over the plan that would unfold once they reached the village. With him was a quadcopter drone that would be deployed high over the village to provide them with a bird's-eye view. He remained connected over a secure audio line to his CO. Even if he wanted to call Sujata to check on that parcel, he simply didn't have the time at that point.

Back in Jaipur, Sujata was growing restless about the promised package delivery. Why was it so late if her husband had said it would arrive no later than noon? She switched on the television and flipped channels distractedly for a while before turning it off. She paced about the house, wondering if she should get dinner started, but decided to wait for the package or a call from her husband. Their flat in Jaipur had been rented only two months earlier, when it became clear that Maj. Satish would be stationed in that city after he completed his Kashmir posting in three weeks' time.

'I didn't want to make dinner,' says Sujata. 'I was getting impatient. The only thought that I had in my mind was, why did he lie about a parcel being delivered? And why wasn't he answering his phone?'

Sujata couldn't wait for his Jaipur tenure to begin. Maj. Satish had been commissioned into the ASC in 2009, in the logistical supply wing, which oversees the enormous task of procurement and distribution of food, rations, fuel and other items nationwide to 1.2 million personnel. A few months into service, he was deployed on a three-year posting to Kashmir with the 1st Battalion of RR operating in Nowgam. Returning home to his village in Haryana's Mahendragarh district for a short break a year into the posting, he had met Sujata.

'It was an arranged marriage, but we took our time,' she says. 'When I first met him, I was shocked. He looked scruffy, dishevelled and very different from the clean, handsome man in the photo my parents had shown me. I think Satish noticed my shock. I felt bad later when I thought of this. When he visited me again two months later, he looked just like he did in the photograph—clean-shaven, sharp and tidy. I was over the moon. My heart said yes.'

They were engaged in 2011 and married on 17 February 2012, nearly two years after they first met. Still deployed in a sensitive area, Maj. Satish would get very little time with his new wife, returning to Kashmir within days of his wedding, where he immersed himself in counter-insurgency operations. On 3 July 2012, he would be part of an operation that would later win him a commendation from the Chief of Army Staff.

'He called me during that operation,' says Sujata. 'I could hear the sound of bullets being fired, but didn't know what they were. I ended the call and told my father that the call had been disconnected because there was a lot of background noise. My father understood what I was talking about. He followed the news and later told me that three militants had been killed in Nowgam. Later that night, Satish called and said he had been injured, but was okay. Apparently, a bullet had also missed his head by a few inches. I didn't know what to think.'

Sujata remembered hearing from her husband's friends about an operation he had been involved in before they met, when a young Lt Satish had bravely stormed a location despite being warned to be careful, and had killed a militant. They had told her he was crazy to be so brave. He had calmed her down when, agitated, she asked him about the incident. He did what he had to do, he told her.

For the young officer, an honour from the Army Chief was all the affirmation he needed to be sure that fighting insurgency was what he really wanted to do in the Army. When he had the time for longer conversations with his wife, she listened quietly, noncommittally, as he described his work and achievements. Unfamiliar with an Armyman's work, Sujata would have trouble understanding and navigating the first few years of their relationship.

'After we got engaged, we didn't talk much because he was deployed in that difficult area, Nowgam in Kashmir,' says Sujata. 'I thought he didn't want to talk to me, and was busy with other things. Then, when I asked around, it became clear that his unit was in a place where there was virtually no connectivity. I would call the headquarters, and if I was lucky, I would be patched through for a two-minute call with Satish. That was very precious time. On some occasions, he would walk for an hour up a hill to a spot where he could get a mobile signal and then call me for a few minutes. That one year he was there was a very hard time. He was gentle with me. But I understood how difficult Army life is.'

In 2015, when her husband was deployed once again with the RR for a two-year tenure in north Kashmir, Sujata was understandably apprehensive. She was now expecting their child and hadn't fully settled into life as a military spouse. And while leaving his pregnant wife for a posting was difficult, his return to Kashmir was a calling Maj. Satish had been waiting to fulfil. For three years as a young Lieutenant in Nowgam, and through stints in Nagaland thereafter, he had yearned for an opportunity for some actual combat against foreign terrorists entering Kashmir.

On 30 March 2015, Maj. Satish arrived in Kupwara to join 30 RR. The CO was anticipating his arrival.

'Satish was joining us after operating in a sector adjacent to ours,' says Col. Rajiv. 'So he was quite clued in as far as the modus operandi of terrorists was concerned. It was apparent to me from the start that this was a bold, brave young man, capable of giving us solid dividends in the fight against terror and militancy.'

With an impressive record of counter-insurgency operations, Maj. Satish was given charge of a 'jungle' company. Troops of 30 RR are divided into four 'companies'— two companies stay focused on road-opening tasks and providing escort protection to convoys travelling on National Highway 701, which connects Srinagar to Baramulla and Kupwara. The other two companies are 'jungle companies', deployed in the rural hinterland in thick forests.

In 2016, a year into the posting, Maj. Satish went home for a short break to see Sujata and their infant daughter. And just when he was about to return to Kashmir, a shooting pain in his abdomen forced him to delay his departure. Diagnosed with acute appendicitis, he had no choice but to report to the Army hospital in Delhi.

'It was quite bad, and we gave him thirty days of sick leave initially,' says Col. Rajiv. 'Once you have surgery, you can't be part of active operations for about six months. And the general practice is to send such officers back to their parent unit to make place for a physically fit officer, so that operations don't suffer. But as the CO, I was sure I didn't want to lose Satish. I wasn't sure how much time he would take to recover. But I was sure this young man had the strength to deliver—if not today, then tomorrow.

Since I couldn't send him out for operations, I placed him as adjutant in the unit.'

As adjutant, Maj. Satish was, in effect, a staff officer to the Colonel. And even though he ached to be declared fit for operations, he used this time to advise the unit's company commanders. Crucially, he also spent time cultivating his best source, a local Kashmiri villager who would prove crucial in the months ahead. The time away from field missions also brought with it a special privilege—the opportunity to invite his young family to visit his unit and see for themselves why he was hardly ever free to talk.

'I had a chance to meet his wife and daughter when they came,' says Col. Rajiv. 'I found Sujata to be a very confident and supportive partner to Satish. She had many questions and was curious about all aspects of the tough job her husband was doing. And you could see she was very proud of him.'

The visit was brief. A disturbed area like Kupwara is, after all, usually out of bounds for families of Army personnel. But Maj. Satish had taken the time to introduce Sujata to his men—the men in whose hands he placed his life as a matter of routine, and whose lives he took responsibility for. The tough RR soldiers she met were an enormous source of reassurance. When his family left, Maj. Satish dived right back into his work.

'Satish stayed highly motivated despite the health setback,' says Col. Rajiv. 'I knew he was disappointed, but he still worked round the clock. Whenever I went on operations, he would always be awake, and when I returned, be up and ready to work with me. Frankly, I don't know when he rested.'

When Maj. Satish was finally declared fit to return to combat in late 2016 and was deployed to command one of 30 RR's jungle companies in Behak Harvet, he placed a cardboard placard above the entrance of his bunker with five words, scrawled with a red marker, that appeared to answer his CO's question: *I RUST WHEN I REST*.

If anyone thought it was a cheesy line, Maj. Satish and his company very nearly had to live by it. His company had to keep a lookout for militant and terrorist activity over a huge area—over 23 sq km and nearly thirty villages—with a large part of it covered in thick forest. From the moment he took charge, inputs began blaring in about the arrival of terrorists from the JeM's Afzal Guru Squad. Intercepts and whispers from sources had revealed that four terrorists were on the prowl. The names they seemed to go by were Saad, Baaz, Maavia and Darda.

'This was clearly a fidayeen squad,' says Col. Rajiv. 'They were highly trained terrorists. They had already ambushed Army convoys. They were also instrumental in carrying out attacks on a police station, inflicting casualties there and elsewhere. They had survived and escaped multiple police and Army ambushes too.'

Adding insult to injury, intelligence intercepts showed one of the terrorists bragging about how to break Indian Army cordons: '*Fauj ka cordon kaise break karte hai, main bataunga* (Let me tell you how to break an Army cordon).'

The frustrating game of cat-and-mouse had also become something of a prestige issue by now. And on Valentine's Day 2017, as his vehicle sped towards Hajin Kralgund, Maj. Satish prayed his source hadn't made an error.

'Satish was after these guys, religiously working day in and day out,' says Col. Rajiv. 'He spent every waking hour taking out parties, laying ambushes or cultivating more sources. When his source finally gave him that specific piece of data, it basically confirmed weeks of work he had done. Finally, he had something he could act on.'

A month previously, in January, on a short visit to Jaipur for a medical check-up and to see his family, Maj. Satish, who rarely went into specific details of operations, told Sujata about the terrorists he was hunting.

'Satish had been after these militants for two months,' Sujata says. 'He started to tell me about the ambushes they laid for the terrorists, but that they were managing to escape. I would always ask why he didn't shoot them or attack them. But Satish would say just one thing—if anything happens to my men, even a single man, I will never be able to face their families. "*Mere bande first hain mere liye* (For me, my men come first)."'

When he returned to Kashmir, he wouldn't call home for days. And when he did call Sujata, it would be for a few minutes late at night.

'It was only on Valentine's Day that he called so many times,' she says.

A few hundred metres before Hajin Kralgund, Maj. Satish stopped his vehicle near the side of the road. On his orders, one of his men got out of the Gypsy and pulled out a cardboard box from the back. Inside the box was a quadcopter drone that they powered on and launched. With a low, whining hum, the drone rose into the air, climbing steadily until the village came into view. Fitted with a camera calibrated for low-light missions, the drone streamed live images of the village to a briefcase-sized monitor operated by Maj. Satish's men, which, in turn, beamed the images to the 30 RR headquarters where Col. Rajiv sat in the unit's small operations room, keeping real-time watch on where his men were headed.

In Jaipur, Sujata continued to dial her husband and wait for the promised package delivery.

'I called my mother to tell her that Satish hadn't called and that he wasn't answering his phone,' she says. 'My mother asked me not to worry and to have dinner. She reminded me that there was nothing unusual about Satish not taking calls.'

Maj. Satish's mobile phone was with him, but it was silent—and there was no time to answer. As they arrived on foot at the periphery of the village, he had planned that his company would split into two groups and approach it from two sides. At every step, the CO, armed with the live drone video feed from the operation site, was kept updated.

'Initially, we placed a bigger cordon around the village,' says Col. Rajiv, explaining the plan as it unfolded. 'Then the plan was for Satish to go with his team and lay a tighter cordon around the house at the edge of the village.'

Hajin Kralgund was one of the thirty villages that fell under Maj. Satish's area of responsibility, and he knew it well. He and his men had made it their job to be aware of the layout, the owners of most houses and the numbers of family members. But even with all that data, a terror encounter in a built-up space with unarmed civilians couldn't be more unpredictable. Sure, the drone provided a highly valuable live feed of the intended encounter site. But another pair of eyes was truly indispensable. A pair of eyes that was on the ground, deep inside the village, secretly watching from a vantage point. This was Maj. Satish's source. In an inexplicable show of faith, he was risking his own life and the lives of his family members by agreeing to provide a live commentary of what he saw. In human intelligence terms, nothing could be more valuable than this.

'While Satish and his men proceeded to form the tight inner cordon, I took the responsibility to coordinate the outer cordon with another team of my men,' says Col. Rajiv. 'The inner cordon had two parties—the one led by Satish laid its cordon around the suspected house in the middle of the village. A Junior Commissioned Officer (JCO) was tasked with leading the second party to cordon the house on the edge of the village.'

Hajin Kralgund was a small village, but it still had a large number of women and children residents, many in houses just metres away from the two houses that had been identified as the terrorists' hideouts. The Army was hoping to complete the operation as quickly and cleanly as possible, with the least amount of bother to residents. Both Col. Rajiv and Maj. Satish hoped that the intelligence checked out and that they wouldn't need to search other houses in the village, because if they did, it would greatly amplify the risk of the mission. And given that the terrorists would have a number of hiding places within the village, a more delicate and dangerous operation couldn't be imagined in the circumstances.

'Satish voiced his confidence again in the input as he and his men walked into the village,' says Col. Rajiv. 'After overseeing the cordon laid at the farther house, he proceeded towards the middle of the village to lay his team's cordon. So far, the input had been that both houses had two terrorists each. But just before Satish and his men reached the inner house, his source came on the line.'

'*Sahab, donon bahar wale ghar ki taraf bhag gaye hain* (Both terrorists have left the middle house and are on their way to the house on the edge of the village),' said the source.

Maj. Satish quickly passed the information to his CO. Col. Rajiv looked closely at the drone's video feed, squinting to see if he could make out anything at all.

'Now we knew for sure that the two terrorists from the inner house were headed to the outer house,' says Col. Rajiv. 'But we didn't have a fix on whether there were two terrorists already in the outer house, or whether they had already left. When Satish called me with an update, I advised him to take the party and join the close cordon of the outer house. By this time, SSP Jeelani had also arrived at my headquarters and was monitoring the operation with me. He was in touch with his sizeable team at the encounter site, who were part of the cordons we had laid.'

Maj. Satish's source had been quite accurate. The two terrorists had indeed made their way from the centrally located house to the one on the edge of the village. At the latter house, where two men had been hiding, only one terrorist remained—the second had broken the cordon and escaped into the forests. Now regrouped, the three Afzal Guru Squad members took positions inside the house.

The element of surprise Maj. Satish and his men had hoped against hope for was gone. This was made abundantly clear by a hail of AK-47 fire from the first floor of the house that greeted them upon arrival.

The house sat in a small bowl-shaped piece of land surrounded by hills, with forested slopes on three sides and a stream beyond its front gate. Inside the compound, the ground undulated in small dune-like folds.

In his pocket, Maj. Satish's mobile phone continued to ring silently. A thousand kilometres away, Sujata's restlessness grew. The sun had set and there was still no sign of the promised delivery. She wondered if that was why she was particularly anxious that evening. Her restlessness was turning into full-fledged fear.

By this time, Maj. Satish had reached the front gate of the house with his buddy soldier. He had sent some of his men to its back to reinforce the rear cordon, in case the terrorists tried to make a break for the hills.

'Welcomed with heavy fire, Satish and his men rapidly took position and returned fire,' says Col. Rajiv. 'With the cordon now as tight as it could possibly get, the three terrorists inside the house realized that their only means of escape was to fight their way out. Otherwise, it would only be a matter of time till they ran out of ammunition.'

For six minutes, the firing from the house stopped and silence descended. Maj. Satish and his buddy used the opportunity to enter the compound through the front gate and take cover behind a small mound of earth. At that precise moment, the three terrorists burst out through the front door, firing indiscriminately. Maj. Satish immediately let out a burst of gunfire, hitting the first terrorist in the head and sending him crashing to the ground. The two others immediately leapt behind a clump of earth to take cover.

What Maj. Satish didn't let his men know immediately was that a bullet had found him too. The officer was wearing his bulletproof vest, but the round had pierced him in the gap between two plates and had ripped through a major artery. Minutes later, when his buddy soldier noticed the Major's blood-drenched side, he insisted they pull back so the injured officer could get medical help. Maj. Satish refused, reassuring the soldier that he wasn't badly injured, and that he couldn't leave at that moment.

The firefight was now a tense, pitched battle. Two terrorists, with a mound for cover, were firing at Maj. Satish and his buddy, who had their own knoll protecting them. Nearly ten minutes later, the terrorists began to fling grenades towards the periphery of the compound, where the other men of the inner cordon stood firing. It became clear that the terrorists were well-armed and had plenty of ammunition and grenades to draw out the encounter. And Maj. Satish knew that the longer they stretched it, the greater the chances were of the terrorists causing casualties among the cordon and finding a way through it to escape into the thickly forested hills of Handwara, which surround the village.

In the crossfire, Maj. Satish heard muffled screams from behind him, outside the front gate. Three soldiers from his company, who had been providing covering fire from a few metres away, had been hit by grenade splinters and were seriously injured. Maj. Satish quickly ordered all three men to be pulled out of the firefight, but chose to remain where he was. By this time, he had lost a great deal of blood and had begun to feel dizzy. He made one final call to his CO, informing him that he was going to mount a flank attack on the two terrorists, in which he would crawl out from his position and creep up on the terrorists from the side where they had no cover. Col. Rajiv, by this time, had arrived at the encounter site with more men from 30 RR, deploying them up on the hills surrounding the house.

'Satish insisted he wanted to get closer and finish them off,' says Col. Rajiv. 'He was the operational commander on the ground and best knew the situation. His assessment was that if he waited any longer, the terrorists would definitely kill some of his men. And I knew that was totally unacceptable to him.'

Unknown to Maj. Satish, the three soldiers injured by the terrorists' grenades would tragically succumb to their injuries. It was when the three men—Paratrooper Dharmendra Kumar, twenty-six, Rifleman Ravi Kumar, thirty-three, and Gunner Astosh Kumar, twenty-four—were hit that Maj. Satish decided to finish the encounter himself.

The CO knew it was a delicate situation. He was speaking to an injured officer in the middle of a firefight. He asked Maj. Satish if he wished to pull back. But the officer requested that he be allowed to stay and finish the operation. Maj. Satish's buddy soldier, who had been ordered to retreat towards the front gate of the house, received a call from the CO asking about Maj. Satish's condition.

'*Buri tarah lagi hai, Sir, par khatam karke hi aayenge* (He's grievously injured, Sir, but he'll pull back only when he's finished them),' the soldier said.

Despite the heavy bleeding, Maj. Satish crawled out from his secure position on his elbows, making his way from the side towards the clump that protected the two remaining terrorists, who continued to direct their fire to the front. Taking aim, his bullet killed one. The other let out a burst of fire, narrowly missing Maj. Satish, and bolted towards the hills, only to be felled minutes later by outer cordon troops waiting for precisely such an eventuality.

With the firefight at an end, two soldiers rushed forward to check on Maj. Satish, who had, by this time, slumped in his position and was in and out of consciousness. They carried the Major out of the front gate, where a Tata Sumo vehicle had been arranged to transport the injured officer to a makeshift helipad that had been coordinated minutes after Maj. Satish had been shot.

His eyes still half-open, it seemed as if Maj. Satish wanted to speak, but didn't have the strength. Nobody had the heart to tell the Major that three soldiers had lost their lives in the encounter. He blacked out as the car sped down the highway towards the helipad. A Dhruv helicopter carried him straight towards the 92 Base Hospital in Srinagar, a facility renowned for being able to repair any man with a pulse. But in that helicopter, shortly after 8 p.m., high above the mountains and forests of Kashmir he had come to love and know so well, Maj. Satish drew his final breath.

In his pocket, his silent mobile phone continued to ring.

At 8.15 p.m., Sujata received a call from a lady officer in the Army asking her how she was. The call was followed by a flurry of other calls from Maj. Satish's colleagues in the Army. Now, breathless with anxiety, Sujata asked one of the callers, a course-mate of Maj. Satish, why everyone was calling her. After a moment's pause, the course-mate informed her that her husband had been shot, but that he was recovering in hospital, that there was nothing to worry about. Sujata hung up immediately, dialling the CO of 30 RR. At this time, Col. Rajiv was still at Hajin Kralgund and couldn't answer the phone.

'I lit a diya in my small mandir,' says Sujata. 'My mind and heart were restless and I knew that something was wrong and that everybody was hiding it from me. Priyasha came to me, wondering why I was praying at that time. I usually pray only in the morning. Then the doorbell rang for the first time that day. I ran to the door.'

A delivery man stood outside with a bouquet and a large red package. Sujata grabbed both, took them to the dining table and set them down. She paused for a moment. Then she carefully opened it. Inside was a heart-shaped cake and candles. She stared at it for a moment, then picked up her phone to try her husband's number again. There was no answer.

'I called every single person I had come to know in the Army over the last two years,' says Sujata, 'literally pleading with them to make me speak to Satish somehow. Most of them told me he was fine and that I should come to Srinagar. I still knew nothing. It was when my father arrived at 10.30 p.m. that my heart sank.'

But even Sujata's father, despite knowing what had happened, would say nothing specific to her, instead calming his daughter and telling her that everything would be all right. He also ensured that the television stayed off. News of Maj. Satish's death had begun breaking on social media shortly before 9 p.m. and on television after 10 p.m.

The next to arrive at the house was another Major from 30 RR who was on leave in Jaipur at the time. He told Sujata he was there to help in any way, and if necessary, would take her to Srinagar to visit her husband.

'Nobody was telling me anything clearly,' Sujata says. 'When I pressed my father, he said the Army had told him that Satish was under observation. Everybody was too scared to tell me the truth. I wasn't even admitting it to myself. My heart was praying that these comforting words were true, that Satish was only injured and that he would return my call soon.'

By midnight, with neighbours and Army personnel at her home but still no clear answers to her questions, Sujata begged her father to take her to Delhi so she could catch a flight to Srinagar the first thing next morning.

'I was on the road at night and tried the CO's number again,' says Sujata. 'A voice at the other end, which I did not recognize, told me not to come to Srinagar. They had obviously heard that I was headed to Delhi to take the next flight out. Then the CO came on the line. His voice was breaking with emotion, and he finally told me that Satish was gone, and that I have to take care of myself and Priyasha now.'

Sujata's father directed the cab driver to change course and head to Narnaul in Haryana, the village where Maj. Satish's parents lived.

'After that, I don't remember anything,' says Sujata. 'I went totally blank. Priyasha was on my lap. I wasn't crying. I was just in a daze.'

Sujata had carried nothing with her but the bouquet of flowers and the Valentine's Day cake.

In Narnaul the next morning, huge crowds had gathered on the road leading up to the home of the Dahiya family. Several officers and soldiers from the Army were there too. That evening, amid loud chants in his honour, Maj. Satish's flag-draped casket was brought home.

Surrounded by mourners and friends from the Army, Sujata's calm finally shattered. In front of television cameras that had streamed into the Dahiya house that evening, she wept uncontrollably. The sound of her wails would be broadcast across the country. Priyasha, too young to fully understand what was going on, would be carried by an uncle to light her father's pyre not far from their home.

'Priyasha lives in the belief that her father is alive somewhere,' Sujata says. 'She asks me sometimes when her Papa will come. I have a few audio and video clips of Satish, which I make her watch or hear every now and then, so she feels she has actually spoken to Satish. I order things online and say her father has sent gifts for her. She has begun to insist now on meeting her father. She is very young. I have to take it slow. Maybe, in a few years, she will understand.'

Sujata left Jaipur weeks later to move to Delhi, where she now lives. She hopes to begin a job soon.

'I take out Satish's uniform every few days and look at it,' she says. 'It has the place marked where he was hit by the bullet. It is washed and cleaned and kept in my cupboard.'

Two days after the funeral, on their fifth wedding anniversary, Sujata would learn from a travel agent that her husband had booked a four-day holiday in April for them at the Taj Vivanta in Goa, a place Sujata had longed to visit but hadn't had the chance. The holiday was to coincide with Priyasha's second birthday. Growing up in landlocked towns, the two had often spoken about a holiday at the seaside.

Meanwhile, search operations for other members of the Afzal Guru Squad continued for nearly two weeks after the Hajin Kralgund operation. It was only twelve days later that Col. Rajiv would get the time to visit Maj. Satish's family in Narnaul.

'His father is a very bold personality,' says Col. Rajiv. 'And Satish was a very good son. The way he looked after his parents was truly commendable. He understood his responsibility to them very well. Whenever he went home, he would find out if there was anything he could do to help the village. A street in the village and a nearby college are now rightly named after him.'

'When I think about the Hajin encounter, a part of me wonders what would have happened if Satish had survived,' says a Lieutenant Colonel from 30 RR who was part of the mission. 'He was obsessively concerned about the welfare of his men. I wonder whether he would have been able to digest the news that three soldiers were lost in the operation. It was the most unacceptable thing to him. That's why his men worshipped him.'

Weeks before the Hajin operation, Col. Rajiv had visited Maj. Satish's highly secured jungle post, a base he had meticulously protected with five layers of fencing.

'I told him we were both at the fag end of our tenures with 30 RR,' says Col. Rajiv. 'I told him it was okay if I wrapped up my tenure without eliminating those three terrorists, but Satish Dahiya would never be okay if he moved on without finishing the job, this hardcore group that had inflicted so many casualties on our security forces. Satish said, "I promise you, I won't leave the *paltan* till I eliminate them."'

Months after the operation, Maj. Satish's source in the Hajin Kralgund encounter resurfaced after having gone underground for safety. In a message sent to another officer designated to replace Maj. Satish in the event of the end of his tenure—or worse—he said Kashmir would miss Maj. Satish.

'He wanted to play his small role in ending the militancy here,' the source said. 'I hope Kashmir will not forget that.'

Maj. Mohit Sharma in uniform and a field disguise

Maj. Mohit at the Academy with his family

Maj. Mohit's bust at a heritage hall
built in his memory at the 1 Para
Special Forces base in Nahan,
Himachal Pradesh

Maj. Mohit's wife,
Maj. Rishma, receiving
her husband's posthumous
Ashoka Chakra

Corporal Jyoti Nirala in full battle gear

Corporal Jyoti with his wife, Sushma, and daughter, Jigyasa

Corporal Jyoti with a group of Garud commandos

The last service photo of
Corporal Jyoti

Corporal Jyoti's wife, Sushma, receiving his posthumous Ashoka Chakra

Lt Navdeep Singh shortly after entering service

Lt Navdeep with his parents at his passing-out parade

Lt Navdeep in Gurez, Jammu and Kashmir

Lt Navdeep celebrating during a break from operations

Maj. David Manlun's
service photo

Maj. David with two Kalashnikovs

Maj. David with his entire family
during a summer break

The *3 Idiots* photo of
Maj. David and his brothers

Maj. David's parents receiving
his posthumous Kirti Chakra

Lt Cdr Kapish Muwal on a break between duties

Lt Manoranjan after combat
dive training

Service photos of
Lt Cdr Kapish and Lt Manoranjan

Service photo of
Capt. Pawan Kumar

Capt. Pawan leaving home to head
to Jammu and Kashmir

One of Capt. Pawan's last photos in Jammu and Kashmir

Maj. Satish Dahiya

Maj. Satish with his wife, Sujata, and daughter, Priyasha

Sujata and Maj. Satish's mother receiving his posthumous Shaurya Chakra

Lt Cdr Firdaus Mogal

Lt Cdr Firdaus with his wife, Kerzin, and son, Yashaan

Lt Cdr Firdaus in his bunk on board a submarine

Capt. P. Rajkumar with a Sea King helicopter

People picked up during the record-breaking rescue flight

Capt. Rajkumar with his flying crew

Maj. Rishi with his AK-47
during an operation

Maj. Rishi with his wife, Maj. Anupama,
an officer with the Military Nursing Service

Maj. Rishi still keeps
a part of his face covered

Flt Lt Gunadnya Kharche

Flt Lt Gunadnya and crew after landing

The moment Flt Lt Gunadnya's An-32 touched down on one wheel

Flt Lt Gunadnya and his wife, Shruti, at Wellington with their daughters

Flt Lt Gunadnya and Shruti's favourite pastime in Wellington

Capt. Pradeep Arya near the China border in Ladakh

Capt. Pradeep with his wife, Deepa,
and their daughters, Dhriti and Dhiksha

Maj. Preetam Kunwar with his family after receiving the Kirti Chakra

Maj. Preetam

Maj. Preetam with his wife, Megha

Sqn Ldr Ajit Vasane with a MiG-29 in Jamnagar

Sqn Ldr Ajit with his wife, Sqn Ldr Rajeev Kaur, and
their son, Rishan

8

'Climb over Me,
Get to the Submarine!'

Lieutenant Commander Firdaus Mogal

Arabian Sea, 220 km off the Mumbai coast
30 August 2010, 6.55 a.m.

'THREE MEN OVERBOARD, SIR!'

Seventy feet from where he stood watch on the periscope tower, Lt Cdr Firdaus Mogal had just witnessed three sailors on the submarine's back being violently flung several feet out into the churning Arabian Sea.

The sun had just risen, and as the submarine violently bobbed and pitched in the swell, it was clear to the Executive Officer (XO in military parlance) that the three heads in the water were drifting helplessly away—and fast. He knew a minute wasted would mean the possibility of losing those men. Using his walkie-talkie, he quickly relayed what had happened to the control room. A reply crackled back in. It was the submarine's CO, informing Lt Cdr Firdaus that two sailors were being sent up to go after the three men who had been thrown overboard.

'There's no time, I'm going after them,' Lt Cdr Firdaus shouted down the shaft to the submarine's bridge. As he did so, he saw two combat divers hastily clambering up the ladder from the control room to join him. As they heaved themselves up through the hatch, the three men felt a familiar wave of vibrations course through the submarine. Their CO had just switched the submarine's engines slowly back on to stand by for the rescue.

167

And just as the three leapt off the back of their submarine into the heaving swell, Lt Cdr Firdous knew he was about to enter a realm he loved and felt most comfortable in.

Mumbai naval dockyard
Fifteen hours earlier

'All set and good to go, Sir,' Lt Cdr Firdaus said, as he welcomed the submarine's CO on board at the jetty. Cdr Gangupomu Murali, the last to walk the gangplank leading into the submarine, returned the younger officer's salute. With the full crew on board, the submarine was ready to depart. The submarine skipper and his second-in-command would be leading a crew of forty on a mission to practise action in a situation that all submariners see in their worst nightmares.

The 211-feet-long and twenty-four-year-old *INS Shankush* dived beneath the surface shortly after sailing out of Mumbai's harbour. The German-built Type 209, one of four attack submarines that the Indira Gandhi government had ordered in 1981, headed straight out into the Arabian Sea for a combat war game that seemed straight out of a Cold War-era film.

INS Shankush was all set to play the quarry in a deadly game of cat-and-mouse, as part of an annual exercise with the French Navy code named 'Varuna'. From the first week of August onwards, the submarine would test the fearsome tracking and detection capabilities of two warships—the Indian Navy's *INS Brahmaputra* and the French Navy's *FNS Dupleix*—both purpose-built to hunt and destroy submarines. The crew of *Shankush*, on its part, would need to dodge the two marauding warships using a combination of silence and evasive electronic techniques. The ships wouldn't be dropping real weapons at the submarine, and *INS Shankush* wouldn't be letting loose any of its deadly torpedoes. But the idea of a war game like Varuna was that the men on board all three vessels performed as if they were in a real war. And pretending isn't difficult. The sound of sensor 'pings' and the distinct tone that blares when a ship's sonar 'locks' on to a submarine, indicating to the crew of the submarine that it has been detected, would make a submariner's skin crawl in any circumstance.

Even the skin of a seasoned submariner.

Lt Cdr Firdaus had opted for the submarine arm of the Indian Navy. A fully voluntary division that permits entry only to sailors and officers who make a certain cut, the submarine arm, like the military Special Forces, requires additional conditioning, both physical and psychological, given the consistently isolated and menacing circumstances that submariners work in as part of their routine duties at sea. It isn't often that military cadets are clear about what they want to specialize in, even if they've chosen between the Army, the Navy and the Air Force. It's rarer still for anyone to join a military academy with the singular intention of choosing to work in submarines.

Lt Cdr Firdaus, on the other hand, had been clear from the day he entered NDA, Pune, that he wanted to be a submariner, spending his years there becoming a masterful swimmer, diver and a prodigious young authority on the history of submarining. When a course-mate asked him why he was so stubborn about joining the submarine arm, cadet Firdaus had regarded him and asked with mock horror, 'How can you want to do anything else?'

When INS Shankush sank below the waves and accelerated out into the Arabian Sea, it was just another day on the job for the young officer. But as his body got used to the familiar, gentle hum of the submarine's diesel–electric motors and the warm glow of the lamps that lined the single thin corridor that ran from end to end, he never forgot for even a moment that he was living a real dream.

Lt Cdr Firdaus and his CO had final discussions with the crew on what lay ahead. As XO, Lt Cdr Firdaus was second-in-command. As *INS Shankush* cruised 50 feet below the sea's surface, he walked the length of the submarine that night, speaking with the crew and conducting a list of final checks. It would be past midnight when the XO returned to his cabin for a few hours of sleep before the next day's drills.

Churning the depths with a low roar, *INS Shankush*'s large rear propeller would push it far out into the Arabian Sea overnight, into a section of the ocean where the submarine would spend the following day, 30 August, practising a few manoeuvres before the arrival of the Indian and French warships.

Back on shore in Mumbai, Kerzin Mogal lay awake. As a submariner's wife, she was used to being cut off from her husband for days at a time. Dinner a few hours earlier with Firdaus and their twenty-month-old son, Yashaan, had been quiet. She wouldn't be seeing him for at least the next ten days. After five years of marriage, words seemed almost unnecessary to fill the silence that hung over a now familiar mood just before departure. Seeing her husband off at the door with a hug, Kerzin put their son to bed and retired to her room with a book. Two hours later, making an involuntary mental note that Firdaus's submarine had probably just slipped beneath the waves, Kerzin fell asleep.

'I remember that it was raining heavily the Sunday that he left,' she says. 'I'm usually a late riser. But the next morning, despite falling asleep quite late, I woke up early and I was very restless. I had no idea why.'

Unable to go back to sleep, Kerzin got out of bed, deciding to start the day. She went about getting ready, picked out a red top for work—she always wore red on Mondays. Then she made another mental note. Firdaus and his submarine were probably far out at sea by now.

By this time, *INS Shankush* had sailed nearly 200 km away from Mumbai. As Kerzin sipped her morning coffee, she couldn't possibly have known that all wasn't well on board her husband's submarine.

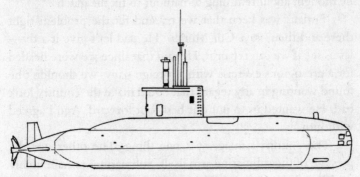

Type 209 attack submarine

There was a problem. A serious one, detected at dawn. An exhaust valve that expelled toxic by-products of the submarine's electric batteries had failed, causing a leak inside *INS Shankush*, a glitch that could be deadly to the crew if left unrepaired. The valve, one of a pair that remains underwater even at periscope depth, wasn't doing its very important job. Cdr Murali wasted no time, quickly ordering the crew to take the submarine to the surface.

Within minutes, the 1800-tonne submarine climbed through the water before gently breaking the surface.

'When we surfaced, we noticed that the sea was quite rough,' Cdr Murali says. 'I knew we had to fix the valve right there and then. I took Mogal with me to the top of the submarine to assess the situation.'

The two men ascended the ladder that led to a hatch at the top of the conning tower, the dorsal fin-like structure on a submarine's back through which the periscope, communications antennae and other sensors jut out of the water, even as the submarine itself remains submerged. It was clear to both the officers that the repair of the exhaust valve would be a stiff challenge in those sea conditions. Cdr Murali asked his XO what he thought about returning to harbour to fix the glitch.

'Firdaus was keen that we try and fix the problem right there and then,' says Cdr Murali. 'He said let's give it a try—let us see if we can repair it. He said that since we were headed for a prestigious exercise with a foreign navy, we shouldn't be found wanting in any regard that could make the country look bad. He wanted us to put our best foot forward. And I agreed with him.'

The country's image was one thing. The other was the prestige of the submarine arm itself. Submarines remain highly stealthy when submerged, but are immediately detectable once they surface. In the restive Arabian Sea, where both China and Pakistan attempt to keep constant tabs on the movement of Indian submarines, sailing the submarine back to base would be a strategic embarrassment. It would be an admission that an Indian submarine, under the watchful eyes of satellites, couldn't complete an exercise with a foreign navy.

Cdr Murali summoned his Engineering Officer, the man trained to oversee the fixing of any technical trouble on a submarine at sea or in port. The three men quickly discussed the operation, deciding that they would try to complete the repair in no more than 20 minutes. The Engineering Officer called three sailors and led them down the outside ladder of the conning tower and onto the submarine's back half. The men were strapped to safety lines as they descended the sides to fix the faulty valve. But to actually conduct the repair, they needed to remove the safety straps since the valve was situated within the submarine's casing. About fifteen minutes into the repair operation, the men were preparing to emerge and strap themselves back into their safety lines, but they didn't see what was roaring towards them.

'You cannot predict waves. This one was 15 feet high and came out of nowhere. Three men were flung overboard,' says Cdr Murali who, by this time, had descended to the bridge, the submarine's control room, to monitor the repair operation while his XO kept visual tabs from the tower.

'Firdaus immediately reported that three men were in the water, with the fourth man not visible,' says Cdr Murali. 'And without a pause, he asked me for permission to go after them himself since there was no time. He said the submarine was stationary, with its engines off, and therefore, he could safely venture after them.'

But something had caught Lt Cdr Firdaus's eye—the fourth man, who had also been flung overboard, was spotted hanging by the side of the submarine, holding on precariously to his safety line. The sailor had injured himself badly and was bleeding from a deep cut on his leg. Lt Cdr Firdaus immediately climbed down the conning tower and rushed forward across the submarine's casing. Reaching down while fighting a ferociously pitching sea, he heaved with all his strength to pull the injured sailor up. Supporting the sailor, since he couldn't walk, Lt Cdr Firdaus rushed him back to the conning tower and had him lowered in for treatment.

'The doctor on board said he needed to be evacuated because he was bleeding very heavily,' Cdr Murali remembers. 'The sea was rough, and it had also started raining quite heavily by then. I knew it would be impossible to send him back to base anytime soon. I held his hand and told him to hold on. I was now doing three things—handling the submarine for the rescue, dealing with my injured sailor, and reassuring the other men that all was in control.'

With one man rescued, Lt Cdr Firdaus cast his gaze away from the submarine to the three men bobbing in the water. Joined by two combat divers, he climbed down onto the back of the submarine and jogged to the far end, as the entire vessel rolled and pitched in the heaving sea. It quickly became clear that the three sailors who had been flung overboard had now drifted too far from the submarine to be thrown a line. And that's when Lt Cdr Firdaus decided to dive into the sea in an attempt to reach the sailors who, by then, had drifted over 100 m from the submarine. The two combat divers jumped into the water after him.

At the bridge, Cdr Murali was faced with a difficult decision. The engines of *INS Shankush* had been turned off for the valve repair operation. And with men overboard, the engines were kept switched off because of the very real possibility of the drifting sailors being sucked into the powerful propeller.

'There were now six of my men in the sea, including Mogal,' says Cdr Murali. 'I waited for the men to drift a certain distance away. Then I switched on the engines to low power, carefully manoeuvring the submarine around in their direction to begin the recovery.'

Two more sailors had been ordered onto the submarine's back to help pull the six men on board. As the submarine edged towards Lt Cdr Firdaus and the two combat divers with him, he signalled to the submarine to proceed forward and rescue the other three men first, who by this time had drifted to over 200 m away.

The submarine gurgled past Lt Cdr Firdaus and the two divers towards the three men. The sea held steady as they were carefully pulled back on to the submarine with some difficulty.

Cdr Murali now had three more men to bring back on board. The wind had picked up and all three had begun to drift similarly. The men were adept swimmers, capable of handling themselves well in rough water, but as the minutes wore on, they would tire. It was imperative that they be brought back on board quickly. As the submarine edged back towards them, the divers gestured to Lt Cdr Firdaus to prepare to pull himself back up on board. But he refused, insisting that he would ascend the rope only after the two sailors were safely back on board.

Back in Mumbai, Kerzin Mogal had just arrived at work.

'I was still extremely restless when I entered the office,' Kerzin says. 'I remember telling a colleague of mine that I thought that day was going to be a holiday. I missed most of my calls that morning and kept mostly to myself. And I had no idea why. I found it hard to focus or concentrate on anything. Something was off. I felt it.'

From the bridge of *INS Shankush*, Cdr Murali edged closer to his XO and the two combat divers in the water.

'Finally, I manoeuvred the submarine close to the three,' says Cdr Murali. 'Mogal told the two sailors to go and board the submarine first and that he would come last. They had been in the water for nearly twenty minutes. All three were tired by this time.'

Realizing that the two combat divers were drifting again despite being highly qualified swimmers, Lt Cdr Firdaus grabbed the rope from the submarine and pushed himself towards the drifting men, offering to be a human bridge of sorts. He shouted to the two men to clamber over him and get to the submarine as quickly as possible. Once again, the two divers pleaded with him to climb on board first. They would manage, they said. But the XO knew they hadn't a chance of being pulled back on board, given how rapidly they were now drifting.

'Do it now! We have no time. Climb over me, get to the submarine,' Lt Cdr Firdaus screamed through the spray.

Finally, they obeyed—they knew it was their only chance of reaching the submarine. Holding on to the XO's shoulders, the two divers pulled themselves into the submarine.

Now, only Lt Cdr Firdaus remained in the water. He began to pull himself up. At the precise moment that he was about to haul himself out of the sea, the swell caused *INS Shankush* to roll violently, hitting the officer in the head and throwing him back into the sea in a splash of blood. It was a devastating knock from a 1800-tonne hunk of metal.

'He was knocked out,' says Cdr Murali. 'I tried to manoeuvre and get him on board, but he was unconscious. One officer and two sailors volunteered and asked me to bring the submarine next to him, saying that they would somehow pick him up. It was clear that someone would have to physically pull him out as he was not conscious. The three sailors who had been rescued by the submarine initially had no choice but to get into the water to pull him out.'

For a few harrowing minutes, the CO wondered about the unrelenting irony of the situation at hand. The unconscious officer was drifting rapidly now in the sea churned by the wind. Over the minutes, he drifted nearly 300 m from the submarine. The three men who went in after him were similarly set adrift in the swell. Even if the submarine was manoeuvred carefully, it would take thirty more minutes to recover Lt Cdr Firdaus and the three men.

The situation was now critical and Cdr Murali knew it was time to call for help. From the bridge, an emergency request was sent to the *INS Shikra* helicopter base in Mumbai, calling for a chopper to be dispatched immediately.

Back on board the submarine's deck, the sailors were ordered a few minutes later to stand by as a Chetak helicopter was arriving to pick up the injured XO. Over a rolling and pitching sea, the helicopter roared in 30 minutes later through the early morning haze and flew back with Lt Cdr Firdaus strapped to a stretcher, still unconscious. Two sailors had been precariously lowered into the churning sea to pick up the officer. The remaining three men were picked up by the submarine.

From the bridge, Cdr Murali conferred with Commodore Mohit Gupta, his boss and the then Mumbai-based COMCOS in the western fleet. Receiving authorization, Cdr Murali turned INS Shankush around and headed straight back to base.

With INS Shankush making an exit from the Varuna exercise, the Indian Navy had ordered another submarine to replace it in the Arabian Sea. The two submarines likely crossed each other that day.

'I was there to receive Mogal at the INHS Asvini naval hospital,' says Commodore Mohit, now a Rear Admiral at the Indian Navy Headquarters. 'When he was brought in, he was still alive. I stood outside the Intensive Care Unit and waited. This was a tough-as-nails officer who had just done something unbelievably brave. I was certain he would make it.'

The first phone call Kerzin Mogal took that morning was from a young Indian Navy officer who worked with her husband. She knew she couldn't ignore a call from the Navy.

'I was informed that Firdaus had been injured and that I should rush to INHS Asvini as quickly as possible,' says Kerzin. 'I wasn't told precisely what had happened, only that I get there as soon as possible. I was in the suburbs and it would have taken two hours to reach the hospital in south Mumbai. I called my mother, who worked in the

Fort area, and asked her to rush there. My son was with my in-laws.'

With a colleague, Kerzin speeded towards the hospital. A series of phone calls to Lt Cdr Firdaus's colleagues in the Navy revealed nothing further.

'There was a lot of anxiety. And a lot of negative thoughts,' says Kerzin. 'The hospital wasn't telling us what was really going on. I guess they needed me to be there. I know their work is dangerous but I had never actually imagined this happening. It's always smooth sailing with these guys. They are such brave souls. They don't tell their wives exactly what happens.'

On the eighth floor of the INHS Asvini naval hospital, a team of doctors battled to revive the injured officer. But scans had revealed a grievous skull fracture. Nobody could have survived such a blow to the head.

A little over an hour after he was flown in, Lt Cdr Firdaus Mogal was pronounced dead.

'As I was crossing Haji Ali, I called Firdaus's colleagues again, yelling and telling them not to lie to me about the situation,' says Kerzin. 'My mother had reached the hospital by then and I was told that she had fainted. I was rushing as fast as I could. Something in my heart told me that when I reached, I would not be seeing Firdaus.'

'Despite the best efforts of everyone, we lost this brave soldier,' says Commodore Mohit. 'His CO knows. His men know. His family knows. And I know—that he did not need to dive into the water to rescue those men. As the XO, he did not need to. That was his super-humanity.'

INS Shankush was headed towards Mumbai at full speed, but had to slow down. A few weeks earlier, a cargo vessel named *MSC Chitra*, coming from Mumbai's Jawaharlal Nehru Port Trust (JNPT), had collided with another merchant vessel, *MV Khalijia-III*, about 9 km off Mumbai, spilling oil and strewing its massive containers over a sizeable area of the sea. This was a navigational hazard, forcing the submarine to approach slowly and with extra care.

'Mogal and the others were picked up around 9.15 a.m.,' says Cdr Murali. 'Then we started back to harbour, reaching around 7 p.m. There were people on the jetty. They informed us that Mogal had not made it. That's when I knew I had lost my brave XO.'

Cdr Murali and the others from *INS Shankush* rushed straight to the naval hospital.

'I wanted to see the body. And I wanted to meet Mrs Mogal and tell her personally what had happened,' says Cdr Murali. 'But the body had been taken home. They wished to hold the funeral two days later. That night, I gathered my entire crew and spoke to them. I told them they had done a brave job that day, and that we had lost a brave brother officer. It was a tragedy.'

But what compelled Lt Cdr Firdaus Mogal to jump into the sea that August morning?

'Imagine how he saw those three sailors struggling—he instantly jumped. It was a flash of leadership. No rational man in his wisdom would have jumped,' says Commodore Mohit. 'It is the eternal spirit of duty that made him jump. He was physically pushing those sailors up, some on his shoulders. But unfortunately, he couldn't save himself. It takes a huge amount of effort to be the one at the top. Even the best of people couldn't do it, it was extraordinary.'

Two days later, Cdr Murali finally got a chance to see the remains of his XO. And to meet his wife, Kerzin.

'I couldn't speak because of the lump in my throat. I tried my best but I couldn't save him. He was brave beyond measure,' says Cdr Murali. 'I remember admonishing the other sailors who were with Mogal, telling them they should have pushed Mogal back in first. They said, "Sir, we tried

that, but Mogal was adamant that he would go only after us."
I told his wife that he could have saved himself by going in
first, perhaps. But he was more concerned about the safety of
his men.'

Lt Cdr Firdaus and Kerzin's son, Yashaan, was barely two
when his father died. Young enough, fortunately, not to know
what was going on, and safely in the arms of a tightly knit
Parsee family. Now ten, he cannot stop talking about a father
he cannot possibly remember, but has heard much about.

'Many people told me I shouldn't be talking to my son
about what happened. But I always felt it was his right to
know what his father did,' says Kerzin. 'Today, Yashaan speaks
about Firdaus very proudly. Even when he was four, he would
narrate in school or to friends how brave his dad was and what
he did. That's how I always wanted him to be. I didn't want
him to be left out because with a father like Firdaus, he has a
legacy. Firdaus hasn't simply left us. We all have to match up
to how brave this soul was.'

In India's small but highly respected submarine arm,
Firdaus Mogal is a name few will ever forget.

'He's definitely considered a superhero,' says Commodore
Mohit. 'You can ask anyone in the submarine arm about the
name Mogal—his memory has not faded. It's been nearly a
decade. We still remember him like it was yesterday.'

To honour his memory, the Navy has named a submarine
simulator complex, marriage accommodation blocks and an
electrical training school in the officer's name. But as with all
military personnel, families and friends of heroes are still the
only ones left to mourn their passing.

'I still tell everybody that if the submarine hadn't suddenly
rolled and hit Firdaus on the head, my husband would have
come back just injured. He would have healed and been with
us,' says Kerzin. 'I can't sit through the stories that are told

of him, and I've read every single one that has been written. They shatter me every single time. He was something else. Firdaus was an angel. He wasn't a human being.'

In the years since his passing, Kerzin Mogal has had time to explore every aspect of her husband's motivation that fateful day. And even though she mourns his loss, she has discovered a strange comfort in what happened.

'I keep wondering how Firdaus would have felt if one of the men had died and he had survived. He would never have been the same again,' says Kerzin. 'He would never have forgiven himself. I've lost my partner, my love, the father of my child. But if anyone else had died in this incident, Firdaus would have been miserable for the rest of his life. Nothing would ever have been the same again for him.'

Lt Cdr Firdaus's family and comrades in the Navy remember him as an officer who unstintingly stood up for the men who served under him.

'"My men are my world," he would say. Everybody will be good to seniors. Real honour is in how you are with your men,' says Kerzin.

Yashaan Mogal is an avid reader. He even reads the Indian Navy journals his mother has collected that contain details of the incident in which his father died.

'Many of Yashaan's teachers say it's amazing how this child doesn't need counselling,' says Kerzin. 'He's a proud and happy kid. He loves talking about his father. When I see and hear that, I feel I can rest easy.'

Kerzin still feels very much a part of the military community in Mumbai. She gets frequent calls from the Navy asking her if she's all right, or if there's anything the service can help her with. She often attends Navy events when she's invited. The one thing she usually declines, though, are the evening functions and dinners.

'I avoid going because I see men in uniform and it's hard for me not to see Firdaus there,' says Kerzin. 'We would go to these together.'

In January 2011, six months after the incident at sea, when Kerzin Mogal arrived in Delhi to receive her husband's posthumous Shaurya Chakra gallantry decoration, a senior Naval officer accosted her at the Rashtrapati Bhavan ceremony.

'He said your husband need not have gone into the water,' says Kerzin. 'His uniform did not tell him to do that. I remember telling this gentleman that he did not know Firdaus. If he were to be in the same situation again, he would go back into the water again and save the six people that he did. Some people are meant to be heroes. It's what I've always said to console and heal myself. Saving those men was his motive. Many of us live without motive. Firdaus just saw it in black and white. He faced no dilemma. He had absolute clarity about what he had to do. I keep saying this—I know in my heart he would have done it again.'

The Shaurya Chakra citation now adorns a wall in Kerzin's living room. It reads:

Lieutenant Commander Firdaus Darabshah Mogal displayed exceptional courage, unmatched show of fearless valour in the face of death and made the supreme sacrifice in saving the lives of six men.

Initially sensitive to questions, Kerzin is now used to them.

'Somebody once asked, when he jumped into the water, did he not think about his child and his wife? And I say, no,' she says.

'I know Firdaus. He was thinking of nothing but his men drowning.'

9

'Just Tell Me when to Begin, Sir'

Captain Pradeep Shoury Arya

Bengaluru
10 May 2017

'Promise me one thing—that you will be alive to receive your medals. And that I won't have to do it on your behalf. Promise me, Pradeep.'

Deepa Arya chuckled nervously. At the other end of the phone line, there was silence. But she could tell he was smiling. It was the sort of verbal ambush Capt. Pradeep Shoury Arya had only been half prepared for in the three years since he began doing what he did.

It was their thirteenth wedding anniversary that day, 10 May 2017. He had promised to celebrate it with Deepa at their Bengaluru home. But his flight out of Mumbai a week ago had taken him in the opposite direction.

Capt. Pradeep disconnected the call from a Special Forces camp in Uri in Jammu and Kashmir's Baramulla area. Contemplating Deepa's words, Capt. Pradeep walked back to the cramped dormitory he shared with three other officers. Unlike them, he knew he didn't fully belong here. For the Captain wasn't an Army officer at all; he was from the Indian Revenue Service (IRS), a comfortably settled tax bureaucrat who had made a career choice that most who knew him would blame on a moment of insanity.

Eight days earlier, on a sultry Mumbai afternoon at his Ballard Estate office, Pradeep Shoury Arya had placed piles of tax papers aside for a quick lunch of his favourite grilled fish. Work didn't stop, though. As he ate, he pored over an International Monetary Fund (IMF) report on money laundering and terror financing, a subject he had grown increasingly obsessed with. Three minutes into lunch, his cell phone rang. It was a call he couldn't dodge.

'Pack your bags, buddy, and take the first flight out of Mumbai. Details after you reach the location,' said the caller. Capt. Pradeep instinctively straightened in his seat, placing his fork with a bit of fish still on it down on the plate with a gentle clang.

The caller was the CO of a Para Special Forces unit operating in Jammu and Kashmir's volatile Uri sector near the LoC—a place where nineteen Army soldiers had been killed in a devastating terror attack that had shaken the entire country eight months before. It was an attack that had sparked the devastating surgical strikes of 29 September 2016, which left thirty-six terrorists and two Pakistani Army personnel dead in one of India's most brutal revenge missions till date.

'On my way immediately, Sir. Jai Hind,' Capt. Pradeep said. If details were to be provided later, it meant there was no room for questions or clarifications now. The only thing to do was to move, and fast.

Except that he was a taxman.

As an Additional Commissioner of Income Tax for International Taxation, Capt. Pradeep couldn't just get up and leave whenever he got a call. He was a Captain in India's Territorial Army, but he still needed leave from his boss in the Income Tax department when the Army needed him. Reserve troops from the Territorial Army, which Capt. Pradeep had joined in 2009, come from all walks of life and are required to operate alongside regular soldiers for at least two months each year, though they are expected to answer calls at any reasonable time. Capt. Pradeep was a reservist attached to a Special Forces unit in the Kashmir Valley. If his full-time work garb involved shirts, ironed trousers and formal shoes, his other job allowed him to wear the coveted maroon beret of India's most lethal soldiers. Capt. Pradeep would jump into combat fatigues in minutes if he could.

But first, he needed leave.

Capt. Pradeep quickly tossed the IMF report he was reading into a drawer. The report was central to his growing expertise in how terror networks raise and move money, and how that financing could be disrupted. The officer's talent for detail in the murky world of terror financing had been recognized a few months earlier, in January 2017, when he was awarded the Chief of Army Staff's commendation for a useful data report he had generated tracking fundraising methods employed to fuel terrorism and anti-state activities in Jammu and Kashmir. The report he had been reading had confirmed many of his suspicions, which he would further study. But the phone call from his CO meant he would have to read it another time.

He moved quickly. A flight to Delhi had to be booked, a promise to be with his wife in Bengaluru for their thirteenth wedding anniversary had to be broken. And a long overdue evening with friends at the popular Leopold Café in Colaba had to be called off. The really tricky part would be seeking leave from his boss, Charanjeet Gulati, the Commissioner of Income Tax. His reasons were solid—a tour of duty in Kashmir—but as Capt. Pradeep walked towards his boss's cabin, he knew he would still have to make a persuasive argument. He wasn't going to be pleased at all, Capt. Pradeep thought to himself as he knocked on the cabin door.

'For heaven's sake, are you saying you are going to be away for a couple of months again? This is utterly unbelievable,' the Income Tax Commissioner spluttered, staring at Capt. Pradeep in disbelief.

'Sir, I am sure we can find a solution,' Capt. Pradeep said quietly, hoping the conversation would end soon so he could go home to pack.

'If you have to go to Kashmir so often, then who will work for the department? Why don't you take a long break and do what you have to do, Arya?' his boss snapped.

'Sir, the call was from the CO himself. I have to reach Uri as soon as possible. You know how things are in Kashmir,' Capt. Pradeep said, a touch of apology in his voice. His boss's irritation wasn't unreasonable, considering Capt. Pradeep had been spending more time with the Special Forces unit than the minimum required under the rules for an Army reservist. Instead of the compulsory two months, he had been out on missions for four to six months in each of the previous two years.

His boss sighed.

'And when do you intend to leave?'

'Tomorrow. As soon as possible, Sir.'

The drive from Ballard Estate to Capt. Pradeep's Malabar Hill apartment overlooking the Arabian Sea took 20 minutes that evening, giving him enough time to make the required phone calls to his family in Bengaluru and the friends who would be nursing hangovers the following morning.

After an early dinner, Capt. Pradeep called it a night. Staring at the ceiling in the dark, he wondered about the reason he had been summoned. He thought of his Special Forces comrades in Kashmir, men for whom a full night's sleep was a rare gift. However, he knew this was likely to be his last predictable night for the foreseeable future and soon fell asleep.

On an early morning flight to Delhi the next day, Capt. Pradeep was typically restless, his mind crowded with thoughts of the new 'adventure' that lay ahead.

'My CO hadn't dropped a single clue. I had no idea what I had been summoned for. And I was restless to get there and find out,' says Capt. Pradeep.

His CO, an Army Colonel, had become something of a cult figure after the September 2016 surgical strikes on terror camps in PoK.[1] He had received a Yudh Seva Medal for the operation that would blast its way into popular culture in the following months and become both a strategic and political buzzword.

The Special Forces unit under the Colonel's charge, to which Capt. Pradeep is attached, played a central role in the blistering covert action behind enemy lines, a mission that drew attention to India's hardened political resolve in the face of repeated terror provocations from Islamabad, as well as its military capability to strike terror havens on the hostile territory beyond the LoC.

Catching a connecting flight from Delhi to Srinagar, Capt. Pradeep settled into his seat for a 40-minute nap. He was certain sleep would be elusive once he landed and made his way to the base he had been summoned to.

'Normally, I would be called to the unit once a month for about a week. But this time, I was told I should be prepared to stay back for a couple of months. That was straightaway unusual,' says Capt. Pradeep. What he was certain about was that he was headed to a site of action.

Darkness had enveloped Uri by the time he reached the quiet and secluded base, where he was greeted by familiar fragrances, a faint breeze whispering through the chinar trees and some of the Army's most elite fighters with long hair and

---

[1] The first and only official account of the 2016 surgical strikes is in the first part of *India's Most Fearless 1*, published by Penguin Random House India in 2017.

full beards, not uncommon among Para commandos operating in Kashmir.

'What took you so long? We were expecting you earlier,' said an officer, high-fiving Capt. Pradeep as he stepped out of his jeep.

'I stopped at Khunmoh [near Srinagar] to meet the boys from 106. You know I always do that,' said Capt. Pradeep, referring to his parent unit, the 106 Infantry Battalion Territorial Army (Para).

'Well, the CO should be here any moment. He's coming from Udhampur,' said the officer.

'I am dying to meet him. Let's stick around till "Tiger" comes,' Capt. Pradeep said.

The Army's Northern Command, headquartered in Udhampur, serves as the nerve centre for the command and control of all Army operations along the LoC with Pakistan. COs from Special Forces and other units are frequently summoned to Udhampur to brief seniors on missions or plans.

Minutes later, the CO's vehicle screeched to a halt inside the base and the muscular six-foot-tall officer stepped out. Respected highly by his men—his credentials burnished even more after the 2016 surgical strikes—the Colonel cut a menacing figure in his battle fatigues, enveloped by an unmistakable aura of authority.

'Good to have you back with us,' the Colonel said, flashing Capt. Pradeep a grin. 'You are curious, aren't you? You were always looking for that great adventure and there's one coming your way.' And without another word, the Colonel walked into the camp quarters.

Capt. Pradeep knew there was no use pushing to know more. He would be told about his mission when the CO was ready, and not a moment earlier. Fortunately, he only needed to wait till dinner to find out why he had been summoned at such short notice, and why he had been asked to stay back almost indefinitely.

At dinner that night at the camp mess, the CO finally got down to briefing Capt. Pradeep and the others.

Intelligence had been gathered that week pointing to unusual activity across the LoC, with military-style terrorist infiltration squads biding their time to slip into Kashmir. The information was apparently solid and required a careful but urgent follow-up with a full-fledged action plan. And Capt. Pradeep was being put in charge.

Capt. Pradeep remembered the jarring images of death and havoc at the Uri Army base from eight months earlier. The base had been struck by a four-man infiltration squad from across the LoC in a nightmarish assault that left nineteen soldiers dead. The pre-dawn strike at the base, rimmed by verdant hills, had taken place in this Special Forces unit's own backyard, and the stinging memories had scarcely faded.

Following India's revenge attacks a few days later, Pakistan was keen to keep the terror pot simmering despite a heightened alert along the LoC.

Capt. Pradeep's CO had told him that the broader intelligence picture pointed to a strong possibility of brazen attempts by terror cells to infiltrate Kashmir in the course of the next few days or weeks.

'The CO gave me a clear mandate to establish a robust intelligence network involving a variety of elements, and simultaneously, prepare my squad to ambush the infiltrators before they could set foot on our soil,' he says.

It was a simple enough job to describe. Capt. Pradeep needed to corroborate intelligence, establish an intelligence network of his own to fine-tune the information and then act upon it with all the force at his disposal. But nothing about it was remotely elementary. Terrorists, aided by the Pakistan

Army and Inter-Services Intelligence, frequently altered plans and locations for infiltration, leaving Indian units guessing till the last moment—sometimes also being caught off guard, with devastating consequences.

As he headed towards the barracks later that night, the single thought that gripped Capt. Pradeep was how a few hours had taken him from a grilled fish lunch in upscale Mumbai to the prospect of a fight to the death in one of the world's most dangerous conflict zones. He contemplated Kashmir's steady and obvious slide back into chaos, with the chances of normalcy dispiritingly remote. The mission at hand for him was but a dot in a larger constellation of threats. But a dot missed, he remembered someone telling him, could make all the difference.

It was early May and the border state was wrestling with what was turning out to be an especially grim year, a tumultuous phase that Pakistani Army-backed terrorists were seeking to exploit to the fullest. Still smarting from the humiliation and damage of the previous year's surgical strikes, Pakistan's Army was ratcheting up efforts to stir up trouble in Kashmir by dispatching commando-trained terror graduates from the camps, running with its full support and funding, in PoK.

'They are up to their old tricks again. But there is no way we will let them succeed,' thought Capt. Pradeep, as he settled into his bunk for the night.

There was nothing remarkable about the barracks at the Special Forces base except its occupants, and the special weapons their dangerous missions afforded them. Capt. Pradeep shared his dormitory with three other officers, and the small attached toilet was the only luxury. It was a far cry from living in one of Mumbai's most exclusive neighbourhoods. He was equally at ease in either world, but secretly loved the austere barracks and the company of these fellow officers he had worked with since he had been attached to the unit in 2015. Their respect for him was inflected with a laughing curiosity—why would a comfortable tax babu living the good life want to be in the Special Forces?

Everyone knew the story, though.

It all began a few years ago with a conversation between the Army's Lt Gen. Subrata Saha, then heading the Srinagar-based 15 Corps, and a senior IRS officer at the prestigious National Defence College in Delhi, where military and civilian officers are groomed for higher leadership positions.

Lt Gen. Subrata, a scholarly three-star General, had just finished delivering a talk on civil–military cooperation when the senior bureaucrat introduced himself to the Corps Commander.

'General, do you know that one of our IRS officers is serving in the Territorial Army? Maybe you can meet him and find a way to put his expertise to the best use,' he said. Lt Gen. Subrata was pleasantly surprised—he didn't know of any bureaucrat who was a military reservist. He made a quick mental note, took Capt. Pradeep's details and a few days later, summoned him to the Badami Bagh Cantonment in Srinagar for a meeting.

When he arrived, the General cut straight to the chase: 'Arya, why don't you consider conducting a study on money laundering and terror funding, and how we can combat these activities? It can be very useful in the context of Kashmir.'

'Just tell me when to begin, Sir,' Capt. Pradeep said.

With the formalities completed a few weeks later, Capt. Pradeep moved to Srinagar for the new assignment. And after Lt Gen. Subrata was transferred to Delhi to take over as one of the Army's two deputy chiefs, the Captain was attached to the Special Forces unit for the next phase of his study, and to also help provide intelligence on terror groups. When he heard about Capt. Pradeep's expertise, the unit's CO grabbed the opportunity with both hands. This man could be very useful, he thought.

'I had had enough of the academic bit and longed to be part of actual operations that the unit was carrying out, the rough-and-tumble of the Special Forces. The peril, the action-packed adventures enticed me,' Capt. Pradeep says.

A notoriously gruelling three-month-long training course followed, which Pradeep describes as the ultimate test of endurance. Upon its completion, he was declared ready to join the ranks of the Special Forces as a Territorial Army officer and be counted among those who would go into combat with them. A higher vote of confidence was unheard of. The Special Forces are not known to outsource. As an outsider, Capt. Pradeep had been welcomed into a unit that normally drew its strength from a nightmarishly difficult training. The tax bureaucrat had proved worthy of the entrance examination. And now he was in.

'One of the critical lessons I learnt during training was that all limits are in our heads. The trainers were ruthless, but they did an amazing job of preparing me to operate at my maximum potential,' says Capt. Pradeep, the training regimen having sculpted his already wiry 5-foot-9-inch frame into raw sinew.

Kashmir had not been far from Capt. Pradeep's mind ever since he had signed up for the Territorial Army in 2009. Regardless of where his work took him, he made sure he kept a finger on the troubled state's pulse. Entries in his personal diary capture how Kashmir was beset with problems at the time, with a sharp escalation in unrest after Hizbul Mujahideen commander Burhan Wani's killing in July 2016, and the flare-up of tensions ahead of the by-elections to the Srinagar and Anantnag Lok Sabha constituencies in April 2017. The diary, his constant companion, details other distressing symptoms of a situation spinning out of control—the swelling crowds at terrorists' funerals, the fury of protesters hurling stones at security men, the surge in anti-India protests, the disturbing images of teenage students clashing with the police, and worse.

'There is no way to sugarcoat the truth that Kashmir was absolutely shaken by a destructive spiral of violence,' says Capt. Pradeep, flipping through the diary.

It was against this backdrop of heightened turbulence in the Kashmir Valley that the operation assigned to Pradeep by his CO assumed greater significance. And he didn't have to be told twice what to do next.

Vital to the effective conduct of army operations is the enormously difficult business of gathering and interpreting intelligence, which requires unsparing effort, skill and patience. The success of a mission depends, unwaveringly, on how good the intelligence is.

The scale of the task before Capt. Pradeep was clear to him from the moment the words left his CO's mouth. And before he hunkered down to sleep that wind-whipped night, Capt. Pradeep wrote a tentative to-do list in the same diary. Activating a carefully cultivated network of informants on either side of the LoC topped the list. He would also need to work with units specializing in diverse intelligence collection disciplines, such as human, technical, communications, electronic and imagery. The different strands would need to come together to form a clearer picture of the mission. The greater the number of strands, the sharper the picture.

Preparing the commando squads for the job ahead was the least of Capt. Pradeep's worries, since Special Forces units train hard every day for some of the Army's most dangerous and secret missions. One of the elements critical to the mission's success would be the difficult task of denying

Pakistani infiltrators the use of well-known routes across the LoC through increased and targeted surveillance. It is no secret that despite the Army's best efforts to hold them off, infiltrators manage to exploit the blind spots produced by the rough terrain to sneak into the state.

And since this was Pakistan the men were dealing with, they weren't just up against terrorist infiltrators, but also Pakistan Army units that actively aided their crossing of the LoC. In the world of Pakistani terror schooling, infiltration operations were the ultimate job placement.

Capt. Pradeep, like all military men operating in Kashmir, was fully aware of the dual face of the adversary—civilian youth honed into dangerous terrorists by a sharp, focused military machinery. And, for the job at hand, Capt. Pradeep knew that the Pakistani Army posts across the LoC in Uri that had steadily provided logistical support to infiltrators could not be allowed to slip under the radar.

'Following through with each element of the broad plan was crucial. We still had a long way ahead of us and had to go about our business keeping a low profile to avoid alerting people across the LoC about Special Forces involvement,' says Capt. Pradeep.

He spent the next three weeks shaping a plan of action, ticking off his to-do list and working to narrow down the enormous amount of information he had collected in a few short days. He knew that this was far from being a 'wham–bam' operation. Success, Capt. Pradeep knew, would rest on a multi-pronged approach that drew on the strengths of key local Army units, especially the electronic warfare detachment, whose primary responsibility was to listen in on terror-related chatter across the LoC. He was assured of their unstinting support.

Before Capt. Pradeep's arrival in Uri, there had been a steady flow of broad, general warnings of a major infiltration attempt by a group of military-trained suicide attackers, aided by a Pakistani Army Mujahid battalion. He knew that such alerts were not uncommon and seldom served as actionable intelligence for a successful operation. It was the dispiriting old maxim of intelligence: only a tiny percentage of all warnings resulted in anything meaningful at all, let alone a successful operation.

'It is no exaggeration that we are swamped with a number of alerts every day. Rarely do one or two inputs out of, say, ten carry any real intelligence value. But no input is ignored,' says Capt. Pradeep.

There were plenty of dots that he had to connect in the right order to generate that elusive big picture of a major infiltration attempt—the where, the when and, crucially, with what strength. For days, Capt. Pradeep thoroughly reviewed volumes of fresh intelligence data and cross-checked it for accuracy with multiple sources, including his informants on the ground on both sides of the LoC. He prayed for a breakthrough.

On 10 May, after he called his wife to wish her on their anniversary and spent some time in the dormitory with the Special Forces men, Capt. Pradeep returned to the camp's war room to continue the hunt for intelligence. By noon, it became clear that the Pakistani Army's 652 Mujahid Battalion, the 'Mountain Tigers' based across the LoC in Chakothi, was very likely to be the unit that planned to 'administer' the looming infiltration. Detailed analysis of intercepted communication by Capt. Pradeep revealed that terrorists belonging to Pakistan's two most formidable terrorist groups, the LeT and the JeM, would be launched from the notorious Sugna post to enter Uri at an appropriate time.

In the war room, Capt. Pradeep also received a crucial audio report from the electronic warfare unit he had enlisted for help.

'*Mehmaan aa rahe hain. Bhejne ki tayyarian shuru karein* (The guests are coming. Begin preparations to dispatch them).' The audio intercept of a piece of communication from the Pakistani Army post to a terror launch pad seemed to confirm, at the very least, that an infiltration attempt was afoot.

'Raw data had been distilled into possibly accurate information. The attackers were coming. The likely route they would take was now practically known. It was hard to predict the exact timing, though,' Capt. Pradeep says.

No amount of intelligence can conclusively establish the precise date and time of infiltration activity. The likelihood of plans changing at the last minute is a near certainty, the modus operandi, in fact, of the Pakistani Army. But what seemed certain by this time was that the countdown had begun.

Briefing the CO that evening, like he did every day, Capt. Pradeep presented his recommendations based on an analysis of all the intelligence he had—what was made available to him and what he had additionally gathered. The 'unwanted guests' were likely to try their luck in the last week of May, he said.

At the base, Special Forces squads were busy doing what they do all year round—training for the worst possible situations and the most difficult missions. Capt. Pradeep remembers the training regimen that involved each commando firing hundreds of rounds every day, irrespective of whether a mission was at hand or not. War readiness was a defining requirement. Once a mission had been assigned, there would be no time to train.

Three squads, consisting of six soldiers each, were now training to be a part of Capt. Pradeep's upcoming operation. Two additional squads would provide backup. As mission leader, he was now armed with enough intelligence to brief the squads about how things were likely to unfold and where they would lie in ambush for their Pakistani 'guests'.

'*Humare paas pukki information hai ki yeh log Sugna post se launch honge. Launch hone ke baad yeh KDK nallah ke raaste se ayenge LoC paar karne ke liye. Hum inko wahin par khatam kar denge* (We have solid information that these people will be launched from the Sugna post. After being launched, they will take the route through KDK nallah to cross the LoC. We will finish them off there),' Capt. Pradeep told his men during a briefing using a sand model of the Uri sector, which contained detailed features of mountains, valleys and the LoC itself. The men knew that the KDK nallah was a notorious blind spot.

The sand model was necessary for such a briefing, even though the Special Forces men knew the area supremely well. This was, in every sense, their backyard. But there could be no mistakes, no assumptions and no short measures before a mission as delicate and dangerous as this one.

'*Abhi yeh clear nahin hai ki yeh fidayeen dasta PoK se kab rawana hoga. Par hum apne kaam par abhi se lag jayenge* (It is not yet clear when the terrorists will leave PoK. But we will begin our work now),' Capt. Pradeep said.

The area was now under intense covert surveillance day and night. With indeterminate intelligence on the date and time of the infiltration, Capt. Pradeep decided to take no chances. On 22 May, he ordered the first of his Special Forces squads to proceed to the likely ambush site along the LoC, near the Indian Army's Chabuk post, to make sure the infiltrators could spring no surprises. The men rolled out from the camp in a jeep that would drop them off near a trail they would trek to get to the LoC. Vehicular sounds needed to be kept to a minimum. Pakistan's own highly evolved intelligence networks could smell a Special Forces man from a mile away.

That morning, Capt. Pradeep had woken up with a stinging pain in his bloodshot eyes. With one squad dispatched to the LoC, and the CO waiting for a morning briefing on his next step, there couldn't have been a worse time to contract conjunctivitis.

'Arya, stay the hell away from me. I don't want to see you within 10 miles of the squads. If you are still harbouring any desire to lead this operation, go see a doctor now,' the CO snapped.

Capt. Pradeep knew he was right. On his way to the field hospital, he felt miserable thinking that the mission may just have ended for him even before it began. The doctor sent him back with a small bag of medicines and much-needed assurance that the infection would go away soon.

'It was a nightmare. I didn't come all the way to Uri to let an eye infection ruin everything,' he says. By that evening, fortunately, the infection had resolved itself.

Preparations for the ambush began in full swing 22 May onwards. The Special Forces squads, fully kitted out with their assault weapons and body armour, were assigned to the operational area in rotation to keep an eye on terrorist movement along the KDK nallah.

'When a Special Forces team waits in ambush, it's not like we just sit in one place. We sit, we move, we sit, we move. It allows us to cover a larger area and hunt better,' Capt. Pradeep says.

Every step had to be taken carefully since the area was peppered with landmines, a legacy from a series of conflicts in 1965, 1971 and even the 1999 Kargil War. It is standard practice for the Army to mark minefields, but these hidden killers are known to drift because of extreme weather conditions, shifting of soil and landslides. Soldiers have blundered into minefields along the LoC, especially in the Baramulla sector, despite mine-risk education to prevent death and injury from these deadly explosive devices.

'A landmine is a weapon of war that treats friends and foes alike. The mines presented a peril to the squads. The men had to proceed with extreme caution,' says an officer from one of Capt. Pradeep's squads.

The next stage of the operation involved planting radio-controlled IEDs along the expected entry routes and testing signal strength to detonate explosives from a distance. Stealth was crucial. Manoeuvres were carried out under the cover of darkness, with the commandos taking every precaution to avoid detection.

Numerous reconnaissance missions to collect intelligence and scout out this particular stretch of the LoC followed. The squads went on night-time patrols, remaining unseen during the day.

'We have a real problem in this sector. Dense foliage across the LoC offers the infiltrators excellent camouflage. We don't enjoy that advantage on our side,' says Capt. Pradeep.

After four days of non-stop alert in the area of expected infiltration, Capt. Pradeep received a late-night phone call on 26 May. It was one of his most trusted informants, a man he had cultivated over two years and someone Capt. Pradeep had been hoping he would hear from. This was a man who operated on both sides of the LoC, but Capt. Pradeep had learnt to trust him.

In a hushed voice, the caller informed Capt. Pradeep that the infiltrators were now being guided by the Pakistani Army's Sugna post and that they would attempt to cross the LoC on the night of 28 or 29 May. The information not only confirmed much of the intelligence Capt. Pradeep and his men had gathered over two weeks, but provided them with that final bit they needed to sharpen their plan of action. A two-day window for an infiltration is a highly specific piece of information, a fragment of data in an otherwise chaotic, unfixable ocean of vague intelligence.

Capt. Pradeep thanked the informant and hung up, immediately ordering four squads to stand by to head to the

Chabuk post the following evening. The post was a 90-minute drive from the Special Forces base.

It was time to move, and fast. Capt. Pradeep made a phone call to his wife, telling her he would be off the grid for the next few days and that he would call her as soon as he was 'free'. Deepa Arya listened in silence, only reminding him of her words from a few days before, 'I'm not collecting your medals.'

As planned, two of the squads would stay at Chabuk for backup and the other two would set out on foot for the last leg to join the squad that had already been positioned in the area on 22 May across the KDK nallah and directly facing Pakistan's Mujahid battalion post on the other side of the LoC. But just when everything seemed to be moving as per plan, the commandos encountered an expected hurdle the next day, on 27 May, which threatened the stealth necessary for their mission.

Sabzar Ahmad Bhat, a Hizbul Mujahideen commander and successor to Burhan Wani, had been killed in a firefight with security forces late the previous night in south Kashmir's restive Tral, a hotbed of Hizbul terror. Bhat's killing had set off a wave of protests across Kashmir.

'Bhat's killing and the ensuing violence was unforeseen. Moving out of the base presented a challenge because of the heightened possibility of being seen. But we somehow managed to reach Chabuk by nightfall on 27 May,' Capt. Pradeep says.

The Special Forces squads were armed with a full array of weapons, including their standard-issue Israeli Tavor TAR-21 assault rifles, Colt M4A1 carbines, Uzi silenced submachine guns, Pulemyot Kalashnikova general-purpose machine guns, C90 disposable rocket launchers, UBGLs and 9-mm pistols. Some commandos carried two pistols, a personal choice.

Each man was armed with six grenades and four magazines of ammunition. They were kitted out for a short, sharp firefight.

From the Chabuk post, large midsummer storm clouds quickly rolled in, raining torrents on the two squads as they departed over slippery ground and up pine-clad slopes towards the LoC.

Colt M4A1 carbine

'*Sir, aaj raat ko contact hone ke kitne chances hain?* (What are the chances of establishing contact with the terrorists tonight?),' asked Capt. Pradeep's buddy soldier, a Havildar whom the officer affectionately called Hero.

'*Ho bhi sakta hai, Hero. Jitna jaldi ho utna accha hai* (It's possible. The sooner the better),' said Capt. Pradeep, remembering that his informant had indicated a window that began the following night. The Havildar's question wasn't surprising. Armed and in position, nothing occupies a commando's mind more than the prospect of coming in contact with the enemy. As soon as possible.

The rain had weakened to a drizzle by the time the two squads reached the appointed rendezvous point, where the first squad, sent there five days earlier, was holding fort barely 100 m from the LoC.

'Sir, we haven't spotted any activity yet. It's all quiet here,' one of the commandos reported to Capt. Pradeep as soon as he arrived. The commando was holding an HHTI, a sensor device that provides clear infrared images in complete darkness.

Capt. Pradeep's informant had said the infiltration would happen on 28 or 29 May, but that didn't mean plans from the other side couldn't change. The squads carried out reconnaissance patrols through the night, taking up their pre-assigned positions long before dawn broke over the hills. If the commandos could prowl in darkness on patrol, daybreak meant complete concealment.

'We had to lie low during the day. There was little else we could do. One wrong move and all the intelligence we had gathered would be useless,' says Capt. Pradeep. Hunkered down only 100 m from the LoC, the day was spent with nearly no movement save for a thin rotation of patrolling commandos to keep the proverbial knife edge pointed and ready.

'Nobody likes the day. It's at night that we go to war,' says an officer from the squad deployed in the area that day.

As the sun set on 28 May, Capt. Pradeep gathered his men for a night briefing. The two squads would be on an even sharper state of alert, if that were possible. The third squad had spread out and positioned itself some distance away to cover more area. He felt an inexplicable pang of certainty that his informant was about to be proven devastatingly correct. Two hours later, he saw the confirmation on a thermal imager in the hands of a soldier near him.

At 10.30 p.m., the dark infrared image of an infiltrator entered the frame, his body heat helping draw a sharp picture against the cold, wet surroundings. In a crouched walk, he was moving forward from the expected direction of the KDK nallah. Within moments, the image of a second terrorist became visible on the thermal imager's monitor, followed by a third and then a fourth. Two more terrorists could be seen 200 m behind them in the nallah.

Capt. Pradeep sent up a silent prayer of thanks to his informant. Like every time before, he was dead on.

As the two squads watched in silence, the six infiltrators trudged forward, hoping to cross the LoC undetected that moonless Sunday night. Each terrorist walked about 12 feet behind the other, to reduce the chances of damage if they were ambushed. Minutes later, the first four terrorists crossed the LoC, pausing briefly to gauge their surroundings. On the thermal imagers, the dark figures hesitated for a few minutes, appearing to assess the air for any telltale signs that they were expected. The Indian squads held their breaths. Capt. Pradeep prayed the four infiltrators wouldn't abort their mission and run back, like several infiltrators had done in the past. But after a few minutes, the infiltrators continued onward.

When they were comfortably on 'our turf', Capt. Pradeep signalled to one of his men to detonate the first IED using the radio-controlled receiver. And then another. Two sharp explosions went up near the terrorists, throwing one of them to the ground. The other five, all supremely well-trained, reacted instinctively by splitting themselves into three groups and taking cover in the thick foliage to better engage their hunters.

When the blast had cleared, and the thermal imager was able to redraw its heat picture of the attack site, it became immediately clear that the terrorist injured in the blast wasn't moving. A second terrorist was trying to pull him away to safety while firing aimlessly in the dark in the general direction of the squad, which hadn't fired a single bullet yet. With his assault rifle, Capt. Pradeep took aim and fired a single shot, killing the second terrorist. The injured terrorist remained motionless. It was likely that he was dead too, though the squad wouldn't take any chances.

The remaining four terrorists were firing a steady stream of bullets in the direction of the Special Forces squads, which had by now dispersed into six smaller groups of two men over short distances up the hill, firing back at the intruders from various directions. As Capt. Pradeep returned fire and the terrorists' bullets hissed around him, he realized that Hero had separated from him and was now dangerously vulnerable. With fire returned, the terrorists had a clear idea of where the Indian commandos were. The chances of their bullets finding targets were higher now, and their vantage points in the foliage meant it was far harder for bullets to find them in return.

'I may kill a dozen terrorists, but if I lose even a single soldier under my command, the mission is nothing but a big failure. It's as simple as that,' Capt. Pradeep says.

Rounds from an AK-47 were peppering the ground near Hero as he lay flat on his stomach, firing back. The Havildar was aware of the approaching fusillade, making a move to get out of the way. At that moment, Capt. Pradeep leapt from his position briefly into the line of fire, before diving for cover behind a large fallen tree. There, he flattened himself against the ground. Stepping on one of the hundreds of landmines dotting that stretch would have left him limbless, if not dead. But the safety of his buddy soldier was now his chief concern.

Partially shielded by the fallen tree, Capt. Pradeep concentrated his fire on the two intruders who were targeting Hero with a hail of Kalashnikov bullets from their position of advantage. The incoming 7.62 mm shots missed Hero by a matter of inches, yet the Havildar held his nerve and fired back at the terrorists. There was no way he was backing out of the firefight.

'*Hero, cover lo! Sab control mein hai!* (Hero, take cover. Everything is under control),' Capt. Pradeep yelled above the sound of gunfire.

The muzzle flash of their AK-47s gave away the positions of the two terrorists. Steadying his breath so he could aim better, Capt. Pradeep pointed his weapon straight into the darkness from which the bullets poured. In a series of short bursts, he unleashed a magazine of ammunition into the foliage. The Kalashnikovs fell silent. Both terrorists had either been killed, or injured enough to stop firing.

Capt. Pradeep leapt once again into the open to pull the Havildar to the safety of cover.

'Every man in my team knows he is being covered by his comrades all the time. He knows he will never find himself alone. This faith is unshakeable and it helps us conduct the toughest of operations,' Capt. Pradeep says.

Twenty minutes from when the first IED was detonated, four terrorists had been either killed or injured. By about 10.50 p.m., the volume of terrorist assault rifle fire had significantly reduced. The next few minutes saw a sporadic exchange of gunfire. The Special Forces squads aimed sustained fire in the direction of the two remaining infiltrators from six different directions.

'The terrorists would fire a burst, and then pause. The pattern was repeated. They were running low on ammunition and were clearly firing only to draw return fire and pinpoint our positions,' Capt. Pradeep says. This was military-style tactical training on display. But Capt. Pradeep noticed something else too.

The spread of the bullets fired by the infiltrators wasn't the typical AK–47 spray. They were using sawed-off Kalashnikovs, with the shortened barrels scattering the bullets wider. The idea was to try and hit a larger area at once, increasing the chances of a bullet finding Indian flesh.

With gunfire now reduced to sporadic pops, the intruders carefully emerged from their hiding positions in the foliage, slipping between rocks down the hill before reaching level ground. Then they started to run back along the trail they had taken towards the LoC, in a clear effort to escape back into Pakistan. As they ran, the two terrorists raised their weapons and opened fire at the Indian commandos. It was clear that the two weren't prepared to fight to the end.

'They wanted to stay alive so that they could return another day. We were not going to let that happen,' Capt. Pradeep said.

Slipping out from their own positions, the dozen Indian commandos trudged down the slopes to the trail and towards the retreating intruders, taking supreme care to duck behind rocks as the Kalashnikovs fired without interruption. As Capt. Pradeep and his men watched, with a six-way line of fire zeroing in on the running terrorists, it became clear that they were now only about 50 m from the LoC. Once they crossed over, the operation would become exponentially more difficult, given that the Pakistani Army was already likely to be on high alert to aid the intruders in any way possible.

Capt. Pradeep shouted to his men, who were close by, that the two intruders had to be stopped at all costs. The teams paused for a few seconds to reorient, slam fresh magazines into their assault rifles, and then took aim as the terrorists sprinted across the final stretch to the LoC. That final burst found the two terrorists. The Indian commandos fired their last shots at 11.15 p.m. No more fire was returned. The last echoes of gunfire and smoke lifted off the mountain as the sounds of the night returned.

But the operation wasn't over yet.

'We had to be certain all the terrorists were dead and more weren't lurking around the corner. We waited till first light to clear up the area. That's standard protocol,' Capt. Pradeep says.

At dawn, the men recovered the bodies of the six infiltrators, along with their AK-47 rifles, dozens of unused magazines, grenades, a satellite phone and Chinese-made pistols—all standard issue kit for Pakistan-sponsored terrorists.

With four commandos still on the lookout for more terrorists, Capt. Pradeep gathered his men for a quick debrief at the site. He congratulated them on a sharp, well-executed mission without casualties or injuries. On their way back to base, he sent a text message to the Colonel announcing the outcome of the operation. After more than three weeks of near-sleepless preparation, the encounter had lasted 45 minutes. Every bit of intelligence gathered by the teams that worked with Capt. Pradeep had proven to be correct. It was a small but ringing success against a machinery that would view the night's proceedings as no more than a temporary setback against an inexhaustible arsenal of human weapons.

But back at the Special Forces camp, celebrations had begun. Capt. Pradeep allowed himself a full bottle of Old Monk rum, his first drink in many years. The CO had also ordered a cake. It was Capt. Pradeep's birthday the following day, 30 May.

In Bengaluru, Deepa got the call she had been waiting for. As their daughters, Dhriti and Dhiksha, slept, Deepa stayed awake—she hadn't closed her eyes with any success for 48 hours. Exhausted but overcome with relief, she listened to her husband matter-of-factly report that he was well and that he had returned to base. Nothing more was discussed.

'The commando missions were completely new to me. I thought I had married an IRS officer,' says Deepa. 'I remember telling him I never signed up for this. He was always very passionate about the uniform, but I had no clue that this was the route he was going to take.'

Being the spouse of an Army officer can be unimaginably hard.

'There are ups and downs, there's pride and there's pain. My heart skips a beat whenever Pradeep calls to tell me that he will be away from his phone for a few days. Yet, I feel proud of his accomplishments and have no regrets. The uniform will always be his first love. The way I look at it is that I should not be the reason for him to not do what he wants to do,' Deepa says.

Eight months after the LoC operation, the government announced India's third-highest peacetime gallantry honour, the Shaurya Chakra, for Capt. Pradeep on the eve of Republic Day in 2018, for prominent acts of courage. His citation for the medal is replete with expressions that describe his actions: 'pre-eminent valour', 'heroic initiative', 'inspirational combat leadership' and 'unmindful of his own safety'.

On 23 April 2018, after President Ram Nath Kovind bestowed the award on Capt. Pradeep, the Rashtrapati Bhavan tweeted, 'He displayed audacity in the face of terrorists' fire and extraordinary valour in risking his life beyond call of duty and eliminated six terrorists.'[2]

At forty-six, Capt. Pradeep, holding a position in the IRS equivalent to a Brigadier's in the Army, was the oldest recipient of a gallantry award at the Rashtrapati Bhavan Durbar Hall that evening. Unlike regular Army officers who walk out of military academies as lieutenants at twenty-one or twenty-two, the Territorial Army allows volunteers to join its ranks till the age of forty-two. Allowing a forty-six-year-old, seconded to a Special Forces unit, to lead a dangerous mission can only be an indicator of the calibre of the officer in question, his reputation, his soldiering skills and commitment.

'Here's a guy, a bureaucrat. A tax official. Who one day packs his bags and goes off to stop terrorists,' says another officer from Capt. Pradeep's unit. 'It's rare to find people outside the uniform who can influence others to get out of their comfort

---

[2] https://bit.ly/2EUxOe8

zones. He could have chosen to be in Mumbai, but here he was, willing to put his life on the line on a godforsaken hill. There has to be something in you if you are ready to take that step.'

He prefers to be addressed as 'Capt. Pradeep', his identity as an Army officer taking precedence over the other hats he wears. His unit comrades don't find this even remotely surprising.

'A bureaucrat sporting combat fatigues is a rarity in India, where the military is neither the first nor an obvious career choice for many. Most of all, the Special Forces are a different species and a prized national asset,' one of them says.

The mission and the Shaurya Chakra have changed many things for the officer. Capt. Pradeep, for all practical purposes an outsider in the Army, is now accorded all the trimmings and respect due to one of their own.

But many things haven't changed at all. Capt. Pradeep continues to divide his time between income tax work and his study of terror financing.

He listens frequently to his favourite Hindi song, which is, '*Main zindagi ka saath nibhata chala gaya, har fikr ko dhuen mein udata chala gaya*'.

And he remains in constant anticipation of that next phone call.

10

'What's Higher than Saving Someone's Life?'

Captain P. Rajkumar

'Laser beam spotted on port bow, Sir!'

The navigator was screaming the words to the pilots, forcing them to throw the helicopter into a sharp left turn and descend from 200 feet towards the storm-churned blackness of the Arabian Sea. What the five men on board the Indian Navy's SK 528, an old grey Sea King helicopter, had been hunting through the furious, beating rain and swells of Cyclone Ockhi had finally been sighted.

As the helicopter shuddered and carefully lowered itself over a sea churned dangerously into a heaving maelstrom by the rain, the flight commander followed the thin, green, barely visible laser beam. Buffeted by 150 kmph wind speeds, he strained to keep the helicopter in control while maintaining a visual lock on the thin green line. With the laser beam flickering and disappearing for whole seconds into the surging sea surface, he knew that if he lost sight of it, this mission would end in at least one death.

At least.

A few feet at a time, the SK 528 descended into an engulfing darkness, broken only by a cone of light from its search lamp that was rendered virtually useless in the storm. At 50 feet, the flight commander paused for a moment, bringing the helicopter into a tense shuddering hover, the roar of the rotors nearly drowned out by the thrashing rain and wind. The four other men looked at him. They knew his dilemma. Any lower in this weather, and there was a good chance that the smallest in-flight emergency would mean disaster. But seconds later, the helicopter heaved and continued its downward drift, the darkness and rain so overpowering that the crew couldn't see the tips of their helicopter's rotor blades.

The elusive laser beam threatened to disappear as the helicopter descended from 50 feet to 40, then to a dangerous 30 feet. In a final push, the SK 528 came to a hover 20 feet over the sea surface, its swells so rough that they threatened to reach up and hit the helicopter's belly. Vulnerable and dangerously close to a catastrophe, the flight commander knew he had bare minutes. As the cone of light from the helicopter's search lamp scanned the small patch of sea below, he saw it.

'Target spotted!' he breathed into his cockpit talkback. Twenty feet below the trembling helicopter, bobbing dangerously in the middle of the sea, was the very object they were looking for.

Six hours earlier

In his green flying overalls, Capt. P. Rajkumar jogged to the SK 528, the Sea King helicopter that was primed and waiting on the tarmac at *INS Garuda*. The Indian Navy's air base at Kochi was on high alert. The Captain's crew was waiting at the chopper as an unusually dark afternoon sky visibly worsened over their heads. The Navy's INAS 336 squadron, of which the helicopter and crew were a part, is dedicated to anti-submarine warfare operations. On that December afternoon, they had been scrambled to embark on a hunt. It wasn't submarines they were being sent after, but fellow citizens.

By 1 December, Cyclone Ockhi was just hours away from assuming its most fearsome form right off the coast of Kerala. Capt. Rajkumar, a decorated Navy pilot, had flown terrifying helicopter missions in the past, including a daring rescue of scientists in Antarctica three decades earlier. But the next 6 hours would dwarf everything else. As he climbed into the SK 528 that afternoon, strapped in and turned the chopper's twin Rolls-Royce Gnome engines on, he had only the barest sense of what lay ahead.

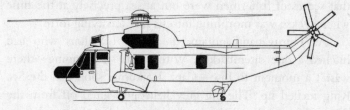

Sea King helicopter

'We're trained for this, but you can never be completely ready for what's in store for you. In the military, we're fatalists. And I'm even more of a fatalist because I'm a Malayali,' Capt. Rajkumar laughs. 'Nobody expected the full force of a cyclone in this side of the country. The meteorological department can cry hoarse as far as the onset of Ockhi is concerned, but on the west coast of India, cyclones are a rare phenomenon. You only hear about them on the east coast. It's only when she hit that it became clear what we were dealing with. And it was not pretty.'

Capt. Rajkumar was flying with co-pilot Lt Cdr Abhijit Garud, navigator and tactical coordinator Lt Cdr Mayoor Chauhan, and two young combat divers, Sumit Raj and Deepak Saini. Also hitching a ride on that 200-km flight to Kerala's capital, Thiruvananthapuram, were a handful of sailors who were required for a separate mission on another aircraft waiting for them there.

Flying south over land, the crew of the SK 528 could easily see the ominous swathe of rain-laden cyclonic cloud on their right, bearing down along the coast. Ockhi had struck two days before and was rapidly whipping itself up into one of the most devastating cyclones of the year. Advisories had been sent out to fishing communities not to venture out to sea and to stay away from the waterline. But a mixture of scepticism— nobody really expected a west coast cyclone to be anything major—and the sobering reality of earning a livelihood meant that scores of fishermen were out at sea precisely at the time when Ockhi was morphing into its full, terrifying form.

At Thiruvananthapuram, the group of sailors who had hitched a ride disembarked. With rotors still running—there wasn't a moment to lose—Capt. Rajkumar soon had the Sea King fuelled up. The big grey helicopter lifted off from the dispersal area and peeled away, heading out directly over the sea.

On a normal day, 2 p.m. would have offered the best flying conditions, with thick sea air giving the helicopter all the lift it needed, and a crisp blue sky offering the crew perfect visibility for an even flight. But on that day, just as Capt. Rajkumar pitched the helicopter forward and speeded out over the Arabian Sea, the crew immediately ran into cyclonic weather with sudden, violent winds and rain that put paid to any visibility they had been blessed with only a few minutes earlier.

'In a typical cyclone like Ockhi, the wind speed picks up, and therefore the sea starts churning and a long swell develops. We knew we were going to face extreme weather. The rain was coming down in sheets, visibility was almost zero,' the Captain remembers.

Very soon, visibility *was* zero. Flying 100 feet over the lashing sea surface, the SK 528 was completely blind. The crew couldn't see more than a few feet beyond the helicopter's windshields and the on-board sensors were tuned to hunting submarines, not finding wrecked fishing boats and survivors in the middle of a maelstrom. Thankfully, the crew had another pair of eyes flying far above them.

Cruising at 1000 feet through the storm clouds was an Indian Navy P-8I, a Boeing 737 aircraft fitted with an arsenal of high-performance sensors and cameras capable of penetrating the worst weather and finding the smallest objects at sea—something the Sea King, flying 900 feet below, could only dream of doing. A small, swivelling camera in a bubble-like container on the P-8I's chin scanned the sea surface in infrared mode, while a team of officers on board scanned the visual feed, hoping to spot a fishing boat in distress.

Or even humans in the water, for that matter.

For 3 hours, the helicopter and the aircraft combed huge sections of the sea roughly 70 km off the Kerala coast. For 3 hours, they found nothing but a roiling sea getting steadily worse.

'The P-8I crew and I knew that with each passing minute, spotting boats or survivors would become increasingly more difficult. But just as we were about to shift our attention to a different part of the sea to look for possible survivors, the P-8I's commander came in through the radio,' says Capt. Rajkumar.

'Boat sighted. Capsized condition. Four survivors visually confirmed,' the P-8I pilot called through the radio, relaying a set of coordinates to the precise location. Daylight was fading fast, but a target had been spotted and the helicopter's crew wasted no time. Still flying at 100 feet, the Sea King banked hard as it changed direction and headed straight for the coordinates of the location where a medium-sized fishing vessel had turned over.

'Unlike thirty or forty years ago, when catamarans and older fishing boats had deep bottom keels that were much more resistant to capsizing, new generation cheaper-to-build fishing boats with their fibreglass hulls are top-heavy, and therefore capsize easily in rough seas,' says Capt. Rajkumar. It was an important nugget of information he had picked up on visits to fishing villages. Now, cruising over a thrashing sea, he knew it meant two things: one, that the time available to rescue the boat in distress was extremely short, and two, spotting them in the water was going to become exponentially more difficult as the minutes passed.

But this needle-in-a-haystack hunt had actually thrown up a target, thanks to the aircraft flying above them. Fully aware of how futile search and rescue operations could be without modern technology, Capt. Rajkumar sent up a silent prayer of thanks for the privilege of precise coordinates to home in on.

The dull grey daylight was fading fast, but as the Sea King swooped in over the coordinates they had locked on to, it was clear that the information supplied by the P-8I was of very high quality. There, bobbing in the sea, was a capsized fishing boat with four persons on top. Fortunately, all four appeared to be in good condition, suggesting that the boat had been out at sea for not more than a day.

'We descended to about 30 feet. The weather was worsening. Our two divers lowered a rescue strop, and we winched the four men up one by one. This was, of course, a time-consuming job and time definitely was at a premium as there was not much daylight remaining,' remembers Capt. Rajkumar.

With the four rescued fishermen on board, the crew of the SK 528 made straight for the coast. By the time the helicopter landed at Thiruvananthapuram with the survivors, it was well past sunset. A difficult mission had been flown with the unlikely bonus of actually finding and rescuing survivors during a cyclone at sea. It was time to switch the engines off and take a break for the night. For one thing, the P-8I that had provided rescue intelligence had flown back to base for the night. And without it, hunting for survivors was virtually impossible. It was a difficult day that had ended with success. There was no reason not to call it a night.

But something nagged at Capt. Rajkumar. And as the SK 528 was refuelled for the second time that day with its rotors still turning, the four other men on board waited for orders.

'My crew understood fully. I did not have to say much. There were no orders or coordinates. We lifted off and headed out to sea for the second time on a hunch and a prayer for those yet to be rescued,' the Captain remembers. 'If there's a very fine line between calculated risk and sheer foolhardiness, we in the military know there's a very fine line between a court martial and a gallantry award.'

In the cabin, combat diver Deepak Saini read the Captain's mind. And then he heard the words.

'We will launch again and search for survivors till the last drop of fuel in our bodies as well as the machine are expended,' the flight commander announced from the cockpit.

'The Captain was determined that we would be angels to someone else that night. He was not ready to give up. And his words energized us afresh,' says thirty-one-year-old Saini, who joined the Navy in 2004 and took the commando diving course in 2010, making him one of a rare breed of sailors tasked with one of the most death-defying mission profiles in the service.

Everything had changed off the coast of Kerala in the hour since the rescue of the four fishermen. The swirling grey of dying daylight had now turned into complete darkness. The only aids the crew had were floodlights and a single controllable spotlight on the helicopter's chin.

'Unfortunately, these lights, when switched on in heavy rain, will only reflect it back to the cockpit, making flying very disorienting. Flying at 200 feet, scanning the night sea in rain, is one of the most challenging tasks out there,' Capt. Rajkumar says. With the sea and sky melting into one endless mass of blackness, the pilots of SK 528 were flying largely with the help of their instruments, most importantly at this time, a radio altimeter that reassured them of their height above the turbulent sea surface.

The SK 528 cruised through the darkness, the bad weather of earlier in the day now working up into an unrelenting viciousness of rain and wind, the endless darkness of the sea and sky only broken by the faint luminescence of waves in violent churn. For a helicopter crew, a more unfavourable set of flying conditions couldn't be imagined.

'We were hunting blind. We had no coordinates. And we couldn't see. This was exponentially more difficult than finding a needle in a haystack,' Capt. Rajkumar now remembers.

The bitter irony of the situation wasn't lost on the crew. They were now searching for something they couldn't see in the first place—and probably wouldn't be able to see even if they flew right over it. But they stayed out over the sea, five men squinting through the darkness in every direction, hoping to see something, anything, combing stretches of inky black ocean on a hunch that there were more people out at sea and waiting to be rescued.

The endless combing of the sea continued for an hour without result. And as the winds picked up, it was clear to the crew that this mission was only getting more challenging. Capt. Rajkumar gathered his thoughts as his co-pilot took control of the helicopter and kept it on course for the search. And that's when a voice with a heavy Chinese accent crackled in on the radio.

The nearly incomprehensible call, inflected with panic, was from a huge 1,00,000-ton Maltese container vessel, the *MV Cosco Beijing*, that had been making its way across the Arabian Sea. The message had come in through Channel 16, the 156.8 megahertz frequency used by merchant vessels. While refuelling at Thiruvananthapuram an hour earlier, Capt. Rajkumar had tuned one of the cockpit's very high frequency (VHF) radios to Channel 16, thereby keeping an ear open for emergency messages from merchant ships. The anguished Chinese voice was distorted and high pitched.

'BOAT! CAPSIZE! FISHING BOAT! CAPSIZE!' came the call through Channel 16 from the *MV Cosco Beijing*. The ship was visible to the helicopter's crew on their radar and had been identified. The call was the first miraculous confirmation to Capt. Rajkumar that his hunch had been correct. He immediately responded to the radio message, confirming that he was headed towards the ship.

Through a series of garbled exchanges deciphered while manoeuvring the Sea King through the cyclone, the crew of SK 528 understood that the *MV Cosco Beijing* had spotted a capsized fishing boat, and was using a laser pointer device to mark its location.

Co-pilot Lt Cdr Garud responded immediately, slowly relaying a message back to the merchant ship. 'This is Indian Navy helicopter on a search-and-rescue mission. Information received on capsized boat. We are heading to your location.'

With the co-pilot in tenuous touch with the merchant ship, Capt. Rajkumar turned the chopper sharply in the vessel's direction.

'We picked up the massive merchant vessel on our radar and speeded towards it. Though the big ship had stopped, it was also rolling and pitching in the churning sea. Its only connection with the fishing boat it had spotted was with the laser pointer. There was no way it could come close to the fishing boat, because that would have been dangerous to any survivor. The safe distance coupled with the heavy rain meant the laser beam wasn't quite reaching its intended target. The huge waves were also constantly hiding the boat. So the man on *MV Cosco Beijing*'s deck was also, in effect, searching for the boat with his laser pointer,' says Capt. Rajkumar.

Arriving within minutes over the huge container ship, the Sea King circled it a few times, its crew hoping desperately to find the tiny laser beam the ship was using to identify the general direction of the capsized boat it had spotted. The sea was so rough, it was very likely that the capsized boat had drifted considerably. But with the Indian Navy helicopter now buzzing over it in a desperate hunt for visual contact, the laser pointer remained switched on.

'Normally, one would not fly this long in such conditions. We had been flying hands-on for 6 hours, without the luxury of autopilot. But in such missions, it's adrenaline that keeps you going, and it's mind over body. In retrospect, you feel you were fatigued, but in the moment, you're not. Your mind is racing, with not a moment to spare,' remembers Capt. Rajkumar.

The flight commander knew it would be much easier to spot the boat from the deck of the ship in these conditions than from a helicopter at 200 feet. The 'slant visibility' at this point was next to nothing over a black cauldron of a sea.

'I had just been circling over the ship for 10–15 minutes, but the laser and the boat were simply invisible to us. We could see absolutely nothing as I manoeuvred the Sea King over the seas around the ship. And it was purely by chance that our navigator saw a flash of the green laser,' he says.

'Laser beam spotted on port bow, Sir!' shouted navigator Lt Cdr Mayoor Chauhan. It was the elusive visual lock the crew had been hunting for. A single laser beam being pointed from the deck of the 1,00,000-ton Maltese container ship, 80 km off the coast of Kerala in the middle of one of 2017's worst cyclones. A single little beam of green light was all that the SK 528 now had to depend on.

'As a submarine hunter, the Sea King has the ability to hover low over the sea surface, but none of those manoeuvres applies in a scenario like this, where you have to slowly descend and depend on excruciatingly delicate hand–eye coordination. There is no autopilot flying here. It's all manual,' Capt. Rajkumar says.

'At such low height, I had to constantly look out and then back at my instruments, because we were flying at very high angles of tilt. In a big helicopter like the Sea King, when you bank in excess of 30 degrees, you lose a lot of your lift power, so you have to compensate with collective power. Piloting becomes much more challenging. So there was no way I could completely ignore the instruments and look for the boat. It was half instrument flying and half visual flying.'

With the laser beam in their sights now, the helicopter swivelled around and headed straight for it, descending slowly. There was no time to lose, but a single hurried step could have meant certain death for the crew of the SK 528.

'Normally, we don't hover lower than 50 feet because there are various criteria that make this a risk, including lift performance and sea spray. In this case, there was no question of staying at 50 feet, because there was sea spray all around anyway. There was no way we could have done this rescue from 50 feet. So we kept descending slowly until we were at 20 feet, which is extremely low over the surface of a swelling sea. It was a constant up-and-down motion for us, because the whole sea would rise and then it would fall. We had to constantly maintain distance between the boat and the aircraft. I knew that if I was not careful with my collective[1] coming up on power, the sea swell could hit the helicopter tail rotor, which was my main worry, and this would have been catastrophic. We had to be extremely sharp while manoeuvring the chopper.'

At 20 feet, a bare whisker in flying terms from the violently undulating sea surface, Capt. Rajkumar finally spotted it.

'It was an unreal moment. By sheer luck, I saw the boat. It had a blue fibreglass hull. And spread across the hull, holding on to a rope for dear life, was a solitary fisherman. From 20 feet above, it was clear that this man wasn't moving,' he remembers.

'I knew if I lost sight of him for even a moment, it would be over. It was extreme, untamed flying, because we were just 20 feet above the boat, which was going all over the place. We didn't know where the natural horizon was. There was the risk of the swell hitting the underbelly of the helicopter or hitting the tail rotor. In daytime, we have a small amount of horizon orientation between the sea and sky. At night, nothing. We could only fly with the reference we had. That was this boat. The boat was moving left, right, up, down, and if I flew looking only at the boat, then I would get disoriented and lose control of the aircraft too. I was looking at the instrument panel for less than a second, then at the boat. And if I looked too long at the instrument panel, I would lose the boat for sure. That's the sort of flying we were doing out there.'

In a shuddering hover at that dangerously low altitude, Capt. Rajkumar collected his thoughts once again. The man on the boat wasn't moving and hadn't responded to the arrival of the helicopter above him. It was clear to the crew that the man

---

[1] The collective lever in a helicopter controls the angle of the main rotor blades, and causes the helicopter to ascend or descend.

was either unconscious or in shock. The horrifying realization also dawned that the man may have been out there for up to three days without water, food or a surface to stand on.

'We realized, much to our dismay, that he was not ready to let go of the rope he had been clutching for at least the last three days. He was a defeated man, both physically and mentally.'

Diver Saini will never forget the moments that followed as he stared down at the boat, with a solitary naked fisherman holding on for life, glaring up with a mixture of yearning and uncertainty.

'High waves and downwash were making the boat drift and making it difficult to hover above it. I suggested to the Captain that we winch down a diver—both of us [divers] were ready to take the risk. The proposal was not approved because of the risk to a diver's safety in the open sea, and that too, on a dark night. The man was staring longingly at us as the last hope of his survival, while above him, discussions were going on about how to pick him up,' Saini remembers.

But how could the crew rouse him?

'There was no question of descending any lower. I was worried about the powerful downwash of our rotors throwing the man off the capsized hull. And if that happened, we would lose him for sure,' Capt. Rajkumar says. His hands on the controls, eyes darting between his cockpit instruments and the man on his doomed boat, the flight commander fought to keep the Sea King in a steady hover.

The first of a series of terrible dilemmas presented itself.

'You think with your mind, you use your logic, backed by knowledge and experience. But there's that other sense which you get. That is often what helps you in a situation where you have to take a decision. If I had used my reasoning and logic, there's no way I would have attempted what happened next.

Because I knew the risks were huge. But I knew we had to. I just knew it,' remembers Capt. Rajkumar.

But before the thought crossed the flight commander's mind, one of the combat divers seated in the helicopter's cabin behind the cockpit shouted.

'*Main jaoonga, Sir* (I will go, Sir)!'

It was Deepak Saini, the younger of the two divers. He already had his black diving suit on. The other diver, Sumit Raj, had prepared the winch and harness. The two young divers were awaiting orders.

'I get emotional talking about it now, because there is disbelief that I even took that decision,' remembers Capt. Rajkumar. 'The most difficult decision for me was to send diver Saini down. It was the only way to attempt any rescue. There was no other way. Sending the diver down was a dilemma for me. He was a young man. I didn't know if he knew the dangers involved. He may have volunteered in his innocence and enthusiasm for the mission. It was very easy for him to step forward. He may not have known the dangers, but I couldn't be excused. I *did* know what those dangers were. It was a gut-wrenching moment for me as I took the decision to send him down. I had to look at the possibility of therefore losing two people at sea—the diver and the fisherman. I knew that if I sent him down, I might never see him again. If I had a small emergency on board—like an engine oil lubricant light coming on, or the rescue hoist not coming up properly, or a vibration developing in the helicopter—there would have been no way to pick up those two people in the water. I would have had to abandon them at sea. I cannot describe how enormous this risk was.'

Capt. Rajkumar hesitated for a moment, turning briefly to look at the two young divers behind him. But that moment of pause, born from a leader's concern for the lives under his charge, dissipated when both co-pilot Garud and navigator Chauhan said taking the risk was the only option they had.

Turning back to his instruments, Capt. Rajkumar wasted no time.

'Roger, lower the diver,' called the flight commander, as he held the SK 528 in its shuddering hover, also issuing instructions to Saini to hold on to the boat after rescuing the fisherman and placing him in the strop harness.

'In that moment, I knew I had to save that fisherman. In that moment, you aren't thinking about yourself. How can you? Here was an opportunity to save a life. Here was my chance to prove all those years of training and money spent to make me a search-and-rescue diver. There was no time for emotion then. It was my job and I did not think for a moment that I had a choice,' remembers Saini.

'I don't know what strength that poor fisherman had left in him as he held on to the rope. The Sea King's downwash can be extremely menacing. At night, if he had slipped off, there would have been no saving him,' says Capt. Rajkumar.

Diver Saini was lowered into the churning sea wearing the rescue harness and with an omni-glow stick so that he could remain visible. He immediately swam up to the boat and grabbed the fisherman, strapped him to the harness and gave the other diver a thumbs-up sign, a signal for him to winch the fisherman up.

'When I swam up to the boat, the fisherman was still refusing to let go. He was totally confused and in fear. In that wild, rough sea, I shouted to him over the sound of the wind and the helicopter rotors above me, trying to calm him down and telling him that we were there to rescue him. He must have thought it was a dream,' Saini says.

Twenty feet above, the Sea King was barely holding steady, thanks only to the flying acumen of the two pilots.

'As I was holding the chopper steady, I was watching Saini as he went about the task of strapping the fisherman to the strop. This young diver, with his entire career ahead of him, had thought nothing of seriously risking his life. As the flight commander, I was immensely nervous about losing him. But I was also immensely proud.'

As the fisherman was winched up, Saini clambered on to the boat, whirling the omni-glow stick in his hand to remain in sight. But a fresh threat had just presented itself.

The winch with the fisherman had begun to swing wildly about halfway up to the waiting helicopter. The other diver was bringing him up carefully, but he had to ensure the fisherman didn't hit his head on the undercarriage. With a measure of difficulty, he was brought aboard the SK 528 without injury.

'We got him on board, removed the rescue harness, made him comfortable,' says Capt. Rajkumar. 'Then we lowered the rescue harness and winched up Saini as well. Thankfully, this wasn't difficult because he was fit and an expert swimmer. It could have been worse if there was an emergency or if we had lost sight of him.'

'I positioned myself on top of the inverted boat, staying calm and remaining positive. As the harness approached the water again, I grasped it and was winched up quickly by diver Sumit Raj. There were huge celebrations in our hearts, but we remained silent. It did not sink in what we had just accomplished,' says Saini.

The rescued fisherman was in shock, delirious and dehydrated.

'He was like a corpse. He was almost dead. More than physically, he was mentally broken. He had given up on life. We could clearly make that out while we rescued him. He had no emotion, he was totally numb. We gave him water and glucose biscuits. He couldn't even eat properly, so we had to do it very carefully because his throat was completely parched. He had been at sea for three days. But had displayed phenomenal strength of mind to not let go and to not give up,' Capt. Rajkumar remembers.

With the all-clear and its doors shut, the SK 528 climbed and turned, speeding immediately towards the coast. Hovering at 20 feet in those weather conditions would have been dangerous even for a few minutes. Capt. Rajkumar and his men had hovered at that sickeningly low altitude for 28 minutes.

Climbing up to 200 feet, the Sea King cruised back to Thiruvananthapuram. On the way, Capt. Rajkumar radioed the *MV Cosco Beijing*, thanking them for the miraculous piece of intelligence and guidance that led to the rescue of one man.

'If the *MV Cosco Beijing* had not spotted the boat, there would be no rescue. Hats off to them. The fisherman wouldn't have had a chance in a million if the Chinese ship hadn't spotted his boat. It was a great humanitarian gesture by them to stop and wait for a rescue.'

Landing a short while later, the fisherman was wheeled away for treatment.

'Funny thing is, we never got the fisherman's name. There was no time. As soon as we landed, he was moved to a hospital for treatment. And frankly, I didn't ask. It never occurred to me. He was a human being and we were doing our job,' says Capt. Rajkumar.

The SK 528's engines had been on for 7 hours with two refuels. The day's mission was now truly over. The cyclone would continue to wreak havoc along the coast for five more days before dissipating. Of a total of 661 missing in Cyclone Ockhi, 261 persons remain missing from the Kerala coast. Official estimates place the damage caused by the cyclone in Kerala alone at over Rs 15,000 crore.

'This was a massive team effort, with contributions from all the men on board. Helicopters are not like fighter aircraft. If I didn't have a competent co-pilot and a smart navigator and brave divers, this wouldn't have been possible,' Capt. Rajkumar says.

What made the seasoned helicopter pilot, trained to take calculated risks, make such an enormous leap of faith?

'The script was probably written by someone who lives up there that this one man had to be rescued. And I had a very small part to play in it. The emotions come in waves once the mission is over. I'm not devoid of them. After landing, I was shivering all over. While flying, you're calm and focused,' he says.

Older and more experienced than the other men who flew with him that day, dangerous flying is scarcely new for Capt. Rajkumar. In 1989, he received his first gallantry decoration, a Nao Sena Medal (NM), for saving four scientists in Antarctica during an Indian Navy expedition.

'I had thought that was the most challenging mission I had ever flown. It was a similar mission in snow-blown white-out conditions. During the Ockhi rescue, I was flying in complete blackout conditions,' says Capt. Rajkumar.

'I can safely say I've come full circle.'

Capt. Rajkumar and the crew of the SK 528 didn't have time for a celebration that night—they were physically and emotionally drained by the mission. And the next morning, they returned to the air for another day of rescue missions over the cyclone-torn Arabian Sea, rescuing eight more fishermen off the Kochi coast. It would be days before they fully took stock of the mission they had flown—India's first-ever helicopter rescue at night at sea.

Saini, whose family in Haryana's Bhiwani live in that curious mixture of anxiety and pride typical of families of military personnel, says the mission was his life's most critical and that he hopes to have the opportunity to do it again.

'What can be a bigger achievement than saving someone's life?'

On Independence Day 2018, the Indian Navy announced that Saini would be decorated with the Nao Sena Medal for gallantry in the mission, his citation recording that he had displayed exemplary presence of mind and bravery in the face of grave danger.

On the same day, the Navy announced that Capt. Rajkumar would be decorated with the Shaurya Chakra, India's third-highest peacetime decoration for gallantry. His citation would note that, 'The bold decision and daring act of the officer enabled saving a human life in extreme conditions and was possible only because of the sheer determination, courage and decision making abilities of the officer,' and that he had displayed 'undeterred commitment to save human life in the most trying conditions accompanied by courage, fortitude and display of valour in the face of danger'.

In Kochi, there literally wasn't a moment to celebrate. In August 2018, Kerala was in the devastating grip of historic floods, a catastrophe that forced the Indian Navy's Southern Naval Command to suspend all training activity and commit all available military assets to rescue and relief operations. On the forefront of this effort, code-named Operation Madad, once again, was Capt. Rajkumar and his trusty Seaking 42B.

On 16 August, the national media struggled to divide its focus between the intensifying disaster in Kerala and the death of former prime minister Atal Bihari Vajpayee. Elaborate state ceremonials for the departed leader diverted the media's attention at a time when the flood situation had become impossible to ignore.

The following day, 17 August, as Capt. Rajkumar and his five-men crew lifted off into the rainy haze over Kochi, little did they know that they were about to break a world record in aviation rescue.

The day started with a gruelling four-hour flying mission in which Capt. Rajkumar and his crew rescued seventeen people from the submerged outskirts of Kochi. After a quick refuel, the helicopter was back in the air to hunt for marooned families scattered across the many devastated colonies beyond the metropolis.

'The weather was dire and marginal for flying with low clouds, poor visibility and rains,' says Capt. Rajkumar. 'After flying for about an hour, we located and winched up fifteen people on board. We were returning to the Kochi base when I sighted someone frantically waving a red flag from a rooftop. I turned the aircraft around in order to investigate. I realized the rooftop of that house was low with tall trees all around the vicinity and it was difficult and dangerous to hover anywhere near.'

Capt. Rajkumar carefully manoeuvred the Sea King close to the roof of the house and winched down a Navy diver. The diver reported back that there were eleven people waiting to be rescued. With fifteen people already on board, in addition to the six crew members, the pilot was faced with a very difficult decision. Daylight was fading, and if Capt. Rajkumar returned to base without rescuing the eleven, they would have had to wait till the following morning. He knew that the rock-steady hover he had managed eight months before out at sea was going to have to return. And this time, with the danger of trees just a few feet away.

'I carefully made the Seaking hover between the tall trees. The winds were gusting and visibility was receding,' says Capt. Rajkumar. 'Winching up one person after the other was a time-consuming exercise and I had to continue maintaining the helicopter's positions in those tough conditions testing the limits of the aircraft.'

As the eleven were winched up from their submerged home, the crew of the helicopter had to carefully rearrange the fifteen who had already been rescued, so everyone could be safely accommodated. The shifting positions made the helicopter's hover much more difficult, the shuddering airframe threatening at any moment to career into the trees.

After many tense minutes, with the eleven safely pulled aboard, Capt. Rajkumar eased the helicopter out from between the trees and peeled away for the Kochi base. He wouldn't know it at the time, but that night, he would be informed that the mission had set a world record for the maximum number of persons rescued in a single helicopter sortie—twenty-six. And this was in a militarized Sea King, not specifically built to carry so many people.

The record, once again, couldn't pose a distraction. Capt. Rajkumar would fly out early the next morning to continue to hunt for marooned persons.

By the time relief operations ended, he had rescued 114.

11

'Half of My Face Was in My Hands'

Major Rishi Rajalekshmy

Tral, Jammu and Kashmir
4 March 2017

'Amma, I may not come back. But be proud of whatever comes to you. Promise me.'

Standing outside a house in Hafoo village in south Kashmir's Tral, Maj. Rishi held his mobile phone to his ear with one hand. In the other hand were 15 kg of plastic explosive, wired and ready to be detonated. Some 3500 km away, in Alappuzha, Kerala, it was a wonder that his mother had even answered the phone. It was 7 minutes past midnight, well past her bedtime.

Hearing the sound of assault rifles firing in the background, Rajalekshmy froze. The phone slipped from her hand and crashed to the floor. She stared down at it. She could still hear her son's voice coming from it, asking if she could hear him. After a few seconds, she heard him abruptly say he would call her back later. Then, the call was disconnected. Rajalekshmy hurriedly bent down to pick up the phone, dialling his number. But there was no answer. Maj. Rishi had silenced his phone and tucked it into a zipped pocket in his combat trousers. And with a bomb in his hands, he had stepped carefully into the darkness, picking his way through the debris and into the house in front of him.

In 3 minutes, standing inside that house on a spring night in 2017, the thirty-one-year-old officer's world would be torn apart. He had called his mother because he had been prepared to die that night. But a nightmare like he had never imagined was about to begin, which would have no end in sight.

That Saturday in March 2017 couldn't have started more differently. Maj. Rishi and his company of men from 42 RR were conducting an early morning medical camp for men in Tral, part of a regular humanitarian outreach programme conducted by the army to establish friendships and trust among the local population, whose free will is frequently held hostage by militant and terror groups. The camp that morning was a busy one, with nearly a thousand men with all manner of ailments from villages in Tral lining up for treatment. As a team of Army doctors examined each one of them, giving them injections or little brown paper bags with medicines and tonics, Maj. Rishi chatted with the men in the queue. Most were from villages that fell in the young officer's area of responsibility. He had met some of them before, played with their children, dined in their homes. They even had a special name for him.

Khan, they called him.

As he handed out glass tumblers of steaming hot tea, he looked at the faces in the queue—young and old, some smiling, some haunted, but nearly all relieved in some measure when they saw him. Maj. Rishi of 42 RR couldn't have been farther from his Kerala home town. In the two years since the Malayali had set foot in Tral, the Kashmiri town infamous as a hotbed of militancy and a safe haven for Pakistani terrorists, he had never felt such a deep sense of comfort and belonging.

Tral had been unusually peaceful that year. Just eight months earlier, one of its most notorious natives, the young Hizbul Mujahideen commander Burhan Wani, had been shot in an encounter 60 km south, in Kokernag. His death had sparked widespread protests, stone pelting and Pakistan-backed revenge attacks in several parts of the Valley. But in Wani's own village and the areas surrounding it, where Maj. Rishi's unit operated, other than sporadic protests, a strange peace had prevailed.

As the day wore on, word of the medical camp spread and more men emerged from their villages, persuading the team of doctors to extend their timing so that all the patients could be examined. It was just after 3 p.m. when Maj. Rishi received a call from Col. Neeraj Pandey, who had taken over as the CO of 42 RR a month ago.

'My CO told me that an intelligence input had just come in regarding Aaqib Molvi, a terrorist commander whom we had been tracking for a long time, a man who had managed to escape against all odds,' says Maj. Rishi. 'I was at the medical camp with all my men, so I quickly mobilized a Quick Reaction Team (QRT) and we proceeded towards Hafoo village.'

The officer's team didn't need to go back to its base first, since RR companies almost always travel with everything they need for an encounter or a cordon-and-search operation (CASO). This includes weapons, ammunition, bulletproof vests and helmets, and the ingredients required to assemble IEDs—bombs customized for a desired objective.

Hafiz Muhammad Aaqib alias Aaqib Molvi was no ordinary terrorist. Like Burhan Wani, he was a young Hizbul Mujahideen commander. A native of nearby Awantipora, he had swiftly climbed the ranks of the terror group. His methods and habits in many ways mirrored Wani's. He had embraced avenues afforded by social media to spread propaganda against the Indian state and to exhort Kashmir's young to enlist with terror organizations, especially in the aftermath of Wani's killing. Photographs of him with kohl-lined eyes, carrying a camouflage backpack and an AK-47 rifle, were regular on Hizbul's recruitment posters and digital feeds. But it was his skill in organizing attacks, and his survival and evasion tactics, that had brought him to the notice of Pakistani intelligence. And that's why, as Maj. Rishi and his men speeded towards Hafoo village, they were informed that Aaqib Molvi wasn't alone. A Pakistani JeM terrorist called Saifullah (alias Usama) was with him.

Intelligence agencies had long suspected that Pakistani terror groups were looking to join forces with the local Hizbul Mujahideen to conduct terror attacks in the Kashmir Valley. Information that a Jaish terrorist was with Aaqib confirmed this. The intelligence input suggested that the two had met a few days earlier at Aaqib's home in the village next to Hafoo. When Maj. Rishi and his men approached, the two terrorists deployed a crowd of stone-pelters and protesters, using the cover and distraction to run to a house on the edge of Hafoo village.

'Stone pelting started as soon as we arrived,' says Maj. Rishi. 'Units of the Jammu and Kashmir Police and the CRPF were quickly deployed to keep the pelters at bay so we could focus on the hunt.'

Maj. Rishi knew this was going to be an extremely delicate operation. If the stone-pelting crowds managed to overwhelm him or pin him and his men down, Aaqib Molvi would simply add another successful escape to his already impressive record. Moving quickly, Maj. Rishi and a soldier from his squad darted into a series of houses to make sure Aaqib and his Pakistani accomplice were not hiding in one of them. Clearing one house after another over the next 30 minutes, the officer emerged into the open, frustrated.

The two terrorists could have gone in any direction. At the far end of the village street he stood in, he could see stone-pelters being held off by a police cordon. Closer to where he

stood, a small group of men stood outside a house. In that kind
of volatile situation, the last thing Maj. Rishi was realistically
hoping for was local help of any kind. But as he watched that
group, their gaze fixed on him, a single pair of eyes silently
turned towards a house about 200 m down the path, in the
opposite direction. Maj. Rishi stopped, turning to look at
the house the man was staring it. When he turned back, the
same pair of eyes was fixed on him. Followed by an almost
imperceptible nod.

Immediately summoning his men, Maj. Rishi jogged
towards the house that had been silently pointed out, ordering
a cordon to be formed around it. If the two terrorists were
indeed inside that house, it was almost certain they would be
armed. Maj. Rishi and his men took protective cover behind
a low boundary wall around the house.

'I shouted out, requesting several times that they come
out, saying we didn't want to kill them,' he says. 'At this point,
we were still not sure if they were in that house. Either way,
I didn't expect them to surrender under any circumstances.
That's not how they're trained. But I had to give them that
chance. The moment after I made my offer, there was firing
from the second floor of the house.'

A fierce firefight commenced, with Aaqib and Usama
shifting positions on the second floor and firing at the cordon
with AK-47s. Policemen joined the operation as well. The
exchange continued in waves for nearly 3 hours—bursts of
fire punctuated by minutes of silence, as the terrorists reloaded
their weapons or planned their next move. It was a stalemate
that would end only if the terrorists ran out of ammunition.
The steady firing from the second floor suggested that the
house they had chosen was something of a safe house, stocked
with rifle magazines—clearly enough to draw out a firefight
for hours.

But for how long? In any encounter, the forces do their best to finish in daylight. Darkness brings with it obvious challenges. Most of all, it gives the terrorists an exponentially better chance to escape through the cordon and into the night. No search operation in the darkness thereafter stands a chance of tracking them down. Something had to be done before sunset.

'I called my CO, letting him know that we needed to step up the offensive,' says Maj. Rishi. 'I told him I needed to get an opening into the house. The best way to do that was with an IED. He approved the idea, so I got moving.'

Maj. Rishi asked the explosives expert in his squad, a young soldier, to quickly construct the IED with 15 kg of highly explosive material. Just before last light, at about 6.30 p.m., the officer picked up the IED. Then, under covering fire from two soldiers off to the side, Maj. Rishi held up a bulletproof shield and stepped lightly over the boundary wall and moved towards the house. Following close behind him was his buddy soldier, Lance Naik Avesh Kumar, who fired in short bursts at the top floor till the two reached the front door.

'The two were still firing from above, so we had to move to the side for cover,' says Maj. Rishi. 'I placed the IED right outside the house, near the front. The terrorists stopped firing for a minute. They were clearly changing positions to protect themselves. They must have known what we were trying to do.'

With hand signals, the officer let the soldiers standing around the house know that he was about to detonate the IED. Then he pushed down on the detonator, which was wirelessly connected to the bomb device. The loud thud of an explosion shook the ground and smashed a big hole in its front wall, causing one half of it to come crashing down. A piece of rock knocked loose by the blast came flying straight at Maj. Rishi, hitting him on the side of the head just below his helmet.

'The stone hit a vein, so I began to bleed almost immediately,' says Maj. Rishi. 'My buddy said he would escort me out so I could get medical help and leave the site. I told him the bleeding didn't matter. It was a small wound. I don't remember even feeling it.'

With half the house now a smoking mess of debris, Maj. Rishi and Lance Naik Avesh carefully returned to their positions outside the boundary wall. After a 15-minute pause, firing resumed from the top floor. If the terrorists were jolted by the blast, they were showing no sign of it yet. And since there were clearly two streams of fire still, it was clear that both Aaqib and Usama were alive and well enough to keep the fight on.

'One of my men helped me bandage my head to stop the bleeding,' says Maj. Rishi. 'I remember that we moved a little distance away to do this, because the firing had started again, very aggressively. The IED had given us an opening into the house, but Aaqib and Usama were still holding out. It was time for the next move.'

Darkness had fallen when the squad received word that Maj. Rishi would approach the house again, this time with an armload of Molotov cocktails. These improvised incendiary weapons, made of bottles filled with petrol and a kerosene-soaked cloth as wick, are famous around the world as a weapon of choice for rioters and guerrilla fighters. It is unclear when these simple devices were invented, but the name, in sardonic honour of Soviet foreign minister Vyacheslav Molotov, was a gift from the Finns during the Winter War, a conflict between the Soviet Union and Finland before the Second World War broke out in 1939. Molotov cocktails were widely used by the Finns to attack Soviet tanks when the latter rumbled in to invade. Eighty years later, nearly identical devices had been assembled in that tiny village in south Kashmir.

Maj. Rishi's squad needed to try smoking out the two terrorists by starting a fire, and Molotov cocktails seemed their best option. The ones they made were with half-filled rum bottles and kerosene-soaked rags.

'I stepped into the compound again and tossed one Molotov into the kitchen area from the outside,' says Maj. Rishi. 'There was an immediate flare-up and the fire caught. There was carpeting and wooden panelling inside, so the fire intensified quickly, with a lot of smoke. I flung a few more of the Molotovs deeper inside the house and stepped away. It was now a proper fire. I was hoping this would force the terrorists to jump down or try and escape. That would be our moment to get them.'

But Aaqib and Usama stayed put. The fire raged for 20 minutes, burning large parts of the house, and then died out. The two terrorists were proving to be extremely resilient and were showing signs of having received the sort of combat survival training that was only possible to get from a military force. It is well known that Hizbul Mujahideen terrorists train at Pakistani Army-run camps in PoK, where the curriculum has rapidly evolved from basic hit-and-run tactics to full-fledged commando-style training. It was clear by now that Aaqib and Usama were among the elite in their batches.

As he watched the fire die out, Maj. Rishi knew that another big move had failed to push the mission to a conclusion. And that each passing hour was making it steadily more unacceptable that the encounter end in failure.

'At midnight, I called my CO again,' says Maj. Rishi. 'By this time, he had arrived at the encounter site. I told him I would like to go back in with another IED.'

Col. Neeraj heard out his officer, perhaps wondering what it was that gave Maj. Rishi the nerve to volunteer to venture into the house again with another IED. The bandage on his head was soaked in blood, but the officer didn't seem even remotely tired or weakened from the blood loss. Col. Neeraj asked Maj. Rishi if he was absolutely sure about the move he was proposing. Surely, someone else from the squad could be sent in to plant the device. But Maj. Rishi politely refused, requesting that he be permitted to proceed inside with the second IED. Col. Neeraj relented.

'I don't remember any fatigue. I was pumping adrenaline and very keen to finish the mission,' says Maj. Rishi. 'I'm not saying I'm a hero or anything, but when you're in the middle of an operation with your men, you don't feel pain. I had forgotten about my head injury.'

Maj. Rishi asked the explosives expert to assemble two IEDs with 15 kg of explosives each. When they were ready, he held a quick briefing with his men, telling them that if the explosions didn't kill the terrorists, they would at least have nowhere left to hide—and would therefore have no option but to attempt to break the cordon and run away into the darkness. Under no circumstances should that be allowed to happen, he told them.

The two IEDs were brought to Maj. Rishi. The moment he picked one up, he felt a strange foreboding. Fighting terrorists in a situation like this was always a life-and-death affair, but for the first time that day, Maj. Rishi sensed personal danger. And that's why, even though he knew his mother would be fast asleep at her home in Kerala, he decided to call her.

'Maybe my mother had an intuition too, and that's why she picked up the phone despite it being so late,' says Maj. Rishi. 'I just wanted to hear her voice. She dropped the phone when she heard the firing from the house starting again. I tried to say a few words to calm her, but she couldn't hear me. I put the phone away and picked up the second IED. There was no time to spare. I knew that back home, my mother would spend the whole night praying.'

The firing from the second floor was coming in a furious non-stop barrage now, without the usual pauses. The two terrorists were alternating their fire, so there were no pauses when one of them reloaded with ammunition. They were clearly becoming desperate and it was likely that they were holed up in a corner on the remaining part of the top floor. With the sort of training they had demonstrated that evening, desperation could make them even more dangerous to deal with.

'I went inside with the IEDs in both my hands,' says Maj. Rishi. 'There was a lot of firing and action. Once inside, I used my walkie-talkie to speak with Lance Naik Avesh, whom I had asked to stay behind, right outside the house. He wanted to accompany me inside to plant the IEDs, but I knew I wouldn't be able to live with myself for the rest of my life if anything happened to him.'

When Maj. Rishi had taken charge of his company in early 2015, 42 RR was going through its darkest phase. On 27 January that year, the unit's then CO, Col. Munindra Nath Rai, had died fighting terrorists in Tral. He had led the operation from the front, but was shot in the head as the hiding terrorists burst out of the house in a bid to escape. Hailed for his leadership in fronting the assault, he will be remembered even beyond the Army, for something else. Two days after his death, images would go viral across the country of his inconsolable eleven-year-old daughter, Alka, saluting her father's casket while screaming lines from her father's parent regiment, the Gorkha Rifles, '*Keta 9 GR ko ho ke hoina* (Is this boy from 9 GR or not)?' and joining in the refrain from her father's comrades, '*Ho, ho, ho* (Yes, yes, yes, he is ours, he's our pride!).' To the Army and beyond, this would be telling of how the officer had ensured that even his children imbibed the fearless spirit that the Gorkhas are famous for.

The 42 RR didn't have the time to mourn, but grieving it was when Maj. Rishi arrived. He had spent the first few days promising his men that he wouldn't let them come to harm, no matter what.

'I told my boys I will never send you back in coffins or with broken limbs,' says Maj. Rishi. 'I might die or take a bullet, but even though you are my strength, I will never let a bullet get past me to you. That was my promise. The battalion was tense and grieving. Before the CO's death, two jawans from the unit had also died in operations. The boys were restless but focused. We trained hard together to get through that phase.'

Two years later, the scene was still Tral. And the two terrorists holed up inside that half-destroyed house in Hafoo were probably contemplating a final bid to escape Maj. Rishi's cordon, a full 9 hours after the encounter began.

'I entered the house with two IEDs, crawling in through the huge hole blown by the first IED. I found a spot near the undamaged part of the ground floor to place the IEDs in my hand. Then I crawled back out.'

Once outside, he spoke on his walkie-talkie with his buddy, calling for a 30-second countdown to detonate the IEDs. The countdown began as Maj. Rishi crept away from the house. Two IEDs would be double the intensity of the first. But from a safe distance, with 10 seconds to go for the detonation, Maj. Rishi clicked his walkie-talkie back on and asked the soldier holding the detonator to pause.

'It suddenly struck me that if I placed the IEDs a little deeper inside the house, they would have a more destructive effect. So I told my men to wait, crept back inside and went to pick up the IEDs. As I was about to, I saw a shadow move down the shattered staircase and instantly, there was a flash of fire. I was thrown off my feet and fell to the ground. In that moment, I fired back at the shadow with a long burst of ammunition, hitting him straight and dropping him right there.'

Three bullets hit Maj. Rishi. One blew his helmet right off his head. Two more bullets hit his nose and jaw, ripping a large part of his face off.

'I was thrown several feet by the impact, but I was lucid. I couldn't tell what damage had been caused, but I realized that I couldn't speak and my vision was a little blurred because of the blood. But I couldn't feel any pain. I started crawling out from the house and I remember thinking in those moments about action movies, where you see people function even after getting shot. I'm telling you that it's possible. I didn't feel weak at all. In fact, I don't think I had ever felt stronger.'

Maj. Rishi saw Lance Naik Avesh run towards him as he crawled out, but raised a hand to stop him. The second terrorist hadn't been accounted for yet and was probably still alive on the top floor. With cover fire from his men, the officer exited the house from one side, dropping off a metre-high platform, and then began moving on his elbows towards the outer boundary wall. Halfway back, Lance Naik Avesh and two other soldiers leapt into the compound and pulled him out. He stood up, and the other officers reeled when they saw what was left of his face.

'I couldn't speak, as a large part of my face had come off,' says Maj. Rishi. 'I signalled with my hands to them that the second terrorist was likely still inside, even though the firing had stopped.'

Unknown to the team, the Jaish terrorist, Usama, had been hit in the firefight and was incapacitated on the top floor. He would die shortly thereafter.

Escorted from the encounter site, Maj. Rishi was bundled into a jeep that sped to a helipad nearby. The Army medic who accompanied him couldn't help but stare at Maj. Rishi's injuries. He knew there was nothing he could do with the emergency equipment he had. This needed specialists. The officer's eyes were open but clouded now, and he was sitting upright. But his face was a bleeding, gory mess of flesh and bone. Loaded into a helicopter a few minutes later, he was quickly flown to the 92 Base Hospital in Srinagar.

As the helicopter flew at low altitude towards Srinagar, a soldier from Maj. Rishi's unit phoned the injured officer's wife. Maj. Anupama Rishi, also an Army officer, was posted at the 92 Base Hospital with the Military Nursing Service. She was awake when the call came through, waiting for her husband to check in with her before she called it a night. Hearing that he was en route and badly injured, she got dressed and rushed to the trauma ward to wait for him.

'When I arrived, I saw Anupama waiting with the doctors,' says Maj. Rishi. 'The doctor who examined me went blank when he saw me. I could tell from his face that he knew there was nothing he could do for me in Srinagar. My eyes were closing because of the blood, but I was conscious. The doctor repeatedly asked me, "Are you awake?" I couldn't speak, so I signalled to him with a thumbs-up. I also took his hand to try and communicate that he was looking too worried.'

The doctors, some of the country's finest and trained to bring back men very nearly from the dead, were on edge. The officer's injuries suggested that he should, at the very least, be unconscious. Maj. Rishi was not only conscious, but lucid too. The doctors continued to speak with the Major, keeping him engaged and telling him to relax. They worried that if he became fully aware of the nature of his injuries—they looked far worse than they felt, apparently, at the time—adrenaline would jog his circulatory system and he would lose blood even faster.

After performing emergency procedures that night to contain the blood loss, the 92 Base Hospital was forced to recommend that Maj. Rishi be sent as soon as possible to the Army's premier Research and Referral Hospital in Delhi. Late the next morning, the Major and his wife would fly to Delhi on an IAF An-32.

The same day, the United Jihad Council, the Pakistan Army's purported umbrella outfit for unified command and control of anti-India militant and terror groups active in Jammu and Kashmir, issued a statement mourning the loss of the two terrorists. It said: 'The two slain militants, Hafiz Muhammad Aaqib alias Aaqib Molvi and Saifullah alias Usama are the two shining stars of Jammu Kashmir who will always shine like gems. Their sacrifices will always be remembered.'

Like the crowds that gathered for Burhan Wani, large crowds would gather at the funeral of Aaqib too. The man who had killed him would see the pictures days later, when he was finally allowed to sit up.

'For forty-five days, I could not speak a word,' says Maj. Rishi. 'I could not breathe through my mouth or nose—I had a tube in my throat. All my food intake was also through a tube. In a matter of weeks, I lost 20 kg. I was reduced to skin and bones.'

When Rajalekshmy saw her son at the Army hospital in Delhi a few days after he was admitted, she said nothing. Her daughter-in-law had requested her not to break down in front of her son.

The injury had brought to a violent stop Maj. Rishi's tenure in the Kashmir Valley. But losing most of his face had, in his mind, destroyed something else too.

'Somewhere deep inside, I had also wanted to be a model, and most of my loved ones knew that. Maybe that's why Anupama ordered people not to cry in front of me. She was very strong. We had laughingly discussed how I would seek permission from the Army to do some modelling. But there I was, totally disfigured.'

One of Maj. Rishi's first visitors was the Army Chief, Gen. Bipin Rawat, himself. The General had heard about the young officer's courage—and condition—and wished to meet him in person.

'When the chief came, my eyes were filled with tears, because I was in a situation where my chief was standing in front of me and I could not even get up and salute him,' says Maj. Rishi.

As the General spent time with Maj. Rishi and his family, he was briefed about the officer's story, starting with how Maj. Rishi had left a 'safe' career in civil government service to join the Army so he could literally fight for the country.

'It sounds clichéd these days, I guess, but it's true—I had dreamt of picking up a weapon and fighting for the country since childhood,' says Maj. Rishi, who has had eight reconstructive surgeries since the incident, and is yet to fully recover. 'Whenever the national anthem is played, I get goosebumps. I don't know what that makes me, but I really wanted to protect this land.'

Rishi had studied engineering in college in Kerala and had been employed as an assistant engineer with the Kerala State Electricity Board upon graduating. A year later, he took a special selection board examination to join Air India as a direct entrant. Posted to Mumbai international airport, he would quickly grow restless, his boyhood dreams of combat and weaponry luring him to IMA, Dehradun. For the first time since his studies had ended in Kerala, he finally felt he was on the path to fulfilment. In 2010, he would be commissioned into the Army's Mechanised Infantry, a regiment raised to provide combat mobility to infantry troops, functioning with armoured vehicle units.

Over the next five years, he would serve in the deserts of Rajasthan, and then be dispatched to the Congo to join India's UN Peacekeeping Force. On a month's break in India, he and Anupama got married. When he returned to India after the mission in Congo, he finally had the opportunity to go down the path he had his heart set on—one that led to the Kashmir Valley. He quickly opted for the RR, arriving in Srinagar in early 2015.

'I told my CO, if you are sending me somewhere, please send me to the ground, and not as staff,' says Maj. Rishi. 'I just want to be with my weapon. With men in the field. My mother had told me, if you want to join the Army, then you have to lead men. Even if you are wounded, you have to lead them. Her words are always with me. Maybe that's why I called her the night of the incident.'

Dispatched to Tral to command a company, Maj. Rishi was soon immersed in the daily tensions of counter-insurgency and anti-terror operations, a universe away from the life he had chosen to leave behind.

'I never thought for a moment about my old life. I feel very strongly for this country, and my weapon is an addiction for me. When you hear bullets fly, when a firefight begins, the rush you feel is incomparable. I always look forward to the next operation.'

That is probably why, a year into his duties with 42 RR, his then CO, Col. Vikram Kadyan, would frequently slap his back and say, '*Kabhi toh darr liya kar* (You should be a little afraid sometimes), you should be afraid of something.'

For all the combat he would be immersed in, Maj. Rishi knew he was in one of the most complicated and difficult places in the country. Before he joined the Army, he had watched the Kashmir conflict fester endlessly, its intensity ebbing and flowing. On the inside and dealing with them first-hand, the complexities were amplified in all their terrifying detail. If fighting terrorists was the job he had signed up for, he knew that an even more difficult duty was to win the hearts and trust of the Kashmiri people. He had been sent into a notoriously hostile hotbed of militancy and terror—Tral, the south Kashmir stronghold of the Hizbul Mujahideen, and a place well known for the implacably anti-Army stance of its people.

'I loved Tral from the moment I set foot there,' says Maj. Rishi. 'There is something magical about that place.'

With a stance that was low on aggression and high on cheerful friendliness, Maj. Rishi embarked on patrols with his men in the villages of Tral, taking every opportunity to befriend residents or help them with their everyday problems.

In late 2016, patrolling soon took Maj. Rishi and his men to Tral's Dadasara village, home to Hizbul Mujahideen's most infamous commander at the time. After they had searched Burhan Wani's family home, his father, Muzaffar Ahmad Wani, a high school principal, stepped up to Maj. Rishi.

'His father offered me *Zamzam ka paani*[1] and made me drink it with him,' says Maj. Rishi. 'It was a very humbling

---

[1] The Well of Zamzam is a well inside the Masjid al-Haram in Mecca, Islam's holiest site. Islamic mythology says that the well appeared by way of a divine miracle to bring forth water from God. The well is visited, and its water consumed annually, by millions of pilgrims during the Hajj or Umrah.

experience. We were there to get information about his son. And we spoke to him about it. But relations remained decent.'

Over the next few months, 'Khan', as Maj. Rishi came to be known among local residents, would become that friendly face in the *fauj*, an officer whose Hindi was tellingly inflected with a Malayalam accent, but who refused to give up on his efforts to improve at the language, even learning bits of the local tongue.

'We established a very good rapport with the people of Tral,' says Maj. Rishi. 'Operations continued, but there was never an attack on my camp. When we patrolled, stones were never pelted at us, like they are in certain other locations. We knew there were tensions, but we were succeeding in convincing perhaps a few that we had good intentions and wanted to keep everybody safe.'

In medical camps, like the one he had organized the morning of his fateful encounter, Maj. Rishi would frequently treat children who would line up with a common winter ailment—burns on their hands from spilling boiling tea.

'I would treat the children and make friends with them while extracting a promise that they would not join militancy. These were just friendly chats, but I know that we were making a connection. I was holding those little hands and treating them. I knew the same hands were highly unlikely to pick up a rock against me. These are really good kids. They have a lot of honour.'

In early 2016, a huge protest erupted at a village in Tral. Hundreds of residents from nearby villages joined in to agitate against power outages in the area. This was an area that came under Maj. Rishi's operational responsibility, even if he had no control over the corruption-ridden civil utility supply system.

'I was advised not to go to the protest area because people there were very agitated,' says Maj. Rishi. 'I remember thinking they had every right to be agitated if they had been deprived of electricity for days on end. With my men, I went there right away. When the protesters saw me, an amazing thing happened. They removed the roadblocks, and they were dispersed by some seniors among them. I went up to the elderly men and told them I would not leave until I had solved their problem, whatever it was. When they told me about the electricity nightmare, I called the District Collector and requested him to urgently send an engineer to fix the problem. He arrived a short while later and sorted out the power situation. I needed the people to know that I lived among them and wanted to serve them.'

The friendships established this way would often lead to awkward, uncomfortable incidents. Many of the elderly men that Maj. Rishi had befriended, and whose trust he had earned, were parents of known militants. When intelligence inputs arrived about their presence in the area, Maj. Rishi would be forced to place those friendships aside, but always with dignity.

'They knew I would never trouble them unnecessarily,' says Maj. Rishi. 'I would bother them at home only if there was a specific input. And they understood my compulsions. Sometimes they would voluntarily give me information, confirming that their militant son had visited but had departed to an unknown location. They were very cooperative with me all throughout. We never irritated them or harassed them.'

Restricted to Delhi as a result of his injuries, Maj. Rishi has had eight surgeries so far, each of them nearly 14 hours long. His face has had to be reconstructed with metal prosthetics, with a new jaw fashioned from bone drawn from his leg.

'It takes almost two months to recover from each surgery,' he says. 'By the time I am strong enough to stand up, it's time for the next surgery.'

The officer needs several more surgeries over eighteen months—and even then, it is uncertain if he will be declared fit for combat again.

'Never have I slept for more than 5 hours,' he says. 'From that to this sedentary life, where there is anaesthesia everywhere I look.'

In August 2017, with a black band covering the lower half of his face, Maj. Rishi would receive a Sena Medal (Gallantry) on India's Independence Day. But the future remains a cruel question mark.

'I want to get back to Kashmir,' says Maj. Rishi. 'I need to get back into combat. I will try all my options, even the NSG. I need to get back on my feet, and with a weapon.'

The morning after the encounter, Maj. Rishi's men and seniors received an unusual barrage of calls from residents across villages in Tral. Word had spread about his injuries. Each one of the callers asked if the young officer would survive. One of them, a teenager perhaps, had broken down on the phone.

'*Khan sahab ko wapas bhejo,*' he said, in faltering Hindi. '*Hum unko theek karenge* (Please send Khan Sahab back. We will heal him).'

12

'I Repeat! Fire in My Cockpit!'

Squadron Leader Ajit Bhaskar Vasane

It was the one place that fighter pilots in the area were forbidden from flying anywhere near. If they saw it on the horizon, standard operating procedure made it compulsory for them to swerve their jets away well before they got anywhere within a 2-km radius. Flying closer than that safety margin could mean serious career trouble. But when the site loomed into view that October afternoon in 2011, sitting in his MiG-29 at 10,000 feet, Sqn Ldr Ajit Bhaskar Vasane knew he had only seconds to make a decision.

A decision nobody in the IAF had ever been forced to make.

The out-of-bounds site to the young pilot's left was easily the most dangerous place to fly an aircraft. It was the world's largest crude oil refinery, the Reliance Industries complex outside Jamnagar in Gujarat's Gulf of Kutch. An aircraft crashing anywhere in the sprawling 7500-acre facility could result in a devastating inferno, the likes of which had never been seen in India. And with over a million barrels of petroleum churned out from the site every day, a fiery visitor from the sky had the potential of sending destructive shock waves throughout India's economy as well as the world's volatile oil markets.

Sqn Ldr Ajit's mind was racing. A paralysing choice had just presented itself to him. He needed to get back to base in

Jamnagar as quickly as humanly possible. *Before he lost control of his jet.* But his cockpit maps had confirmed that the shortest flight path back wouldn't just require him to violate the 2-km safety restriction, it would actually take him directly *over* the refinery. If he obeyed protocol and flew just outside the 2-km radius, in the increasingly likely event that he lost control of the jet, there was still every chance that it might helplessly career out of the sky and drift straight into the refinery complex. The third option was to risk himself and the aircraft and fly a long circuitous flight path away from the refinery and back to base.

As he struggled to decide, Sqn Ldr Ajit wondered if the aircraft would hold on. If it would stay in one piece. If he would stay conscious. Because, despite over 600 flight hours logged in a decade of flying fighter aircraft, he had never been strapped into a more hostile cockpit.

Nine minutes earlier, at 3.30 p.m., Sqn Ldr Ajit had roared into the air in his MiG-29 from the Jamnagar Air Force base, the country's westernmost military air station. A second MiG-29 with his wingman, Sqn Ldr Rohit Singh, lifted off seconds later in pursuit. Climbing into a perfectly clear sky, the two pilots from the IAF's 28 Squadron were out to perform a supersonic intercept mission, a simulated confrontation to rehearse how they would respond[1] if a Pakistani military aircraft were to violate Indian airspace.

The two fighter pilots throttled up on their jets to position themselves 80–100 km apart from each other in a patch of

---

[1] Intrusions, while rare, are far from unlikely. In August 1999, shortly after the Kargil war, a Pakistan Navy Atlantique-2 maritime reconnaissance aircraft that repeatedly violated Indian airspace off the Gujarat coast was shot down over the Rann of Kutch by an Indian MiG-21 jet.

designated training airspace at a height of 30,000 feet, where Sqn Ldr Ajit would simulate a hostile air intruder and his wingman would rehearse an aggressive interception, and if necessary, a shoot-down. All electronically, of course. If this were a real-life interception, Sqn Ldr Rohit would likely fire, as a last resort, a Russian Vympel R-73 heat seeking air-to-air missile at the unwelcome intruder. That morning, both MiG-29s in the air were armed with missiles, but there would be no firing—the brutal air drill was purely to hone the flying reflexes of the pilots, and the time-tested standard operating procedures, in the event of a hostile air intrusion.

Back in Jamnagar, a young Flight Lieutenant from the squadron manning the air traffic control cleared the two pilots to begin their manoeuvres. The 28 Squadron, operating a pack of eighteen MiG-29s, is codenamed 'The First Supersonics' for being the first squadron to be equipped with a fighter that could break the sound barrier, the MiG-21, in the late 1960s. The MiG-29 could easily throttle up to over twice the speed of sound, but the two pilots would be keeping their velocities in check. The IAF does not permit supersonic flights over populated areas as the deafening 'boom' that fighter jets produce when they break the sound barrier can shatter glass panes on the ground and cause panic.

Sqn Ldr Ajit pointed his jet west to fly a long, curved loop 120 km from Jamnagar and back towards the mainland to simulate the intrusion. He squinted as he pulled up, bringing the aircraft head-on with the sun, flooding the cockpit with blinding light. The pilot adjusted his oxygen mask and pulled down the integrated tinted visor on his helmet, crucial to protecting the eyes during such flights.

Suddenly, the MiG-29's head-up display (HUD), a pane of glass sitting on top of the aircraft's 'dashboard', which superimposes aircraft instrument readings and mission data onto the pilot's viewpoint, flickered and blanked out. As the name suggests, an HUD allows a pilot to keep their 'head up' without having to lower their gaze at maps or instruments on the cockpit panel. The HUD going blank wasn't, by itself, a catastrophic emergency. But what had caused it was something unheard of. Something that had never been documented or reported before on any MiG-29 anywhere in the world.

At 30,000 feet, Sqn Ldr Ajit called out to the young Flight Lieutenant at Jamnagar base air traffic control.

'Finback 1 reporting fire in the cockpit,' Sqn Ldr Ajit said over the radio, keeping his voice as casual as possible. It was important not to cause panic if there was no need to. Except, if there was ever a cause for panic in the cockpit, this would be it.

The stunned radar controller wasn't sure if he had heard Finback 1, Ajit's radio call sign, correctly.

'Finback 1, did you just say fire? Can you confirm it?'

Sqn Ldr Ajit replied, 'I repeat, there's fire in the cockpit.'

'This is not engine fire?'

'No, I repeat. It's cockpit fire,' said the pilot. 'Turning urgently back towards base. Need guidance and permission to descend.'

'Finback 1, base 08085 [80 degrees and 85 km away]. Let's get you out of there, Sir. Let's get you home.'

Flying 60 km to Sqn Ldr Ajit's left and on the same radio frequency, his wingman, Sqn Ldr Rohit, heard the terse radio exchange. With permission from the ground, he immediately swerved his jet rightward to get closer to his friend, to see if he could help from the outside. As he banked towards Finback 1, he wondered just how he would be able to help at all.

When the HUD had flickered off, Ajit had immediately spotted the reason—a small fire right below it. At first, he thought he was hallucinating. It could be a symptom of hypoxia from decreased oxygen supply owing to a possibly faulty oxygen supply system. The condition can have deadly consequences—a fighter pilot's mind can blank out completely, for instance. They could even begin to imagine things or experience spatial disorientation, rendering them incapable of taking informed decisions in an unforgiving environment.

'A fire in the cockpit? No way,' remembers Sqn Ldr Ajit about that day. 'I was certain that classic hypoxia was messing with my mind. I thought someone had just lit a matchstick in the cockpit and offered me a cigarette.'

The fire had started small, about the size of an index finger, but was quickly growing. Ominously, it was filling the cockpit with thick, black smoke. But the most obvious danger flowed through the MiG-29's shuddering airframe—over 4000 litres of fuel in a series of tanks in the fuselage and wings that could easily ignite if the fire spread. It would take just a small lick of flame in one of those tanks to destroy the aircraft in seconds.

Sqn Ldr Ajit knew that the first thing he needed to do was check his oxygen supply. He could still breathe through the thickening smoke, but not for long. And it was imperative that he rule out hypoxia, so he could get busy dealing with the emergency at hand. The drill had to be followed. He tilted his head to the left to check the oxygen regulator in the side console. There was no malfunction visible. The system appeared to be generating a steady supply of oxygen. So this wasn't hypoxia. This was a real fire in the cockpit, and it was spreading fast.

'Good news, I wasn't hallucinating,' says Sqn Ldr Ajit. 'Bad news, I was now positive I had a proper fire in the cockpit and had to do something about it before it was too late.'

In seconds, the fire spread to the visor attached to the HUD. The thick dark smoke swirling within the cockpit carried with it the odour of burning plastic. Worse, the smoke was depositing a layer of soot on the aircraft's glass canopy, blocking out the pilot's frontal visibility.

'The time lag between spotting the fire and taking recovery action was less than 60 seconds,' says Sqn Ldr Ajit. 'It's a different matter that that one minute seems almost eternal when you're in the air. Ask any fighter pilot. They'll tell you that 60 seconds in an emergency is longer than a year on the ground.'

Guided by the radio controller at Jamnagar, Sqn Ldr Ajit had carefully manoeuvred his jet and was cruising in the direction of the base. Deprived completely of outside visibility, he was now peering through the thick smoke at the clouded cockpit instruments. He would have to fly the fighter plane with a burning cockpit for another nine minutes if he was to make it safely back to the base, where preparations for an emergency landing had begun.

Hearing about the emergency, more officers had rushed to ground control at Jamnagar. But there was little they could do. Sqn Ldr Ajit chuckled over the radio as he updated the team on the ground. Both he and the men on the ground knew the next few minutes could either end in a messy disaster, or give the IAF a new entry for its flight safety manual. Either way, there was no advice, no precedent. And no earlier record of such an emergency that he or the ground team could fall back on. The pilot knew this was entirely on him.

Even with the daunting uncertainties he was faced with, Sqn Ldr Ajit was sure about one thing. That he would not eject from the aircraft. The option had been presented to him from the ground, but he had calmly declined. Yanking the ejection handle would have given him a possibly safe emergency escape, blowing away the aircraft's canopy, the rocket-powered Russian Zvezda K-36 ejection seat with an attached parachute violently firing him out of the MiG-29. But Sqn Ldr Ajit wasn't so sure.

In the next few minutes, Finback 2 arrived alongside the troubled MiG-29. Sqn Ldr Rohit was still not fully aware what his friend was going through in his cockpit. He looked out of his jet at Finback 1, hoping to get a visual confirmation that things were in control. The sight was a shocking one.

'I couldn't see Vasane,' says Sqn Ldr Rohit. 'The cockpit was filled with smoke and the front portion of the windshield had deposits of soot. I don't know how he was sitting inside that cockpit and flying the aircraft.'

He was right. Sqn Ldr Ajit had, by now, been forced to resort to desperate measures to contain the fire and put it out. He had first tried to douse the spreading flames with his hands. The plan didn't work as the strands of molten plastic adhered to his fire-resistant gloves and he could feel his fingers getting singed.

'I swiftly took off my gloves and tried using them as a duster to smother the fire,' says Sqn Ldr Ajit. 'Nothing seemed to be working. The intensity of the fire kept increasing. My hands were being badly burnt.'

The pilot's eyes had begun to sting and water because of the smoke, and the irritation was growing with every passing second. His helmet's anti-glare visor provided no protection against the dense smoke. For the moment, breathing wasn't as much of a problem in the smoke-filled cockpit as he had his oxygen mask on. But visibility was totally gone. All he could see was a blanket of grey before his eyes. The cockpit panel, with its bright screens, was no longer even faintly visible.

'My vision was now blurred and there was a heavy deposit of soot on the windshield,' says Sqn Ldr Ajit. 'It was all covered in black. I was flying totally blind.'

About 40 km from Jamnagar, Sqn Ldr Ajit was advised by the radio controller to descend to about 10,000 feet. Making any abrupt moves with the aircraft was out of the question. The pilot carefully pushed his stick forward, easing the aircraft into a slow descent. If the cockpit fire was eating away at the insides of the aircraft, its structural integrity could be compromised. Fighter aircraft are made of some of the sturdiest materials in the world, but a fire could easily cause the sort of damage that would seriously hamper flying stability. Worse, it could take control completely out of the pilot's hands.

As the pilot weighed his options, the thought of jettisoning the MiG-29's canopy crossed his mind. On one hand, it would immediately help with the smoke situation. But on the other, there was every chance it would make matters much, much worse. For one thing, blowing off the canopy would suddenly bring a roar of noise from the wind—the MiG-29 was still flying at over 600 kmph.

'In that sound blast, I would not be able to communicate with the radar controller or my wingman,' says Sqn Ldr Ajit. 'I would essentially be flying the aircraft on my own. I was tempted, because the smoke had by now nearly blinded me, but I knew I would be deprived of whatever help I was getting from the ground.'

A sudden rush of wind could also fan the fire into a larger blaze and push it to other parts of the aircraft. It was out of the question, the pilot decided. He had no choice but to continue flying the jet with the canopy firmly on for as long as he could bear the now-choking fire and smoke. What he therefore decided was to fly blind, almost fully dependent on his radar controller.

The toxic plastic fumes became thicker and continued to build up inside the cockpit as the fire quickly spread to other parts of the panel, melting them and distorting the instrument frames. It had now become unbearable. Bits of smoke had begun to seep into the pilot's oxygen mask from the gaps, causing him to cough and wheeze through the cloud, forcing him to again attempt to put out the fire with his now-burnt gloves. But the fire was there to stay. Trying to douse it in any manner was futile.

'Picture a fighter cockpit. It's a really small, confined place stuffed with a whole lot of things, including the pilot. And then there was the fire. It could do a lot of bad things and really fast,' Sqn Ldr Ajit says.

It had been seven minutes into the emergency when the radio control piped up again. He wanted to check if the fire had shut off any of the aircraft's vital systems. Even if the flames hadn't eaten into the fuel tanks, they could still destroy the complex electronics that kept the aircraft stable and the systems that kept the engines running. Losing system indicators was bad enough. Losing the systems themselves would have meant Finback 1 possibly falling out of the sky, with no more options left to the pilot.

'I had begun to see the lack of a catastrophic explosion or deviation as a stroke of luck,' says Sqn Ldr Ajit. 'But I was sure that luck wasn't going to last. Fire does not cooperate. It does not wait for you to take a decision. If the fire killed my systems, none of my flying skills would be of any use. With my instruments and visibility gone, I was entering a situation where I would have no clue about how high and how fast I was flying, and what the engine was doing or, for that matter, the other systems required for landing.'

Finback 1's cockpit had become a terrifying workplace for any fighter pilot, irrespective of his training and experience. If one of the MiG-29's two Klimov RD-33 engines failed, there would be no instrument forewarning in the cockpit. It is instruments that routinely tell the pilot about engine power and revolutions per minute (RPM)—information that is vital to the pilot.

'If panic were to set in, this would have been a good time—at this point, I was desperately concerned about the fire depriving me of vital inputs,' says Sqn Ldr Ajit.

Descending to an altitude below 10,000 feet quickly was critical at this juncture. At that height, Sqn Ldr Ajit would have the option of activating a ventilation system to drive the smoke out of the cockpit.

'The air-conditioning system on the plane has options of "normal" and "flood". Additional air flows inside the cockpit when "flood" is selected. I needed to descend below 10,000 feet for this option to work effectively,' says Sqn Ldr Ajit.

Strapped in his seat in the burning cockpit with the sun blazing behind him, Finback 1 continued its descent, with Finback 2 flying above and to his left.

'I could see Vasane's plane below mine, but I didn't know what exactly was going on inside,' says Sqn Ldr Rohit, who was flying Finback 2. 'The MiG-29 technical handbook lists several emergencies such as engine failure, flameout and loss of oil pressure. We know how to deal with those issues. But a cockpit fire was something new. How do you handle a problem that has never been encountered before?'

As the pair of MiG-29 jets cruised towards their Jamnagar base guided by the radar controller, the cockpit fire assumed its worst form thus far. For the first time in the minutes since the emergency began, Sqn Ldr Ajit wondered if ejecting from the jet was the only way to survive. Ejection seats in modern fighters have a success rate of more than 90 per cent, but pilots can end up with broken spines because of the sudden explosive force that rockets them out of the cockpit.

Even as the fumes choked the pilot, activating the ejection sequence was near unthinkable. Because emerging over the horizon just then was the Reliance Industries refinery complex, which is south-west of Jamnagar city. The heat inside the cockpit was now painful and it had become difficult to breathe. If the human instinct to survive overwhelmed everything else, a pilot in such a situation would bail out of his aircraft. Self-preservation, after all, is the most powerful impulse in all human beings. It would matter less at that point that the blazing wreck of his aircraft could glide unstoppably like a missile into the world's largest crude oil refinery to spark what would almost definitely be an inferno of historic proportions.

'The radar controller was continuously giving me the course and distance from the base,' says Sqn Ldr Ajit. 'If I were to draw a line from my position to the base, the flight path ran right above the refineries. I had been operating from the Jamnagar base for nearly three years and I knew I was in the danger zone. You just can't crash your plane there. I am not supposed to violate the 2-km rule under any circumstances. So there was absolutely no question of not adhering to the restriction on a day when my plane could explode any moment. I decided not to eject until it was absolutely necessary. And by this time, I felt I was mere seconds away from that situation.'

Fully aware of the consequences of his aircraft crashing into one of the refineries below, the pilot of Finback 1 took the most difficult decision of his flying career. Informing the radio controller that he was concerned he would soon lose control over his jet, Sqn Ldr Ajit peeled away to the right, putting 10 km between his aircraft and the refinery complex. He had chosen to take a longer route back to the base, adding excruciating minutes to his flight time.

'In my mind, it was the only way to ensure that there wasn't a bigger tragedy on the ground,' says Sqn Ldr Ajit. 'The refineries were my big worry. I kept thinking, what if my aircraft suddenly turned left and I was unable to control it? In a matter of seconds, the plane could have crashed into one of the refineries, causing unimaginable damage. I just wanted to land my aircraft soon.'

Slowly descending to below 10,000 feet, the pilot set the MiG-29's air-conditioning system to 'flood' mode, hoping to drive the thick cloud of smoke out of the cockpit. It didn't help, but with wisps of smoke dragged out of the cockpit, it stopped the smoke build-up from intensifying any further. The aircraft had begun to shudder slightly, indicating possible internal damage. Sqn Ldr Ajit still held off on ejecting—he made a mental note to be fully prepared to make that split-second decision, if required. Fighter pilots don't eject at the first sign of trouble. They are trained to calmly follow drills to avoid casualties on the ground as a priority, even if that means putting their own lives at enormous risk.

Under the guidance of ground control, Finback 1 continued its descent. The Jamnagar base was finally now on the horizon, except that Sqn Ldr Ajit couldn't see it. He and his wingman had flown identical missions several times before and were fully familiar with the ground features that would lead them back to the base they had departed just 15 minutes ago. But with his visibility completely compromised, Sqn Ldr Ajit listened carefully for visual cues from his wingman flying above and behind him now.

Still flying blind as he lowered his landing gear and came in for a final approach, Sqn Ldr Ajit finally spotted the runway. A tiny keyhole-sized gap in the smoke had opened right above his HUD, affording the smallest glimpse of the outside world for the first time since the fire had ruined his visibility. With a rush of confidence, reducing his speed to 280 kmph, Finback 1 descended the final few metres to touch down on the Jamnagar tarmac.

As the aircraft sped down the runway, Sqn Ldr Ajit saw a pair of crash tender trucks positioned alongside the far end, ready to douse the aircraft with high pressure water jets, if necessary. Sqn Ldr Rohit watched from above as the stricken MiG-29 jet deployed its chute and rolled to a halt.

'I breathed a sigh of relief in the cockpit,' says Sqn Ldr Rohit. 'It takes exceptional skill, presence of mind and plenty of guts to fly and land a doomed plane safely. I sent a word of congratulations from the air before circling around and bringing my own jet in.'

The fire in the cockpit was still burning as Finback 1's canopy finally opened, rapidly dissipating the smoke that had collected inside. Quickly unstrapping himself, the pilot climbed out of the aircraft. He had flown in a crippling blanket of smoke for nine minutes, but as Sqn Ldr Ajit stepped out of the aircraft, he found himself reaching into a zipper in his overalls for his pack of cigarettes. Picked up by a jeep, he lit up on the short drive back to the operations room, where he would brief his seniors about an emergency none of them had ever encountered before.

The MiG-29 was put down as 'unserviceable' in the aircraft's logbook. Over the next two hours, Sqn Ldr Ajit would brief his Flight Commander, the CO, the Chief Operations Officer and the Air Commodore commanding the Jamnagar fighter base about those nine minutes. He was the first Indian fighter pilot to encounter what had just happened. And he had managed to not only survive, but bring the aircraft safely back to base. If he had ejected—and nobody would have blamed him had he chosen to—the mystery of the cockpit fire would likely have remained unsolved, throwing into peril the flight safety of the fleet going forward.

By the time he was done with the briefings, the MiG-29's technical crews were waiting to get a low-down on the unprecedented emergency—a crisis that had brought the base to a virtual standstill for two hours.

'I had to explain everything to the technical guys so that they could identify the glitch and fix it,' says Sqn Ldr Ajit. 'It was in their hands now. I told them everything I had experienced. It was up to them now to ensure that the same thing never happened again.'

The one thing the young pilot hadn't done was call his wife, Sqn Ldr Rajeev Kaur, also an Air Force officer posted in Jamnagar. The two had met and fallen in love three years ago, when they were posted at the Adampur fighter base in Punjab. It was their first posting after joining the Air Force as officers. When Sqn Ldr Ajit survived that cockpit fire, they had been married for a year.

Sqn Ldr Rajeev, part of the IAF's accounts branch at the base, had gone to the office of the Jamnagar base commander at around 4 p.m. that evening to get a file cleared. It was there that she heard hushed whispers among the staff that a MiG-29 piloted by her husband had managed to land at the base a few minutes earlier after a critical emergency in the air.

'In the waiting room, the base commander's personal assistant told me about the incident,' says the pilot's wife. 'I asked him for details but he said, "Oh, nothing to worry about." Then my husband's flight commander, Wg Cdr Shekhar Yadav, entered the room. I asked him the same question. All he said was, "Don't worry, nothing serious," and went in to brief the base commander.'

Extremely anxious about what could have possibly happened, she began to dial her husband's phone, fuming that he hadn't called her on landing. After several attempts, he answered. She demanded to know what had happened and why nobody was sharing any details with her.

'*Yaar, kuch nahi hua hai* (Nothing has happened),' Sqn Ldr Ajit said with a chuckle. 'Who told you all this? I am having chai in the squadron. Don't worry. All is well.'

She was enormously relieved that he was back on the ground, but resented being kept out of the loop. At dinner that evening, she probed her husband a little more, perplexed that he wasn't more forthcoming with details of the mid-air drama.

'It was a routine sortie,' her husband had said, taking her hand from across the table. 'I am here having dinner with you. Everything's okay. Can we talk about something else, please?'

Sqn Ldr Rajeev would learn the full story only by chance that weekend at a party hosted by the Jamnagar base commander and his wife to celebrate their wedding anniversary. At the party, the chief operations officer of the base, a Group Captain, asked her if she had taken a look at the aircraft her husband had flown five days earlier.

'You must go and see that aircraft if you haven't already,' the Group Captain said. She had almost forgotten about the incident by this time. 'It was only then that I got to know about the scary emergency. I remember losing my cool with him for keeping me in the dark. I told him this was not done. How could he not tell me? But I realized later that he was dealing with it as well, and didn't want me to worry. But nobody can stop worrying. Fighter pilots can be crazy. Mine definitely is.'

That night, Sqn Ldr Ajit was allowed to sleep only after he recounted, in the minutest detail, what had happened on his flight that October afternoon.

'The briefing I gave her was probably more detailed than the ones I gave to my seniors after landing,' Sqn Ldr Ajit smiles.

The emergency on board Finback 1 had become the talk of the entire flying branch of the IAF that week. If the pilot needed a few days to calm down and recover, he didn't give any such indication. Sqn Ldr Ajit was back in the cockpit of a MiG-29 the day after the incident, out on another training mission.

'I was only doing my job, which is to train every single day through the year. I don't think it was an event to celebrate, or for that matter, to even thank God for keeping me safe. I never thought it was a big deal,' he says.

Sqn Ldr Ajit may not have thought it a big deal, but it was more than that for the IAF. Awkward about the sudden flood of attention he was receiving, the pilot wouldn't know at the time that the calm resilience he had displayed in the air for nine hellish minutes would earn him a Shaurya Chakra, the country's third-highest peacetime gallantry award, ten months later.

Posted out of Jamnagar a few months after the incident, to Tambaram in Tamil Nadu to train as a flying instructor, Sqn Ldr Ajit would learn about the decoration headed his way as he sat down to dinner with his course-mates one night.

'I had completely forgotten about the incident,' he says. 'I had moved on. And here I was, fielding congratulatory calls all night. I must admit it felt good, but I still say I was just doing my job.'

On the eve of Independence Day 2012, the government announced the gallantry decoration for a pilot who had displayed 'nerves of steel and unwavering commitment to the mission assigned to him'. His Shaurya Chakra citation would heap praise on him for handling a critical emergency that was 'neither documented nor had occurred before in a MiG-29 aircraft'.

He would play down the courage he displayed in the air when he spoke to his colleagues and his wife, but the Shaurya Chakra citation was unequivocal in its praise:

'Amid rapidly increasing intensity of fire and at great personal risk, he initiated emergency recovery of the aircraft. With exceptional presence of mind and courage of highest order, he elected to avoid flying over various petrochemical installations in the vicinity of the airfield, even though this prolonged flight endangered his life,' reads the citation. 'Despite limited visibility due to soot deposits on the windshield, Vasane skilfully positioned the MiG-29 jet for an emergency landing that he executed flawlessly. Throughout the flight, he maintained extreme calm and composure, devotion to duty and thorough professionalism in keeping with the highest traditions of the IAF.'

That August of 2012 was special for another reason. Sqn Ldrs Ajit and Rajeev had a baby boy eleven days before the Shaurya Chakra announcement. Little Rishan hasn't heard the full story yet. His mother says she will ensure he does, though, and soon.

Back in Jamnagar, Air Force specialists had finally managed to get to the bottom of the mysterious cockpit fire on Finback 1. A team from the IAF's base repair depot in Maharashtra established that the source of the fire was a short circuit involving a use-and-throw component in the HUD system. The lesson was a major reminder of how every single component on an aircraft—no matter how small or seemingly insignificant—could literally bring it down if it failed to do its job.

The findings were shared with MiG-29 bases across the country. Three months after the Jamnagar incident, in January 2012, a similar fire broke out in a MiG-29 cockpit at the Adampur fighter base while the jet was still on the ground for safety checks. The repeat incident forced the Air Force Headquarters in Delhi to order a comprehensive safety audit of the MiG-29 fleet to fix the problem. No such incident has been reported in the last seven years, but maintenance crews remain alert nevertheless.

In 2007, four years before Sqn Ldr Ajit's close call in the air, the Indian government decided to upgrade its entire fleet of MiG-29s with new engines, radars, weapons and modernized cockpits. The upgrade programme of seventy-eight aircraft is now nearing completion, though the IAF is still fighting a troubling decline in its combat aircraft strength. The IAF remains the only air force in the world still operating old MiG-21 jets, and is hoping to retire them soon with the arrival of the indigenous Light Combat Aircraft Tejas, the Rafale from France and new fighters that it hopes will be built in India.

Even as successive governments try to modernize the Air Force, pilots don't have a choice but to wait for better and safer aircraft in the interim.

Posted as a flying instructor at an air base in the country's east, Sqn Ldr Ajit—now a Wing Commander—frequently flies with trainee pilots, men who've heard about the Jamnagar incident and almost always ask him about it. His reply is brief and almost always the same: 'Fly with all you have.'

13

'Not a Sound until They Enter the Kill Zone'

Major Preetam Singh Kunwar

Near Badori, PoK
23 May 2017, 10 a.m.

The six men stepped out furtively, one by one, separated by a minute each, from a bunker built into the side of a hill. The advancing summer had turned the blanket of ice into rivulets of snowmelt, but the remnants of a harsh winter still clung stubbornly to the terrain. The six men had draped shawls over their phirans to keep warm; they wore camouflage fatigues and combat boots underneath. They stood for 10 minutes on a ledge cut into the mountainside, talking and sipping steaming hot tea from glasses passed around by one of them. Behind them, to their right, rose the towering Badori mountain, 3700 m high, with a couple of Pakistani Army posts that used its height for an unmatched view of the Uri sector. And 5 km ahead was the place the men were headed to next.

The LoC.

A small, rectangular gadget, an eyepiece, sat on a short tripod less than 2 feet high as an Indian Army soldier on his stomach peered through it. He scanned the area before him slowly, focusing the lens until he had the sharpest picture he could get from that distance. On an LCD screen, the six men appeared as dark, fuzzy blobs, flickering as the thermal imager captured their movements, a flourish of warm, dark pixels against the cold white of their surroundings. The soldier lowered the imager and looked straight out over the LoC. If those dark figures really were who he thought they were, then they were at least a month early. The soldier quickly picked up his communications console and sent a coded message to his base, which was then relayed to other Army units operating in the area. What it said was: 'Six men in view near Badori. Five kilometres inside. Suspected infiltration team. Maintaining surveillance.'

The soldier was part of a reconnaissance unit at a forward post in the Uri sector, manned by men from the 4th Battalion of one of the Army's most decorated infantry regiments, the Garhwal Rifles. In the 1962 war with China, 4 Garhwal Rifles fought overwhelmingly large Chinese forces in the North-east, inflicting significant damage and earning themselves a rare battle honour. They would thereafter be known as the Nuranang Battalion, in honour of a fearsome, courageous battle that the men from the unit fought in Nuranang in Arunachal Pradesh. Fifty-five years later, the unit was watching over a critical length of the frontier in Jammu and Kashmir. And at an enormously tense time.

Eight months earlier, Indian Army Special Forces units had crossed[1] the LoC in Uri and neighbouring sectors to strike at terrorist infiltrators. The mission was, in part, an act of revenge against Pakistan-sponsored terror groups for a commando-style attack by the LeT on the Indian Army's Uri Brigade headquarters, in which nineteen soldiers were killed. The revenge mission resulted in thirty-six terrorists and two Pakistani Army personnel killed across four infiltration launch

---

[1] The only first-hand account of the 2016 surgical strikes, by the Major who led them, is in *India's Most Fearless 1*. At the time of the publication of this book, the account is also being produced as a major web series.

pads. Over the next eight months, through a typically cruel winter, the Indian Army nursed no illusions that the surgical strikes would put an end to the flow of terror. It was only a question of *when* the infiltrations would begin again. And the six dark, pixellated figures that flickered on the soldier's thermal imager confirmed that it was finally time.

At his unit's Alpha company base in Uri's Rustom post, thirty-four-year-old Maj. Preetam Singh Kunwar listened carefully to the incoming message. No one from the unit had had any rest for weeks. Ten days ago, intelligence networks had begun to buzz[2] with the possibility of infiltration just over 10 km away, along the LoC in the Chakothi area, where a parallel operation to intercept infiltrators had begun. The sighting of six more infiltrators near the Badori mountain proved one thing—the final week of May 2017 was about to see the first big burst of infiltrations since the 2016 surgical strikes.

'The surveillance detachment had observed five to six people,' Maj. Preetam says. 'They alerted everyone over radio and line communications about these men. Our CO, Col. Samarjit Ray, then asked the same surveillance detachment at the LoC to check if the people were still there and whether the suspicious movement was still on. The jawan had first observed that movement at 10 a.m. on 23 May and reported it to everyone in the area. He was ordered to stay put and keep his sights fixed on those men.'

At noon, another report came in from the surveillance unit at the LoC. The thermal imager was able to paint a slightly more detailed picture than before, but it still couldn't give precise information on what the six men were doing. The soldier reported that it wasn't possible to tell if the men were carrying weapons or equipment, but that they were repeatedly

---

[2] See Chapter 9.

moving in and out of a *dhok*, a mountain hut constructed by local shepherds.

'*Bande uss dhok ke andar-bahar jaa rahe hain* (The men are going in and out of the dhok),' the soldier reported.

At 12.30 p.m., the CO, Col. Samarjit, sent out a communique to the unit's company commanders, including Maj. Preetam at Rustom, ordering them to be on maximum alert. The Rustom post sat on top of a snow-blown mountain, with other posts on spurs on the ridgeline ahead of it.

'Col. Ray told us there was something fishy on the other side,' Maj. Preetam says. 'He told me to gather as much information as I could about what was happening across the LoC.'

The first person Maj. Preetam called was a source across the LoC, asking him to check as quickly as possible who the six men in the shadow of the Badori mountain were, and to get back with any information about their movements. While he waited, the officer also activated his local sources and intelligence units, a network significantly weaker in that area than the one commanded by the Pakistani Army and the terror groups it armed. Asking a source in PoK about the specific presence of a certain group of men *always* ran the risk of alerting the other side and compelling them to change their plans.

An hour later, Maj. Preetam's PoK source called back, telling him that the group of men had crossed the Haji Pir pass, a veritable gateway for infiltrators looking to cross the LoC and make their way into the Kashmir Valley. Half a century earlier, in the 1965 war, Indian forces had captured this very pass, situated between the Poonch and Uri sectors, but had returned it to Pakistan following the Tashkent peace negotiations the following year, a decision that is widely rued even today by Army veterans and strategic thinkers. It is through the Haji Pir pass that the lion's share of Pakistan-sponsored terrorist infiltrators reach the LoC.

'I was told that a group had crossed the pass, but there was no way of knowing what their intent was,' says Maj. Preetam. 'This intelligence input was corroborated by other agencies and my people on the ground on both sides. We didn't need to wait long for another input to come in.'

That night, the surveillance unit at the LoC kept its thermal imagers trained on the location they had been monitoring. For the second time that day, the six figures emerged from their mountain dhok. The moment the new input was relayed back to base, the CO felt all doubts vanish about what was afoot. Immediately, he sent out orders to tighten the entire anti-infiltration grid, which included a sprinkling of forward bases and patrolling teams that would now step up their readiness to the maximum level.

'We set up extra anti-infiltration posts, sent out more patrols and placed more ambush units out there than usual,' says Maj. Preetam. 'There was little sleep that night. Every man in the sector wondered if this was going to be the infiltration that would break the eight-month lull that followed the surgical strikes.'

The following morning, 24 May, CO Col. Ray arrived at the Rustom post. In the operations room, he met Maj. Preetam and another young officer, the commander of the battalion's Ghatak[3] platoon. On a laptop screen, Col. Samarjit showed the two officers a video clip from the thermal imager used by the surveillance unit the previous day.

'The CO asked me what I thought,' says Maj. Preetam. 'I said those people had no business being in that area in the month

---

[3] Every Indian Army infantry battalion has a 'Ghatak platoon', comprising men trained in special operations and reconnaissance. It is often this platoon that leads offensive operations as 'shock troops'.

of May, as infiltration groups usually assemble at their staging areas only after June, when the snow has melted. He agreed. He also informed us that fresh intelligence had come in indicating that the infiltrators could take any of a number of routes to cross the LoC. So all units in the area needed to stay awake at all costs.'

Already in a high-pressure stand-off on a daily basis, in May 2017, the Army units in Uri were being tested to their limits of preparedness. The loud political narrative in Delhi surrounding the surgical strikes had painted a picture of an Army that Pakistan messed with at its own peril. On the ground in Uri, soldiers and officers knew that the swell of public attention meant that it was even more imperative that not a single infiltration attempt be allowed to succeed. The daily dance of life and death at the LoC had become tinged with an element of prestige, fuelled by political pronouncements of how the Army had been given full tactical freedom to avenge any 'misadventures'[4] by Pakistan.

Maj. Preetam decided to leave his base and lead a reconnaissance party to the LoC. Before departing with eight men from his company, he again checked in with his network of sources, both local and in PoK. Everything he heard only confirmed what was, by this time, beyond any real doubt—that the six pixellated figures captured by the Army soldier's thermal imager the previous day were set to be the first terrorist infiltrators since the 2016 surgical strikes.

'I had been the company commander in that area for over eighteen months, and I knew it like the back of my hand, be it the terrain, the likely infiltration routes or even the phases of the moon,' says Maj. Preetam. 'I checked with my men and assessed which areas were vulnerable and needed to be

---

[4] The word 'misadventure' would be used by the Army Chief, Gen. Bipin Rawat, days after taking office in December 2016, and would be repeated several times the following year.

covered better. We had a shortlist of such patches, the nallahs that had to be covered to prevent infiltration. The entire 161 Infantry Brigade (under which the 4 Garhwal Rifles Battalion operated) was on high alert.'

At 3 p.m. on 24 May, Maj. Preetam and his squad rolled out from their post, arriving 4 hours later at a point 500 m from the LoC, immediately spreading out to get a wide view of that stretch of frontier.

'If the infiltrators were on the foothills of Badori, this was one of the routes they were likely to take,' says Maj. Preetam. 'There were two-three nallahs in this area. I had eight other men in my squad. We were fully equipped.'

The squad had arrived armed for a big fight. They carried AK-47 assault rifles, MGLs, UBGLs, night-vision goggles, grenades, Motorola radio sets and enough rations and ready-to-eat meals to sustain them for a few days. As the sun set, they pulled on their night vision goggles, which allowed them to peer across the LoC to a distance of about a kilometre.

'We had positioned ourselves on a spur to cover the maximum area possible,' says Maj. Preetam, who was using his night-vision goggles to keep a close watch on the two nallahs that flowed in across the LoC in the kilometre-long stretch that he and his men were now keeping tabs on. 'We sat there through the night on 24 May, but didn't see a thing.'

Switching between surveillance and quick naps, Maj. Preetam's squad watched the LoC till the sun rose. Early in the morning of 25 May, a radio message came in from the surveillance unit that had first detected the infiltrators two days earlier.

'Six persons detected leaving Badori foothills, moving towards LoC,' the message said. 'Movement being kept under observation to the extent possible.'

The foothills of Badori sat at an elevation that allowed the Indian Army to get a glimpse of the infiltrators. But once they began to move, folds in the mountainous path and patches of thick foliage soon engulfed them. They were last sighted crossing a nallah on their side of the border.

The Ghatak platoon had placed itself a short distance away along the LoC, on another likely infiltration route. Later that morning, Maj. Preetam, still scanning the stretch of LoC in front of him, called his CO back at the Rustom post.

'I asked for permission to move closer to the LoC,' Maj. Preetam says. 'I was now certain that I wasn't going to be able to detect anything from where I stood. I needed to get a better view of the LoC stretch we were monitoring. Col. Samarjit said it's fine, you and your squad can move ahead. But he had one major concern that he warned us about.'

Tracts of land close to the LoC on both sides are infested with landmines, planted over the years by both armies as a deterrent to attempts to cross the LoC.

'Move ahead if you have to,' Col. Samarjit said over his Motorola handset. 'But I'm telling you right now—I don't want any landmine casualties. *Operation shuru hone se pehle hi mine casualty ho jaaye* (Mine casualties even before the operation)—that's not happening. Make sure each of you treads the ground very carefully.'

Maj. Preetam and his men were wearing anti-mine combat boots, reinforced footwear with a multilayered composite armoured sole built to dissipate the blast of a landmine and spread it outwards. But these were heavy and didn't exactly lend themselves to rapid movement.

'The boots affect mobility, no doubt,' says Maj. Preetam. 'They definitely slow you down a bit and are nowhere near as comfortable as our regular combat boots.'

The landmines pose a real threat. The Army has maps of where these mines are, but the shifting of soil has meant that mines might have moved many feet over the years and could be lethal to infantry troops. A landmine had struck during the 2016 surgical strikes—a Lance Naik from the Special Forces suffered a serious leg injury in a landmine blast when his team was returning from across the LoC after the offensive operation. Two months later, in November 2016, a soldier of Maj. Preetam's own battalion had lost his left leg in a mine explosion in that very sector. Maj. Preetam had seen it happen.

'The minefield was an enormous challenge,' says Col. Samarjit. 'I made it clear I didn't want any blood spilt before the operation began. It hadn't even been a year since we nearly lost one of our boys.'

'I cannot forget that sight,' Maj. Preetam says. 'My men were also aware of that incident. It never left our minds. So when the CO kept telling us to beware of the mines, he knew what he was talking about.'

The dilemma that morning was real. Maj. Preetam needed to lead his men closer to the LoC while crossing, quite literally, a minefield. They also needed to do it as quickly as possible. And with only eight men on the squad, he couldn't afford[5] to lose a single man.

Wondering how they could safely cross the mined stretch in the shortest possible time, the solution presented itself in the form of a six-foot log they found lying on the descent from their position.

'My buddy soldier, Lance Naik Sukhpal Singh, saw that log and had a flash of inspiration,' says Maj. Preetam. 'It was

---

[5] No troops are dispensable in any sense, but in mission planning, an expected casualty count is realistically considered to enable pragmatic, objective-oriented decisions.

basically a simple improvisation. He picked it up and suggested that we use it as a bridge to navigate the minefield.'

Lance Naik Sukhpal quickly demonstrated what he had in mind to the rest of the squad.

'We will not put the other end of the plank on the ground but place it on a small boulder or a helmet—like a small makeshift bridge,' the soldier said. 'And then we will walk across it to ensure we aren't putting our feet on the ground.'

The idea was clever, though complicated. But with no other option, Maj. Preetam ordered the squad to begin the breaching operation.

Before they began, the officer placed an arm around Lance Naik Sukhpal's shoulder, reminded of the time they had stared death in the face together. In 2011, while deployed in the Keran sector of the LoC in north Kashmir, Maj. Preetam, then a Captain, had saved young Sepoy Sukhpal's life during an anti-terror operation. The act had only cemented an already close bond.

Early in the morning on 25 May, aided by the log, the Alpha Company of 4 Garhwal Rifles stepped into a minefield.

It would turn out to be a deeply tense operation, with each man on edge, sweating even at that altitude as they placed the log carefully, hoping it wouldn't be on a mine. The log allowed them to reduce the risk of a mine explosion significantly, but didn't eliminate it completely.

'The innovation ensured safety, but it really slowed down our movement,' says a soldier from the squad. 'We were moving ahead at a snail's pace, one man covering six feet at a time. We took almost 5 hours to cover around 350 to 400 m. We were very mine-conscious and took every precaution possible as we approached the LoC. The moment we got close to the LoC, Maj. Preetam started scouting for an area that would give us both good cover and an unrestricted view.'

By noon, having finally crossed the mined stretch, the squad took up its new positions. Only minutes after they had done so, Maj. Preetam's radio crackled.

'Spotted and in sight, two men in the nallah straight ahead,' said a soldier, who was looking through his binoculars from an elevated position.

The two men the soldier had spotted were about 75 m away across the LoC. Maj. Preetam had split his squad into four buddy pairs, each positioned 30 m apart to provide a 90-m breadth of cover.

'The moment he gave me that information, I immediately changed my position and moved closer to him,' says Maj. Preetam. 'This was the first time I was observing likely terrorists from such a close distance. I felt an adrenaline rush. I instructed my squad to hold fire, and not to open fire until I said so. We sat in our positions and observed them. The two men retreated a short distance.'

Maj. Preetam then called his buddy, Lance Naik Sukhpal, and told him that the two of them would be moving about 40 m closer to the LoC, descending from a spur. He ordered the remaining three pairs to remain in their positions.

'We took our chances without the log, since there was very little time, and because there's little possibility of mines sticking to a slope,' Maj. Preetam says. 'From our new position, closer to the LoC, we could see not only the two men who had been spotted a few moments earlier, but also three more. So there was a total of five, and three of them were carrying weapons. It was now clear that this was the same terror squad that had left the Badori foothills the previous night and was now approaching the LoC.'

Maj. Preetam radioed his CO. When Col. Samarjit was informed about the sighting of five likely infiltrators, he ordered Maj. Preetam and Lance Naik Sukhpal to retreat to their earlier position immediately. Gathering a QRT at Rustom, Col. Samarjit immediately departed the post and made for the LoC to join what was clearly turning into a major operation.

'Looks like they plan to take one of the three nallahs to cross the LoC and come to our side, Sir,' Maj. Preetam told his CO. 'I have a hunch about which nallah they will use, but we are watching all three to be safe.'

At 3 p.m., suddenly, the five terrorists retreated and disappeared from view. Col. Samarjit ordered Maj. Preetam's squad to retreat further, to the position they had taken up before crossing the mined area. Using the log once again, the eight men crossed back over the minefield in failing light, reaching their earlier position by nightfall.

'We took positions there and sat throughout the night—it was extremely cold,' says Maj. Preetam. 'Once again, we kept an uninterrupted watch across the LoC.'

The squad had been outdoors in the cold for over 48 hours since they left the Rustom post. At first light the following day, 26 May, Maj. Preetam took five men and used the log to return across the minefield for the third time, towards the LoC. Two men were left behind at the position from where the first two terrorists had been spotted in a nallah the previous day.

The hours rolled by, with no sign of the men who had been spotted 24 hours earlier. Then, at 4 p.m., three figures came into view.

'It was sudden and very clear—we detected three people about to cross the LoC with weapons and rucksacks,' says Maj. Preetam. 'They were barely 40 m away. We decided not to engage them because we were not certain how many of them there were.'

At 40 m, and undetected, Maj. Preetam and his men had a clear shot of the three terrorists and could have finished them right there. But the officer waited. And there was good reason.

Forty metres. Close enough to hear their footfalls splashing in the nallah.

'We could see only three men—but if there were six or eight of them, the remaining guys would retreat the moment firing began,' says Maj. Preetam. 'I wanted to wait until the full group showed itself. Maybe there were six or eight or ten. It was hard to say. If we opened fire at the three we could see, the remaining would easily escape. We didn't want that to happen. We would lose the element of surprise and alert the Pakistani Army post 500 m away. It would have been ready to provide firing support to the infiltrating group, which is their standard operating procedure.'

Once again, Col. Samarjit ordered Maj. Preetam and his men to fall back. The CO and his team had reached a nearby post, taking position to block another infiltration route.

'As we fell back this time, we decided not to use the log as we wanted to retreat quickly and without a moment to lose,' says Maj. Preetam. 'There was a sense of urgency and I decided to take that risk. I didn't have the luxury of wasting 4 or 5 hours. Once we crossed the minefield, we went straight to link up with our CO and his squad. We were now in a place that the infiltrators needed to cross, no matter which route or nallah they chose.'

The three infiltrators who had been spotted crossing one of the nallahs that day had stopped and waited after they crossed, observing the stretch of LoC ahead of them. Col. Samarjit's team had already blocked one of the nallahs.

'I told my CO that they have crossed the nallah, and now their intent is clear,' Maj. Preetam says. 'They are terrorists about to infiltrate. It was still hard to say which route they would take from where they had stopped, as there were two more nallahs ahead, giving them two more possible routes. But we had both covered now. All possible infiltration routes were closely guarded.'

The men of 4 Garhwal Rifles were now simply waiting for the full group to cross the LoC and reveal its true numbers.

'My buddy and I had taken position on one side of a nallah,' says Maj. Preetam. 'Our CO was on the other side. The complete area was covered. At around 6.30 p.m., as the sun was setting, our squad spotted five men. They were walking with weapons in one hand and walking sticks used for hiking in another. They had rucksacks slung on their backs.'

Five men. *Thirty metres away.*

Maj. Preetam radioed his CO. Col. Samarjit immediately told the squads that no one would open fire until Maj. Preetam gave the go-ahead as he was the closest to the approaching terror group.

As Maj. Preetam and Lance Naik Sukhpal fixed their night-vision-aided gaze on the five figures stepping slowly towards the LoC, another terrorist stepped into view behind them.

'So six were visible now,' says Maj. Preetam. 'The sixth guy was far behind. The first five men were walking 5 m behind each other, but the sixth man was about 20 m behind the fifth. I thought that the sixth man was perhaps leading another squad. There was a possibility that we were dealing with a dozen well-equipped and trained terrorists.'

It was perplexing. Why was the sixth terrorist walking so far behind the group? Again, Maj. Preetam told his squad not to open fire till all six men had crossed the second nallah. The men were climbing up a small spur. They would need to descend from it before crossing the second nallah that was covered by Col. Samarjit's squad. The moment they crossed the nallah, they would be in the field of fire of both squads.

They were being lured into a kill zone they had shown no signs of having noticed yet.

Just as the terrorist group entered the second nallah, the sixth man splashed through the water to catch up with the first five, now marching with a distance of 5 m between them. Crossing the second nallah, the terrorists stopped for a moment. And their postures completely changed.

'As we watched, they crossed the nallah and immediately assumed tactical postures,' says Maj. Preetam. 'They were now holding their weapons in an offensive posture, each of them scanning the area carefully, I could tell. Perhaps they knew that they could be ambushed any moment and were prepared to fight back. They knew they were in the danger zone now. They didn't know we were waiting for them, but they had clearly been trained not to let their guard down for even a moment.'

As CO of the unit, Col. Samarjit had his weapon pointed and ready. He didn't have a moment to think of anything else, but couldn't help remembering that this group of infiltrators were the first since the 2016 surgical strikes—it was beyond doubt that they weren't coming in for small kills. They had to be stopped at all costs.

'I remember thinking—these guys are looking to infiltrate, and then they'll recruit a whole lot more people and head straight for the Valley to create mayhem,' says Col. Samarjit. 'We had to stop them, no matter what.'

Maj. Preetam and his buddy soldier were in a position to cover an area between the two nallahs, where both merged into a single large stream. In the dark, with their night-vision goggles strapped on, the squad watched as the six terrorists stepped through the middle nallah into the Indian side, climbing a spur and passing Maj. Preetam and his buddy.

'The moment they crossed me and my buddy, I looked at my watch—it was 7.13 p.m.,' says Maj. Preetam. 'That was the time I radioed all squads to open fire.'

The men had been out there for two days, tracking the terrorists from a stone's throw away, but hadn't fired a single bullet so far. Finally, they had their orders.

'Every man was waiting for this,' says Maj. Preetam, who opened up his AK–47 with a furious burst of fire directly at the six terrorists. 'We had already decided that we would open fire when the first terrorist crossed the first buddy pair. And the other buddy pairs would engage when they saw them. All the infiltrating terrorists were now in the range of our men. They didn't get much reaction time because they were climbing up a spur when we opened fire. But remember, they were very well trained. Like commandos.'

AK–47 with under-barrel grenade launcher

The six terrorists stopped in their tracks, taking cover, with two of them firing back in the darkness. The Indian squads were well concealed, so the two terrorists fired randomly.

Maj. Preetam realized he needed to move if this operation was to end well.

'From the place where I was firing and carrying out surveillance, I didn't have much cover,' he remembers. 'This was from where I was informing the other pairs about the number of terrorists that had passed me and my buddy. The plan was that the moment the crossfire started, I would change my location.'

The lead infiltrator and the man behind him were killed in the opening minutes of the ambush. The third and fourth terrorists scrambled to take cover behind a boulder, disappearing from the line of sight of Maj. Preetam and his buddy soldier. The fifth and sixth terrorists were being fired at by the other pairs. A full-fledged firefight had erupted by this time.

'Sukhpal and I crawled for about 25 m to take position on slightly higher ground to see if we could engage the two terrorists who had hidden behind the boulder,' says Maj. Preetam. 'We took cover behind a tree with a thick trunk, from where we spotted both of them. We could see the muzzle flashes of their rifles as they stuck their weapons out to fire at us.'

As the crossfire intensified, the sixth terrorist was spotted climbing up the hill towards Maj. Preetam and his buddy. He was crawling quietly, without firing, hoping to sneak up on the two and kill them at close quarters.

'*Uss ko dikh gaya tha ki maximum firing kahaan se ho rahi hai* (He could make out where the maximum fire was coming from—our position),' says Maj. Preetam.

The terrorist got to his feet and began running towards the officer and his buddy. Just as Maj. Preetam and the soldier began to move from their position, a grenade fired by one of the terrorists from behind the boulder landed a few metres away.

'I think he must have seen us as we also had to stick out our rifles from behind the tree trunk to fire at them,' says Maj. Preetam. 'The blast was deafening and for a few moments, I could neither hear nor see anything. The grenade exploded very close to us. Splinter *kaanon ke itne paas se gaye ki mujhe unki awaaz aa rahi thi* (The splinters were flying so close to my ears that I could hear them). I screamed out to Sukhpal to see if he was okay. He asked me the same question. We were both okay.'

The sixth terrorist, who had been running towards them, was shot down by another buddy pair who had seen him when he got to his feet. Three terrorists were now dead, with three left. At this point, Maj. Preetam left his cover briefly and stepped closer to the boulder that still hid two terrorists.

'From 15 m away, I lobbed a grenade at them,' says Maj. Preetam. 'They were both killed by that grenade. After throwing the grenade, I was still firing in their direction, and so was Sukhpal. Firing from behind the boulder had stopped totally.'

There was now only one terrorist left, and he was approaching Col. Samarjit's squad. Maj. Preetam quickly radioed his CO to tell him, asking him to throw grenades in his direction. Col. Samarjit's buddy soldier flung a grenade directly at the approaching terrorist, while the other squads fired towards him. The terrorist crumpled to the ground just as he was about to break into a run for the final stretch to the CO's squad position.

All the six terrorists were dead. They had been drawn into a kill zone and eliminated in under 15 minutes. The ambush site had been designed in such a way that there was no real place for the infiltrators to hide for any extended period. They had been, in effect, lured to a place from which there was no escape. From any one point, the terrorists were visible to at least one of the buddy pairs, allowing for two pairs of eyes to be fixed on them no matter where they tried to run or hide. By the time the assault rifles finally fell silent, the sky was overblown with clouds and it had begun to drizzle.

'I radioed my squad to check if everyone was okay,' says Maj. Preetam. 'My CO was doing the same. There were seventeen of us in that operation. My team of eight, which included me, and our CO and his QRT of eight soldiers. That area, in the shape of a bowl, was covered by these seventeen men. We enjoyed the advantage of height. The ambush site was chosen very carefully. And we got the results we wanted.

We were still very alert, because you never know—there might still have been some more people hiding somewhere. We told our surveillance detachment to keep the area, that section of the LoC, under watch to see if more infiltrator squads were coming. All our men were still behind cover.'

The squads then launched quadcopter drones equipped with thermal cameras for an airborne sweep of the area—a final effort to ensure they hadn't missed a terrorist or two. With the all-clear from above, the squads settled down on the mountainside to wait the night out.

At first light on 27 May, the men of 4 Garhwal Rifles began searching the ambush site to retrieve the bodies of the six terrorists. Standard operating procedure needed to be followed in every case.

'First, we took headshots from up close to make sure they were dead,' says Maj. Preetam. 'Terrorists trained by the Pakistani Army frequently use their bodies as booby traps. We use a rope and hook to move the bodies. We throw the hook hoping for it to catch on the body. If not, we go close to the body and anchor it and then pull the body from a distance of about 25 m. If there is a grenade under the body, it will explode.'

The search and retrieval of bodies continued till early in the afternoon. The men looked at each other, and then to their company commander as they completed the 'mopping up' operation, which involved special surveillance by two buddy pairs to ensure that the ambushers weren't ambushed by any more infiltrators.

'As a company commander on the ground, my top priority was that there should be not be a single scratch on any of the men I am leading,' says Maj. Preetam. 'This was a highly dangerous mission, and we needed to stay motivated as a team. Imagine the scout out front. He knows the area is infested with mines. But he follows my word because he trusts me. No mission is possible without the trust of your men. And it was that trust that allowed me to plan the mission in such a way that all of us stayed alive.'

With the mopping up operation complete, the squads finally received word that they could return to Rustom post.

'This was an operation that stood on a razor's edge,' says Col. Samarjit. 'This terrain was tricky. The minefield threat was real. The terrorists were very well trained. And we still managed to ensure there wasn't a single scratch on any of the men. It was a very clean operation, although Preetam and his buddy, Sukhpal, exposed themselves to a lot of risk during close-quarter surveillance of the infiltrators and by frequently relocating their ambush site.'

Back at Rustom post a few hours later, Maj. Preetam, Col. Samarjit and some of the team gathered in the operations room for a debrief about the mission and to take stock of what they had accomplished. If there was a unanimous takeaway, it was fire discipline.

'If you lose the element of surprise, chances are you will end up getting killed,' Maj. Preetam says. 'I made it very clear that no one will open fire till I order them to. Imagine you are observing two or three guys with weapons and they are a few metres away. You know that either they are going to kill you or they will get killed. That is the time you have to be in control of the situation. You cannot suddenly become trigger-happy and fire. Had we done that that day, we would have got only three of them. The remaining would have escaped. It is easy to forget how crucial and indispensable fire discipline is.'

He may have been the one issuing orders to his men to hold their fire, but Maj. Preetam would remember how it was his own momentary lapse of fire discipline that had cost him at least seven terrorists two years earlier, when he operated as part of the Army's 28 Division in Kupwara. An early burst of fire had sent a large group of terrorists scurrying back across the LoC, depriving the squad of a major encounter. The squad had waited 96 hours for the terrorists, but a few bullets fired too early had brought the operation to an end in minutes. A major infiltration had been foiled, but the terrorists had got away alive—certain to attempt another infiltration at a future date. That day, Maj. Preetam had decided he would never make the same mistake again.

The other major lesson from the debrief was the intricate detailing and design of the operation. The large number of moving parts—when and where the terrorists would cross, the number of terrorists, how well they would be armed, and whether they would split up after being challenged, to name a few. Luring them into a zone of no escape was therefore both critical as well as an enormous challenge. And with all of these difficult variables, there were still the minute levels of planning that needed to be built into the operation even as it rolled out. Fighting effectively at night, for instance, was a certainty, and the squads were armed for it. But they needed to take it a step further to face an infiltration squad.

'The moon was in its first quarter at the time, so there was not much moonlight,' Maj. Preetam says. 'It's almost pitch dark and an intense firefight is on. So how do I spot my buddy? We can talk over the Motorola radio sets, but what if I need to know his exact location? We had passive night-vision goggles, which emit an infrared blip when you press a button on the side. Those IR lights can be seen through passive night-vision sets only. You can see a red dot. So the moment I see a red dot, I know it's a man from my squad. This is how we knew who was where.'

There was the additional challenge of targeting the terrorists accurately in the dark.

'We were also carrying laser pointers with us,' explains Maj. Preetam. 'Say, your buddy has spotted some movement, but you haven't—he will direct you to that movement with the laser light. The fifth terrorist was killed with the help of a laser pointer. One of the buddy pairs directed the laser at him, and following the pointer, the CO's buddy lobbed a grenade and killed him. We had kept it simple. No one would laser in the direction of our parties' positions. *Jahan mein laser karunga, wahan bina soche ya time waste kare wahan fire karna hai* (Where I point the laser, just fire in that direction without thinking or wasting time). It was a simple plan. Once the target is painted by the laser, just fire or throw a grenade.'

The six terrorists killed that night were all Pakistani nationals from the LeT. Their rucksacks contained enough rations and ammunition for a major strike—bigger than the September 2016 attack at the Uri Brigade headquarters. The encounter had ended so quickly. The Pakistani Army post that had been expected to wake up and attempt to help the terrorists hadn't fired a single shot. It wasn't clear why, though it was likely that the post had let its guard down and was unable to focus fire before the encounter ended.

Back at the Rustom base that evening, the rest of the battalion was waiting for the return of the squads. Celebrations erupted, but had to be kept brief—the surveillance unit, still at the LoC, had radioed in, alerting the men to the possibility of more infiltration attempts. The alert would prove true the following day, but in a stretch of the LoC over 10 km west of the Rustom post's area of responsibility.

On a visit to the Kashmir Valley five days later, the Army Chief, Gen. Bipin Rawat, took a chopper out to the Rustom post to meet the men who had foiled the first infiltration since the 2016 surgical strikes. Rawat had played a part in the surgical strikes as Vice Chief at the Army Headquarters in Delhi.

On 14 August 2017, the government announced that Maj. Preetam Singh Kunwar would be decorated with the Kirti Chakra, the country's second-highest peacetime gallantry award. He would find out about it only the following day.

A few days earlier, in August, a soldier from the unit, Kuldeep Singh Rawat, had been killed by a Pakistani Army sniper not far from where the 26 May infiltration attempt had taken place. The entire unit had been drawn into the imperative for revenge, an impulse which, at the tactical level, doesn't normally escalate into a larger confrontation.

'We were focused on avenging our boy,' says Maj. Preetam. 'On the night of 14 August, I was out on a patrol in the same area. On 15 August, I began getting congratulatory calls for the Kirti Chakra. It was a good day. On the same day, we sniped three Pakistani Army men. That was a very special Independence Day. It was a doubly joyous day, more so because we were able to take revenge.'

'My boys were so aggressive that they did not allow the Pakistanis to retrieve the bodies,' says Col. Samarjit, describing an anger it is hard to imagine outside the confines of the bonds that functioning in a single Army unit can engender. 'If they tried to retrieve the bodies, my boys would fire at them. They gave up after trying several times. Finally, it happened only after their Director General Military Operations called his Indian counterpart.'

The Kirti Chakra citation would record that Maj. Preetam had shown 'great courage and valour' in the 'highest traditions of the Indian Army'. Like most heroes, the officer plays it all down.

'I don't think I did anything extraordinary,' he says. 'I signed up for this job and did what I am expected to do.'

Col. Samarjit, who was decorated with a Sena Medal for the operation, feels differently.

'That night, Preetam came very close to being awarded an Ashok Chakra, posthumously,' he says. 'That was the kind of risk he took to make sure we were able to kill all the intruders. The terrorists were barely metres away from him. No man in that operation would have been surprised if we had lost Preetam that night. His courage was extraordinary.'

Maj. Preetam's buddy, Lance Naik Sukhpal Singh, and Col. Samarjit's buddy, Havildar Brijendra Lal, received Sena Medals for gallantry in the operation.

Back home in Dehradun, Maj. Preetam's father, Narender Singh, a retired soldier from the Garhwal Scouts, couldn't have been happier about his son's mission. On the evening of 27 May, when Maj. Preetam called his wife, Megha—after being off the grid for three days—to tell her about the operation, she had been overcome with relief and had broken down. Her father had come running, his heart in his mouth. Taking the phone from his weeping daughter's hand, he exhaled when he heard the voice at the other end.

'The day the operation took place, I was very restless,' says Megha. 'I couldn't sleep the whole night. I guess it was intuition that not all was well with Preetam. Maybe he was caught in a difficult situation. When he finally called and told me he was okay, I just couldn't hold on, and I began to cry. My father then hugged me and said, "You should be proud of what your husband has done for the country."'

Megha Kunwar says that ever since her husband has been deployed in Kashmir, she sits in their home's puja room and meditates twice a day, morning and evening.

'I had spoken to Megha before the operation—I told her I had been given some extra responsibilities and I would be unreachable for a few days,' says Maj. Preetam. 'That's what I tell her when I am going out to conduct operations. When I came back on 27 May, I saw around forty missed calls from her and a barrage of WhatsApp messages on my mobile. You can tell your family that everything is going to be alright, but you can never really convince them. As we lie exhausted in our bunks, getting the deepest sleep so we can perform well the next day, our loved ones are sitting far away, having sleepless nights. That thought never leaves our minds in forward areas.'

'Every time he doesn't take my call, I am on the verge of a breakdown,' says Megha. 'One day, one of his unit officers told me, "Ma'am, don't worry if he doesn't call you, but pray *karo ki aapko unit se koi aur kabhi call na kare.*" That day, when he called me after the operation, he had dialled from a different number. I was praying that I hear his voice at the other end. I remember praying fervently till I heard his voice.'

'Of course, I feel pride every single day, but let nobody fool you about our fears,' says Megha. 'The fear I feel as the partner of an Army officer in Kashmir is a constant, daily, hourly fear. It never goes away. It is a constant companion. It is part of the deal.'

Their son, Abhiraj, now four years old, has been told about his father's mission.

'He always asks me, "*Papa, aapne chheh bhooton ko kaise maara* (How did you kill the six ghosts)?"' says Maj. Preetam.

'What struck me most about Kunwar was his unshakeable cool in a very tense situation,' says Col. Samarjit. 'His radio messages from a position just metres away from the terrorists were always conveyed in the calmest manner. There was not a hint of fear or anxiety in his tone. Through the firefight too, he didn't get even slightly jittery. It takes nerves of steel to hold yourself together like that. If he had not, both he and Sukhpal would have been lost. The terrorists were so close to them, perhaps not even 5 m away. He took an unimaginable risk. It was profoundly brave.'

At the time of this being written, the 4 Garhwal Rifles has completed its tenure in Kashmir and is being moved to the decidedly more tropical climes of Port Blair in the Andaman and Nicobar Islands, where there's a far lower chance of snow, and where starlight keeps even the darkest nights bright enough to see. Not surprisingly, though, Maj. Preetam isn't enthusiastic.

'I've got to be honest—I'm not really looking forward to it,' he says. 'I will miss Kashmir. That's where I wish to operate. It's the reason I joined the Army.'

At a ceremony at the Rashtrapati Bhavan where her husband was decorated with the Kirti Chakra in 2017, Megha sat in the audience sending up a prayer.

'I was thanking God from the bottom of my heart that I was attending this function *with* my husband,' she says. 'There were families who were receiving posthumous awards. I couldn't imagine being in that position. And yet, how difficult is it to really imagine? The unthinkable plays in our minds, invades our peace every minute of every day, doesn't it?'

As they walked out of the Rashtrapati Bhavan that evening and waited for their car to pick them up, Megha held Maj. Preetam's hand and whispered, 'Listen, enough. I don't want you to serve in Kashmir any more. Do you hear me? Enough.'

Maj. Preetam smiled and held her close.

14

'You Cannot Sustain Fear of Death'

Flight Lieutenant Gunadnya Ramesh Kharche

Airspace over Tamil Nadu
6 February 2012

'Would you rather die in a big fireball? Or in a mangled mess?
Take your pick.'

K-3060's co-pilot, Sqn Ldr Aditee Bhangaonkar, found
herself smiling at the question. She turned to the flight's
captain, sitting to her left in the cockpit, his words helping
break the tension, even if only for a few moments. He
chuckled into his headset, which was the only way the people
in the cockpit could hear one another over the roar of the
twin Soviet-built turbo propeller engines. Except, like his co-
pilot, Flt Lt Gunadnya Ramesh Kharche knew that there was
nothing even remotely amusing about their situation.

It was simple, really. The aircraft couldn't land. Not
without ending up in either a deadly fireball or a mangled
mess, as its captain had joked. And the realization had taken
the crew of the Antonov whole minutes to digest.

As Gunadnya's nervous humour hung heavy in the cockpit,
he manoeuvred the aircraft for a pass over the air base they
had departed from 2 hours earlier. He needed a few moments
to process the K-3060's terrifying situation. As he banked the
aircraft sharply to the right, the base popped into view below
them. The pilots and navigator saw it instantly—a large crowd
had gathered on the apron near the air traffic control (ATC)
tower. It looked like every soul at the air base had dropped

whatever they had been doing that busy Monday morning in February 2012 and gathered near the runway. Right next to the tarmac, the pilots spotted three crash trucks, their lights flashing and engines running.

Two hours had changed everything.

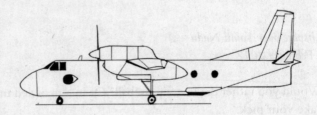

An-32 military transport aircraft

At 11 that morning, as the K-3060 had taken off from the IAF's Sulur air base near the ancient city of Coimbatore in Tamil Nadu, the pilots remembered noting what perfect weather it was for the sort of flying they were about to embark on. The Soviet-era Antonov An-32 transport plane had been its usual reliable self— rugged, rough and reassuringly loud. Apart from co-pilots Flt Lt Gunadnya and Sqn Ldr Aditee, the crew included navigator Sqn Ldr Saumitra Mishra and flight engineer Sergeant Shailendra Singh. As the aircraft roared off the runway, the pilots pulled the 20-tonne airplane into a gentle climb to 1000 feet, levelling out at that altitude. The crew from the 33 Squadron, nicknamed 'Soaring Storks', was on a 'low-level navigation mission' that day, which meant they would stay at a low altitude and practise a series of manoeuvres to test flying capabilities, navigation skills and, quite simply, to keep the complicated and skill-intensive daily business of operating aircraft in shipshape.

'It was a beautiful day. No clouds, bright sun, cool weather. Perfect for flying,' recalls Gunadnya about that February morning in 2012.

Cruising at 1000 feet, the crew had pointed the aircraft south, flying it out over a relatively low-population area, quite a distance away from the Coimbatore metropolitan area, which was to their west and which was Tamil Nadu's second largest city after its state capital, Chennai. Flight paths for military air missions are usually carefully chosen to avoid built-up and densely populated areas. It was especially so that morning, since the crew of K-3060 was flying low.

Flying low wasn't a problem at all. The An-32 has endeared itself to generations of Indian pilots for its forgiving toughness and stability even during risky, low-level flight missions. It is the An-32, after all, that transports the bulk of military personnel and material to forward bases in the north and the north-east, frequently flying through narrow valleys and navigating past lofty ridge lines. Some would say the An-32 is an ungainly sight, with its narrow fuselage and hulking shoulder-like engine pods. But to the men and women who fly them, there are few aircraft more cherished than the An-32.

The K-3060 may have been over two decades old, but it was still a reliable airframe that had given its current and past crews little cause for worry. It was already in line for an elaborate upgrade. Three years earlier, in June 2009, the Indian government had engaged a Ukrainian firm to give 105 IAF An-32s an additional fifteen years of service. This would be done by overhauling each aircraft from the inside out, fitting them with better engines, modern navigation and survival electronics, advanced new sensors and a superior cockpit. The aircraft would also receive better ergonomic and functional seats for the pilots and crew. The plan was to squeeze a valuable decade and a half out of a rugged fleet of planes by making them more modern, safer and easier to fly. The K-3060 was in queue for the big makeover, but that wouldn't stop normal, daily missions like the one it was on that morning.

'We had planned to fly for 3 hours. Everything went perfectly smoothly,' says Flt Lt Gunadnya. 'Until, of course, it was time to return to base.'

Their mission complete, Flt Lt Gunadnya ordered his crew to prepare for the return leg of the journey. The aircraft was eased out of its already low altitude to about 800 feet. It was gently descending as the pilots manoeuvred it into a return flight path towards Sulur. Over the radio, co-pilot Aditee notified air traffic control at Sulur that they were returning to base. With a clear flight path back, it was time to lower the K-3060's wheels. The An-32 has three wheels—two tough main landing wheels that pop out from the engine pods in the wings, and a smaller nose wheel that is mostly used to steer the aircraft on the ground. Gunadnya pushed a rectangular white button on the cockpit panel to trigger the clanking hydraulic sequence that would see the landing gear being lowered in a ballet of moving mechanical parts.

And that's when it happened.

'I waited for the three indicator lights on the cockpit panel to tell me that the landing gear has successfully been lowered. Three green lights in a triangle,' Gunadnya says. 'The nose wheel had lowered fine. Check. The right landing wheel had landed fine. Check. But the cockpit indicator for the left wheel glowed orange, not green.'

Gunadnya's first thought was that it could be an electrical malfunction. It was rare, but not unheard of, for cockpit indicators on old aircraft to return incorrect information owing to something as simple as a short circuit in the wiring. Perhaps the left wheel had indeed lowered successfully, but failed to trigger an electrical signal to the cockpit. Gunadnya quickly leaned towards the cockpit's side windshield, twisting backward while trying to check visually if the plane's left wheel was down. From where he sat, he couldn't tell, so he ordered Flight Engineer Shailendra to go to the flight cabin and look through one of the tiny porthole-style windows. Shailendra returned with the confirmation Flt Lt Gunadnya had been dreading. The entire wheel was indeed stuck in the engine pod in the wing, and had failed to descend.

Sqn Ldr Aditee suggested recycling the undercarriage—raising the wheels and attempting to lower them again, in the hope that all three would descend. It was aviation's equivalent of that old solution to a stubborn computer problem: reboot. In the event of a hydraulic fault, it was possible that the jammed wheel would come unstuck and descend without further trouble. With the wheels whining back up into place, the crew held its breath as Gunadnya waited 15 seconds before pushing the landing gear button again. The hydraulics whined again as the wheels descended into landing position. When Gunadnya turned around in his seat for a confirmation from the flight engineer, he only saw a 'thumbs down' gesture. It hadn't worked.

'We tried everything to lower the undercarriage. Nothing worked,' says Sqn Ldr Aditee. 'And finally we decided to leave the undercarriage in the same position. This was when we all finally came to know that we had to face this situation.'

'This was now a real in-flight emergency,' says Gunadnya. 'We immediately informed ground control that we had an undercarriage emergency and that we were looking at our options.'

Gunadnya and Aditee took a deep breath, looking to each other for a moment. Both knew that an emergency of this kind had never happened in the Air Force. Both also knew that with fuel and time running out, they needed to battle it the only way pilots really can—solve one problem at a time, then move to the next.

'Let's fix this,' Sqn Ldr Aditee said, still smiling. 'Let's take this one step at a time and fix this.'

Eight years earlier, Aditee had dreamed of flying fighters, but had to settle for transport aircraft when she graduated from the Air Force Academy near Hyderabad, since rules stopped women from flying fighters. When journalists chatted with her about whether women would ever be allowed to fly fighters in the IAF, she had confidently declared, 'Only a matter of time.' She was dead-on. Five years later, the very same military flying academy that had no choice but to place Aditee in an An-32 cockpit would graduate its first batch of women fighter pilots after the government changed rules, opening fighter cockpits to women pilots for the first time.

She wasn't flying fighters like she had hoped to, but eight years into service as a Short Service Commission officer, Sqn Ldr Aditee was still living the dream, plunged, alongside the much larger number of male pilots, into the daily rigours of transport aviation, a stream she would quickly learn brought with it its own set of tough challenges. That morning, as she smiled to herself in the cockpit of the K-3060, wondering how she and the pilot were going to land a 20-tonne airplane without all its wheels down, she thought about that old familiar yearning for the thrill of aviation. And like the men on board with her, Sqn Ldr Aditee was fully aware that this could be her final landing.

Except, they couldn't land.

'Looking back, I know that death was, in fact, a sure possibility,' says Sqn Ldr Aditee. 'But there was a lot of communication going on among all of us. All the crew members, the ATC, our CO too had come on RT. We were discussing everything. This kept the atmosphere in the cockpit very positive.'

On the ground at Sulur, the base commander, Group Capt. R.C. Mohile, had rushed to the ATC tower to be in touch with the pilots of K-3060. He knew that it was a highly experienced crew in the aircraft now circling the base. As a proficient An-32 pilot himself, it would have seemed logical for him, an older and more experienced pilot, to guide the aircraft's crew out of their increasingly critical situation. But years of established protocol stipulate that beyond exception, the captain of the aircraft in distress has the final word on the course of action. Group Capt. Mohile could talk to his crew, but he knew that the ultimate decision on what to do lay with young Flt Lt Gunadnya. As it happened, it was an enormously difficult decision.

'How are the hydraulics doing?' Mohile's voice came in through the radio. Gunadnya quickly updated the senior officer on the aircraft's mechanical status.

The An-32's Russian flight manual offered an emergency solution to the landing gear problem. It recommended that if any of the wheels failed to deploy, standard operating procedure would be to retract all wheels and land the aircraft on its belly. Before the actual touchdown, the crew needed to turn off the aircraft's engines 50 feet above the ground. This, according to the manual, was to minimize the possibility of an impact fire.

'So the manual told me to descend slowly, pull back my landing gear, switch off my engines at 50 feet, and kiss the ground,' Gunadnya says. 'Ground control reminded me that that's what the Russians had recommended in such a situation.'

Except, Gunadnya remembers thinking, if he switched off the engines at 50 feet, it was certain to him that the crew would all be dead that day.

'Switching off both the engines simultaneously in the air at 50 feet seemed like a very bad idea,' he says. 'The aircraft would go out of control without engine power. If you switch off the engines, the An-32 becomes one big asymmetric mass of metal and it would become very difficult to control it. And everybody in it would die. It would be practically crashing the aircraft. This was my overwhelming sense.'

A thirty-year-old pilot was basically about to toss a carefully crafted aviation safety manual into the dustbin. With voices from ground control reminding him of the manual's prescription for the mid-air predicament, Gunadnya finally spoke out. Politely, but firmly, he told his crew as well as ground control that he disagreed with what the Russians had prescribed.

Now, An-32s are trusty Cold War-era birds with strong bones and a reassuring ruggedness. That was one of the reasons why the safety manual actually recommended a last-ditch belly landing. The aircraft were tough. But it was the final 50 feet of descent with engines off that had led Gunadnya to dismiss the idea entirely. In those 50 feet, headwinds beating against an unpowered aircraft could easily throw it off course, sending it careening dangerously into the scrub.

The alternative that Gunadnya was proposing was even scarier.

'Everybody was trying to sort out the issue, but the aircraft was in my hands,' says Gunadnya. 'So I announced that we would land the aircraft on one wheel, and hold it up on that wheel for as long as possible.'

If the aircraft were a tricycle, Gunadnya had basically recommended hitting the runway while doing a 'wheelie' on just the right wheel.

A few seconds of silence followed from ground control as the words sunk in. To many in the ATC tower at Sulur, the young pilot had just ditched an admittedly dangerous but prescribed recovery mechanism in favour of what looked like certain suicide. Gunadnya turned to his crew, searching for the tiniest semblance of affirmation. Almost imperceptibly, the others nodded back.

Let's do this.

Gunadnya's 'wheelie' plan was an enormous risk. It would require a magical level of cooperation from several hundred mechanical parts of the aircraft landing precariously on a single wheel. And there would be no practice run. The crew of the K-3060 would have one single chance to get it right. The reason for that was another sharp irony in the air that day. The pilots had enough fuel to last at least 20 more minutes—plenty of time in the normal course to practise-land a few times, if necessary. But for the sort of landing that Gunadnya had decided on, they wouldn't have a second chance. Therefore, they needed to empty their tanks to minimize the possibility of ending up in a big fireball on the ground. The An-32 doesn't have a mechanism to jettison or eject fuel in emergencies, so the crew needed to keep flying until their tanks were nearly dry before they attempted their one shot at a single wheel landing.

'There was consensus in the cockpit that we preferred not to die in a fuel fire,' Gunadnya says. 'Anything but a big fireball.'

The K-3060 needed to stay in the air for another 18 minutes. Gunadnya put the airplane in a long circle around the base, burning off fuel and waiting till the tanks were nearly dry. From the cockpit window, the 'X' of Sulur's two intersecting tarmacs glimmered under the hot afternoon sun. From the crowd that had gathered near the ground control tower, it was clear that the entire base had heard about the K-3060's unprecedented predicament.

From the ground, the base commander and a few other officers used binoculars to look up at the An-32 as it circled the base.

'So he advised us what we should do and we told him what we planned to do,' says Sqn Ldr Gunadnya. 'We did not get a yes or no, but he's in a position where he can't give a yes or a no. My ground controllers were also awesome. They reassured us about everything. When we were flying, we could see that the whole Air Force station had gathered on the tarmac. All the safety services were lined up for any eventuality. It was in a controlled procedural manner, the way it is in the Air Force.'

'It was a very disturbing sight,' says an officer from the Soaring Storks squadron who was at the ATC tower that afternoon. 'Hearing about it from Gunadnya and team was one thing. Seeing the aircraft fly by with just one landing wheel deployed was a shock to everyone who was watching. Many prayers went up in that moment.'

Over those 18 minutes, Gunadnya wondered quietly to himself if he was making a mistake. He had overruled the rule book and chosen to ignore gentle words of advice from ground control, including those of the boss of the Sulur base. This was his call. His crew completely supported his decision. But he knew the decision was his alone.

'Doubt can be a paralysing thing when you're in a cockpit. It can disorient you,' says Gunadnya. 'But there was something inside me that was just totally sure that the path I had chosen was the way to go.'

Sqn Ldr Aditee glanced over at the pilot.

'In my mind, I was very clear that we were not going to die,' she says. 'For me, that day, death was never a possibility. It may be hard to believe and I do not have any explanation for this feeling. But I was very confident. And it was not that I was trying to show calmness.'

'My co-pilot and I shared a very high comfort level. She trusted me completely,' Gunadnya says. 'A crew's lives were in my hands. I couldn't for a moment show fear or hesitation. If I did, it would spread to Aditee and the others. When the emergency first surfaced, Aditee had smiled and said, "Okay, this is new! Let's fix it!" We were a great team.'

Gunadnya worked to control any semblance of agitation that could have surfaced in his manner. Barely a few years into his service, he had been thrust into a difficult leadership position that involved keeping everyone's emotions in control in the face of likely injury and possible death.

'The fear of death cannot persist. You can't sustain fear of death for an hour,' says Gunadnya. 'That old cliché is true. I saw my whole life pass before my eyes when we reached the point of no return. The others were stressed when I looked at them, because they didn't have anything in their control. We're from the same squadron, but in the aircraft, what can you do except trust your captain? We're all personally connected. My crew reassured me and I reassured them.'

Aditee's voice cut through the pilot's thoughts.

'This is going to work,' she said, sensing Gunadnya's quiet tension. 'Time for final approach.'

The aircraft was now on its final minutes of fuel. The margin for error at this point was zero. The K–3060 made a loose final turn from the south-west and headed back towards the base, this time in slow descent from 800 feet. As the aircraft flew lower and slower, turbulence buffeted its frame unequally, since it was slicing through the air with one landing wheel down and another up.

'We turned for the final and then gave a call for the final approach,' says Gunadnya. 'When we descend from 1000 to 800 feet, and then to 500 feet, we give a call. We usually say, "Three greens, landing clearance requested." We only had two greens and one amber. The ground control noted our request for the record. They had never received a request to land in such circumstances before.'

In 40 seconds, the Sulur runway loomed into view. Descending to 100 feet, the crew lowered the aircraft's flaps to slow it down to about 250 kmph, the slowest it could fly for a landing. Gunadnya tightened his fists around the flight control stick and turned to look toward his co-pilot. Aditee gave him one final nod, then took the aircraft down to 50 feet.

'My speed was 250 kmph. What I didn't realize at the time was that I was flying with mixed controls. And now, if one wheel is not there, that means that amount of drag is not there. So, to maintain the same flight profile, you have to apply rudders. There's no autopilot capable of helping you land in such a situation,' Gunadnya says.

There was another reason for Gunadnya's decision not to switch off the engines at 50 feet, as prescribed by the Russian flight manual.

'We needed to reduce the aerodynamic forces on the aircraft at slow speed and increase drag as much as possible,' Gunadnya says. 'We needed the engines on because we needed to "fine" the propellers to increase the aircraft's drag. Therefore, there was no question of switching off the engines as prescribed by the Russian manual. I needed the advantage of drag. Switching off the engines would kill my drag, and the momentum of the aircraft would have thrown it out of control. Drag was our friend. And we needed every ounce of it.'

On any other day, Gunadnya would have had the luxury of touching down further along the runway, even near the middle, since the An-32 didn't need a lot of length to slow down after landing. But on this day, if there was one overwhelming certainty, it was that once K-3060 touched down, it was only a matter of moments before it would veer off the runway. If Gunadnya landed the aircraft too far down the runway, he ran the risk of the aircraft running off the track and ploughing into air base buildings or even the parked aircraft to the left. If the aircraft was going to veer off to the left, it needed to be into the open area filled with red earth near the beginning of the runway.

Twenty feet above the ground, Gunadnya and Aditee could see the full runway before them, the flashing lights of crash vehicles far in the distance. A final prayer went up before the crew took the K–3060 to the tarmac.

'Landing was the most difficult part,' remembers Sqn Ldr Aditee. 'We had spent a lot of time in air. And we had rehearsed the entire procedure. Now there was no turning back.'

From ground control, a video camera filmed the aircraft's approach. Officers present remember the cold silence that descended on the tower and the crowd below as the K–3060 descended the final few feet to the runway on its right wheel. The crew's singular aim was to bring the aircraft down on the tarmac's centre line with the aircraft's nose up and to control it against all the physical forces that would begin to act on it.

Seconds later, the wheel touched the tarmac. A collective gasp went up from the crowd as the aircraft shivered unsteadily for a moment.

'We could not believe what we were seeing. For a few seconds, the aircraft was on one wheel. It was moving at 250 kmph on one single wheel,' says an Air Force Sergeant who had been deployed at the far end of the tarmac to film the landing.

In the cockpit, Gunadnya was leaning forward, his face a grimace of concentration as he fought to hold the aircraft steady while it screamed down the runway, dangerously balanced on one wheel.

'As we roared forward on one wheel after touchdown, there was immediate danger,' Gunadnya says. 'The cantilever beam of the An–32's wings could have turned viciously 180 degrees. It could have broken or toppled over. Anything could have happened in those very tense moments. I was using every bit of my strength to steady the aircraft as much as possible.'

The aircraft screamed down the runway. But as drag began to kick in and shake the aircraft dangerously off its path, Gunadnya shouted to his co-pilot to 'withdraw' the propellers.

'Two seconds after touchdown, I felt myself losing control of the aircraft,' says Gunadnya. 'I could not hold it because as the air speed forces reduced, the ability to control it was gone. Like trying to steer a stationary car. Aditee had withdrawn the propellers. There was nothing more we could do now but hope for the best.'

Control of the aircraft was out of Gunadnya's hands now. For 5 full seconds, the K–3060 shuddered precariously down the runway on its right wheel as the crew battled to keep it steady and slow it down. And then it began to tilt dramatically, as predicted, to the left.

'Kharche was flying very well. He was doing a great job. I was following him on controls,' says Sqn Ldr Aditee.

Gunadnya remembers, 'I had briefed the whole crew that the moment we crash, the flight engineer will jump out of the emergency exit first, followed by the navigators, Aditee and, finally, me. The emergency exit on the An-32 is a small square opening, large enough for barely one person.'

As the aircraft veered with a roar off its course and off the runway into open shrubbery, Gunadnya sent up one final prayer. If the remnants of fuel did spark a fire now, the crew would have just seconds to get out of the aircraft—if the fire didn't cut off their exit entirely, that is. The crash tender trucks would still take at least 2 minutes to safely approach the aircraft.

His hands still clutching the aircraft controls even if there was nothing more he could do, Gunadnya watched in horror as the K–3060 careened to its left, its wing tip hitting the runway in a flash of sparks, turning the aircraft now violently to the left and into the muddy scrubland off the tarmac. The aircraft thudded on for 50 more feet before it finally came to a stop.

Gunadnya immediately received word on his radio that three crash tenders were speeding towards the aircraft. Both Flight Engineer Shailendra and a voice from ground control confirmed that, miraculously, there were no visible fires. Switching off all the aircraft's systems, Gunadnya gave the order for his crew to exit the aircraft from the emergency slot.

'Nobody said a word for the first few minutes,' Gunadnya says. 'We exited the aircraft in silence. Then we walked a few feet away and turned back to look at the plane. It was sitting on its belly, its left wing touching the ground.'

Almost immediately, Gunadnya's mobile phone rang. It was his wife, Shruti. She had chosen to remain in Mumbai at their family home while her husband was deployed with the Soaring Storks in Sulur. Gunadnya heard an anxious voice as he took the call.

'Where are you? I've been calling you for so long. Your sortie should have been over by this time. What happened?' Shruti asked. Her husband chuckled gently into his phone, assuring her that all was well. It would be days before Shruti would find out what he had managed to do that afternoon.

After a medical team quickly attested that the crew had sustained no injuries, a pair of jeeps picked up Gunadnya and his team and transported them to a briefing room with the base commander and other senior squadron staff. Every last person at the Sulur base was sure they had witnessed history that afternoon. But they also knew how close the crew of the K-3060 had come to a fiery death. The Air Force would need to dive deep into every second of what happened in the air. It would check every bolt, every wire on board the K-3060. And it would investigate Gunadnya's own leadership in the cockpit to judge whether his decision to disobey a flight manual was worthy of praise or punishment. But for the rest of the day, after the crew had logged their flight and changed out of their olive-green overalls, ruthless process would have to make way for some welcome revelry.

A large cake was wheeled into the mess that night as the base celebrated the 'rebirth' of the crew of K-3060.

'We were elated. There's a tradition that if you survive an aircraft accident without injury, you celebrate a birthday. A rebirth, really. We cut the cake and there was a huge party that night. There was joy, but also a sense of disbelief that we were safe. It was unreal for both us and those who had received us,' Gunadnya says.

Gunadnya's deadly tribulation in the air may have ended miraculously without damage to life or limb—or even much damage to the aircraft itself—but when the sun rose the following day, he was about to receive a heavy reality check in the form of orders for a Court of Inquiry. This was due process, but on the line would be the young pilot's fledgling career. Gunadnya had been in service just over five years.

An Air Marshal-rank officer, the chief of the Southern Air Command headquartered in neighbouring Kerala, landed in Sulur early on the morning of 7 February, kicking into motion an accident investigation the likes of which the IAF had never handled before. For a whole month, Gunadnya would be summoned to provide detailed testimony and a defence of his actions in the cockpit. He would be cross-examined and interrogated so the Court of Inquiry could draw up a complete, detailed picture of what had happened on board the K-3060. Ten days into the inquiry, Gunadnya was permitted to fly again.

'They basically had to judge whether I was right or wrong. They needed to fix some learnings for the future. And I was at the centre of what happened. Thankfully, the Court of Inquiry gave me a tentative green light to fly after ten days,' says Gunadnya. 'This did not mean that I was in the clear, by any means, but simply that as a pilot, I was allowed to continue my daily flying duties.'

The Court of Inquiry interviewed the other members of Gunadnya's crew, officers who manned the Air Traffic Control at Sulur and senior officers from the Soaring Storks squadron. When the inquiry was complete, Gunadnya waited for their judgement.

'I was expecting trouble. I had deviated from established procedure, but hadn't violated any norms. It was complicated. I ignored the Russian procedure and did what I thought was best. I explained my decision to the best of my abilities. But I was aware that deviating from tried-and-tested procedures is no joke. And no matter, a very serious view can always be taken. I could be in a lot of trouble,' Gunadnya says.

Three days after the Court of Inquiry ended, Gunadnya was headed out of the flight operations room towards the flight line for another sortie, when he received a call on his mobile phone. It was Group Capt. Mohile, the base commander.

'Good news and bad news, Kharche,' Mohile said. 'Which one do you want first?'

'Bad,' Gunadnya said. 'Always bad first, Sir.'

'Okay, the Court of Inquiry has concluded that the decision you took in the cockpit wasn't the correct procedure,' Mohile said.

Gunadnya stopped in his tracks, thunderstruck. Were they really going to bring the axe down on him? After all that?

'And there's good news after that, Sir?' he asked.

'The Court has recommended no action against you. You're in the clear. Congratulations. Have a safe flight,' Mohile said. The Court of Inquiry, as it happened, would make highly nuanced conclusions about the K-3060 incident.

What Gunadnya didn't know was that other wheels had quietly begun to turn, between the Sulur base, the Southern Air Command and the Air Force Headquarters in Delhi. The K-3060 incident had become a hot topic of conversation among aviators and the IAF's senior leadership. By the end of March, despite the Court of Inquiry ruling that the captain of K-3060 hadn't followed established procedure, Flt Lt Gunadnya's name was recommended for a Shaurya Chakra, India's third-highest peacetime gallantry award.

'The Air Force still maintains the diktat that the flight manual is our Bible and that I should have followed it. The rationale was that every other pilot hereafter will have doubts about procedure and instead apply his or her own mind. The Air Force was very mature in making a decision of this kind, and yet awarding me for the decision I took,' Gunadnya says. 'They saw merit in what I had done in my situation. They deemed it worthy of reward.'

Weeks later, Gunadnya would be part of an IAF team visiting Ukraine to inspect the An-32 upgrade programme that had been contracted in 2009. While there, he would get a chance to speak to the Antonov company's test pilots.

'We had a philosophical talk. They agreed with me, mostly,' says Gunadnya. 'They said manuals exist, sure, but when you sit in an aircraft, your decisions are over and above the flight manuals—always. They told me what I did was probably the better way to do it.'

Sqn Ldr Aditee has since retired from the IAF and now lives in Pune. The video of that landing remains on her phone, and she looks at it often.

'Most of the time, aircraft emergencies require immediate action. Like in the case of engine fire or engine failure. The crew has to complete the actions without even thinking. To prepare ourselves for such emergencies, we practise a lot,' she says. 'However, our situation was very different from this. We had to spend a lot of time in air. We had to burn maximum fuel and land with minimum weight. We had never really practised something like this. In this type of scenario, all the crew members had to be in the situation for longer duration. If someone panics, there are chances of the situation going out of control. So it was very important to maintain calmness in the cockpit. Kharche and I kept flying alternately to avoid stress and fatigue. We kept talking with each other and with the ATC. I kept asking our flight engineer to keep calling out engine parameters, to keep carrying out visual checks. The navigator kept watch on fuel and aircraft endurance. This was just to keep everyone occupied. This was a very different and unique situation we were put in. But in the end, teamwork is the most important thing.'

Meanwhile, there was the question of damage to the aircraft itself. The K-3060 had taken an obvious beating as it had landed on one wheel and veered off the runway into muddy no-man's land. But the aircraft had sustained surprisingly little real damage. Test pilots from Kanpur flew down to Sulur to conduct an elaborate check of the aircraft's stress points and mechanical systems. With some minor tinkering at Sulur, the aircraft was flown to Kanpur for more detailed structural testing. Months later, it returned to service.

'It's an amazing aircraft. I actually flew that same aircraft later when I was deployed for a UN Peacekeeping mission in Africa,' Gunadnya says.

Six months later, on India's Independence Day, Flt Lt Gunadnya, who had by then been promoted to the rank of Squadron Leader, arrived in Delhi to receive his Shaurya Chakra gallantry decoration from the President of India. The citation would recount his actions on board the K-3060:

Flt Lt G.R. Kharche carried out a safe emergency landing with only starboard main wheel and nose wheel. The aircraft landing was controlled in the most courageous way and the aircraft suffered minimal damage. After landing, the action to evacuate the personnel on board were carried out most efficiently under his supervision. Flt Lt G.R. Kharche displayed qualities of exceptional courage and extreme professionalism during handling of such a grave emergency inspite of limited experience. His actions not only saved the lives of personnel onboard but also recovered the aircraft with minimal damage. For the display of exemplary courage and composure in handling an extremely rare emergency, Flight Lieutenant Gunadnya Ramesh Kharche has been awarded Shaurya Chakra.

'I can never forget that there were two things that happened that day. We brought the K-3060 down safely,' says Gunadnya. And the other?

'And the K-3060 had also brought us down alive.'

Acknowledgements

In the nearly two years since we wrote the first *India's Most Fearless*, it has become plainly clear that this is no longer just a book series. When we hear from readers across the world every day, we're constantly reminded that these stories have a life of their own beyond the written page.

For this second book in the series, we wish to thank, above all, the chiefs of our three armed forces—General Bipin Rawat, Air Chief Marshal Birender Singh Dhanoa and Admiral Sunil Lanba. They saw how readers received the first in the series and were even more generous to our inquisitive pursuits with the second. Our deepest thanks especially to Major General A.K. Narula and his team at the Additional Directorate General of Public Information (ADGPI), Group Captain Anupam Banerjee and Captain Dalip Kumar Sharma.

Our gratitude to Swati Chopra, our editor at Penguin Random House, who, like us, has been drawn irreversibly into the lives of the heroes you read about in this book.

Our families—Torul, Tavleen, Aryaman, Agastya and Mira—and our parents who literally provide the world necessary to write such a book.

Thank you to our dearest friend Sandeep Unnithan, a powerhouse of information and talent that we are so proud is now a part of India's Most Fearless.

To officers and soldiers, Special Forces men and doctors beyond counting who helped in ways small and big, who cannot be named for reasons operational. You know who you are and what you've done for this book.

Our thanks to our readers who've received *India's Most Fearless* with an unending store of love and praise—even now, we forward your messages of love to the heroes and their families. We can't wait to do the same with this book.

It is to that latter—the heroes and their families—that we give thanks above all. Nothing continues to astonish us more than the graciousness, generosity and modesty of men and women who've accomplished things beyond common understanding. As we tell the heroes or those they leave behind, the best way we can say thanks is to never stop writing.